Crime and Empire 1840–1940

D0218009

Crime and Empire 1840–1940

Criminal justice in local and global context

edited by

Barry S. Godfrey
Graeme Dunstall

WILLAN
PUBLISHING

Published by

Willan Publishing
Culmcott House
Mill Street, Uffculme
Cullompton, Devon
EX15 3AT, UK
Tel: +44(0)1884 840337
Fax: +44(0)1884 840251
e-mail: info@willanpublishing.co.uk
website: www.willanpublishing.co.uk

Published simultaneously in the USA and Canada by

Willan Publishing
c/o ISBS, 920 NE 58th Ave, Suite 300,
Portland, Oregon 97213-3786, USA
Tel: +001(0)503 287 3093
Fax: +001(0)503 280 8832
e-mail: info@isbs.com
website: www.isbs.com

First published 2005

ISBN 1-84392-108-1 (cased)
ISBN 1-84392-107-3 (paperback)

British Library Cataloguing-in-Publication Data
A catalogue record for this book is available from the British Library

Cover photograph © Mary Evans Picture Library, original photograph by Watts & Skeen,
reproduced in *The Queen's Empire*. The photograph shows inmates at Burma's Rangoon gaol
in 1900, forced to work the prison's giant treadmill.
Typeset by GCS, Leighton Buzzard, Beds
Project management by Deer Park Productions, Tavistock, Devon
Printed and bound by T.J. International Ltd, Trecerus Industrial Estate, Padstow, Cornwall

Contents

Foreword

Carolyn Strange

Who cares about criminal justice history? Ask this question half a century ago, and only a few lawyer-historians, and even fewer scholars working in other disciplines, would have raised their hands. Ask it at the end of the twentieth century and a growing range of historians, along with criminologists, sociologists and anthropologists, would have piped up. This collection of essays shows that the response is quite different today; not only is the range of scholars intrigued by the criminal justice past growing but the general public is keenly interested in the history of the courts, the police and criminal sanctions. So-called 'cold cases' involving unsolved crimes have become prime-time fodder, while lavish historical documentaries dwell on famous trials and grisly punishments. Suddenly, it seems, everyone is interested in the history of crime and criminal justice.

This is particularly the case in countries where European empire builders brought law, European-style, to territories previously governed by traditional rulers and rules. The legacy of colonisation is disputed dryly in civil and constitutional courts in land claims cases but it is also contested passionately on talk-back radio shows and in the popular press. It is not surprising that indigenous peoples have called upon present-day governments to redress wrongs of the past; what would have surprised the old imperial administrators of criminal law is that many of those wrongs were committed by colonisers who considered that they were doing right by the law.

'Just how unlawful was criminal law in the past?' is a question that has invited spirited rebuttals from imperial apologists, who assert that the introduction of European legal systems (and British law in particular) was a gift of civilisation in colonial settings. Against them a much greater group of scholars have rejected the question for different reasons, preferring to examine carefully the records of criminal justice administration through official sources, such as trial transcripts and gaol registers, but also to approach the past imaginatively, through diaries, photos, architecture and uniforms. For the contributors to this volume, then, the question is not whether criminal justice modelled on British customs and policies was 'good' or 'bad'; instead, it is *how* were crime and justice conceived of and managed in the heyday of British imperialism?'

The answers are rarely predictable. As always, history, even of the recent past, is an object lesson in the strangeness and familiarity of earlier times. Key institutions established in the period covered by this collection – the penitentiary and the professional police – persist in modified modes in our own time, while other practices, such as public executions and the criminalisation of certain 'tribes', seem safely and squarely in the remote past. Interpreting continuity and rupture invites reasoned speculation, an intellectual practice that earlier criminal justice historians typically rejected in favour of making definitive assessments of the past. Another shift from earlier modes of historical inquiry is the express engagement with queries about the present, whether it be current bids for indigenous self-determination or inquiries into systemic abuses of police power. In a period when memories of the troubled and troubling past threaten to eclipse scholarly analyses of criminal justice history in public policy debates, collections such as these are timely; in other words, they are as important to the present as to the past.

Carolyn Strange
Centre for Cross-cultural Research
Australian National University
January 2005

Notes on the editors and contributors

Editors

Barry S. Godfrey is Senior Lecturer in Criminology at Keele University. He teaches and researches crime and policing in the later nineteenth and early twentieth centuries. He has edited *Comparative Histories of Crime* (2003) with Clive Emsley and Graeme Dunstall. A co-authored book (with Paul Lawrence) will be published in 2005, and a monograph entitled *The Rough: Marginal Criminality 1880–1939* is currently being written.

Graeme Dunstall is Senior Lecturer in History at the University of Canterbury, New Zealand. He researches and teaches New Zealand social history and criminal justice history. His publications include *A Policeman's Paradise? Policing a Stable Society 1918–1945* (1999); jointly editing *Comparative Histories of Crime* (2003) with Barry Godfrey and Clive Emsley; jointly editing *Southern Capital. Christchurch: Towards a City Biography, 1850–2000* (2000); and a contribution to the *Oxford History of New Zealand*.

Contributors

Sarah Anderson is a PhD candidate in Criminology at Victoria University of Wellington in New Zealand, and is currently exploring the relationship between literature and the history of the prison, with her main research interests being in the history and sociology of punishment, and popular culture.

Mark Brown teaches criminology at the University of Melbourne. He has written on a number of aspects of corrections and penology, including contemporary understandings of risk and the so-called dangerous offender. Since 1999 he has been engaged in research on the penal history of British India and is currently writing a book focusing on the notorious 'criminal tribes' of north India.

Jane Buckingham completed her PhD in History at the University of Sydney in 1996 and is Senior Lecturer in South Asian History at the University of Canterbury, New Zealand. Her area of specialisation is the medical and legal history of India.

Catharine Coleborne is a Senior Lecturer in History at the University of Waikato, Hamilton, New Zealand. She is currently engaged in a two-year Marsden funded project (Royal Society of New Zealand) to examine families and insanity in colonial Australia and New Zealand to 1914. Her publications include the co-edited *'Madness' in Australia: Histories, Heritage and the Asylum* (2003). Her book *Reading 'Madness': Gender and Difference in the Colonial Asylum in Victoria, Australia, 1848–1880s* will be published in 2005.

Helen Dampier is currently completing a PhD in Sociology on 'Women's Personal Testimonies of the Concentration Camps of the South African War, 1899–1902 and After' at the University of Newcastle. She has a substantive interest in South African history, and is generally concerned with the use of life writings as historical sources.

Clive Emsley is Professor of History and co-Director of the International Centre for Comparative Criminological Research at the Open University. His publications include *The English Police: A Political and Social History* (2nd edn, 1996), *Gendarmes and the State in Nineteenth-Century Europe* (1999) and *Crime and Society in England, 1750–1900* (3rd edn, 2004). He has been President of the International Association for the History of Crime and Criminal Justice since 1995.

Julie Evans is currently Australian Research Council Postdoctoral Fellow, Department of History at the University of Melbourne, where she will take up a lectureship in the Department of Criminology in 2005. She is co-author of *Equal Subjects, Unequal Rights: Indigenous Peoples in British Settler Colonies, 1830–1910* (2003). Her monograph on race and colonial governance will be published in 2005.

Jeremy Finn is an Associate Professor of Law at the University of Canterbury, Christchurch, New Zealand where he has taught since 1978. He has written extensively in areas of legal history, contract law and criminal law. He has a particular interest in the statute law of the British self-governing colonies in the nineteenth century.

Mark Finnane is a Professor of History at Griffith University, where he is Dean of Graduate Studies. He has published widely on the history of policing, punishment, the social history of mental hospitals and the history of violence. Currently he is writing a biography of Sir John Barry, the pioneering Australian criminologist and historian of nineteenth-century punishment.

Richard S. Hill is Director of the Treaty of Waitangi Research Unit at the Stout Research Centre for New Zealand Studies and Associate Professor at Victoria University of Wellington. He has written four books on nineteenth- and early twentieth-century policing in New Zealand, and has recently published a history of Crown–Maori relations in the first half of the twentieth century: *State Authority, Indigenous Autonomy* (2004). He holds degrees from Canterbury University, including Doctor of Letters, and has been a senior manager and Chief Historian in the New Zealand Crown's processes for settling Maori claims relating to the state's past breaches of the Treaty of Waitangi.

Anna McKenzie is a PhD candidate in Criminology at Victoria University of Wellington, New Zealand. Her thesis is an investigation into the development of the system of penal governance for women in New Zealand from the nineteenth through to the late twentieth centuries. Her research interests include the sociology and history of punishment and penal systems, and the penal governance of women.

Stefan Petrow lectures in Australian and British history in the School of History and Classics at the University of Tasmania, Hobart. His major publications include *Policing Morals: The Metropolitan Police and the Home Office 1870–1914* (1994), *Going to the Mechanics: A History of the Launceston*

Mechanics' Institute 1842–1914 (1998) and *Hobart 1846–2000: A History of the Hobart City Council* (with Alison Alexander, to be published in 2004). His current research interests include the police in Tasmania and a biography of Governor William Denison.

John Pratt was educated at the universities of London, Keele and Sheffield. After graduating in law, he obtained an MA and PhD in criminology. He is now Professor of Criminology at Victoria University of Wellington, New Zealand. He has published extensively on the history and sociology of punishment, including *Punishment in a Perfect Society* (1992), *Governing the Dangerous* (1997) and *Punishment and Civilization* (2002). He has also co-edited *Dangerous Offenders: Punishment and Social Order* (2000, with Mark Brown) and *Crime, Truth and Justice* (2004, with George Gilligan). He is a co-editor of *The New Punitiveness* (2005) with Mark Brown, Wayne Morrison, David Brown and Simon Hallsworth. Since 1997 he has been editor of the *Australian and New Zealand Journal of Criminology.*

Carolyn Strange has taught and written on the history of criminal justice in Canada, Australia and the US, focusing particularly on imprisonment and punishment. More recently her work has explored the variety of media and genres in which the criminal justice past is taken up in the present. She is currently Graduate Director at the Centre for Cross-Cultural Research, Australian National University.

Dean Wilson is a Lecturer in Criminal Justice and Criminology in the School of Political and Social Inquiry, Monash University. He has published widely in the areas of the histories of criminal justice and surveillance and social control. His book on the history of policing in Melbourne, Australia, tentatively entitled *Policing the Colonial City*, is soon to be published.

Acknowledgements

The editors would like to thank all those who took part in the British Academy sponsored Comparative Histories of Crime conference held in Christchurch New Zealand in October 2003; also the History Department of the University of Canterbury for its assistance with this conference, and, of course, the contributors to this volume.

Chapter 1

Crime and empire: introduction

Graeme Dunstall and Barry S. Godfrey

This book offers a contribution to the comparative histories of crime and criminal justice within the legal regimes[1] of the British empire during the nineteenth and early twentieth centuries. An overarching theme is the transformation and convergence of criminal justice systems during a broad shift from legal pluralism to the hegemony of state law in the European world and beyond. In this context, the essays present a variety of approaches, ranging from 'global' discussions to local case studies, and reflecting current criminological, historiographical and post-colonial issues.

Significant changes in European criminal justice systems during a 'long' nineteenth century are the focus of Clive Emsley's essay. Within empires and nation states, a multiplicity of legal codes and infra-judicial methods were largely superseded by uniform (often Napoleonic) codes, new and increasingly centralised prison and policing systems, and changing perceptions of criminals and explanations of criminality. Clearly the degree and effect of transformation and convergence in legal regimes varied within Europe according to local traditions and political circumstances. Within the United Kingdom, for example, neither the English nor Scottish common law systems of criminal law were codified, although much of English penal law was consolidated in statutes by the mid-nineteenth century. In terms of the three types of policing systems that were present in France and which became common on the Continent (Emsley, 1999), Ireland had only a gendarmerie (the Royal Irish

Constabulary), Scotland had only municipal civilian (borough and county) forces, while England had a state civilian force (the London Metropolitan police) and municipal civilian forces, but lacked a gendarmerie. England's relatively decentralised policing system did not imply a weak state, however (Phillips, 2004). By contrast with the English experience, infra-judicial methods of resolving offences and disputes remained much more significant in parts of southern Europe, notably Corsica and Sicily, and epitomised the French and Italian states' weakness in those regions.

Until the mid-twentieth century at least, the dominant view of the changes in English (and more broadly European) criminal law, policing and punishment was that they were (in Emsley's words) 'progressive and increasingly driven by humanitarianism and rationality'. Certainly, as Sarah Anderson's exegesis of a mid-Victorian English novel suggests, contemporaries who exposed the abuse of prisoners could still believe in the potential of professionally administered and centrally controlled institutions to be humane and reforming. However, as John Pratt's historiographical discussion of punishment shows, the traditional accounts of benign motives and improved conditions came to be challenged by others who critiqued in a variety of ways the intentions and outcomes of nineteenth-century European penal reform.

European imperialism saw the transfer of legal codes, and policing and punishment systems, to a wider world as part of the processes of colonial state-building. In fact, the transition from legal pluralism to the hegemony of colonial state law was generally a slow and often incomplete process in the many and varied contexts of the British empire (Benton, 2002; Mommsen and De Moor, 1992; Mann and Roberts, 1991). Colonial law, and more particularly the European concept of the rule of law, could be (and was) a key coercive instrument in the dispossession and subjugation of the colonised to the authority of the colonial state. But law (and the ideology of the rule of law) could also be a resource for the colonised in their disputes among themselves and with the colonisers; it could be a mechanism for protection, resistance, adaptation and collaboration (Mann and Roberts, 1991: 3, 35; Benton, 2002: 254–60; Ward, 1995; cf. Kelsey, 1984). In assessing the nature of British authority in the colonial context – and how far the 'customary' law, policing and punishment practices of the colonised were adopted, modified, transformed or superseded by British law and institutions – a broad distinction can be made between an empire of dominion (involving imperial authority over a non-British population and where legal pluralism was relatively strong) and white settlement colonies – notably Australia and New Zealand where settler self-government was achieved during the 1850s and legal pluralism was officially discountenanced.

Legal pluralism, allowing a role for Hindu and Muslim law, can be seen to have been a key strategy of British rule in India. Nonetheless, from the late eighteenth century, there was growing British control over the content and administration of criminal law – with the principles of English criminal law being eventually embodied in the Indian Penal Code and Code of Criminal Procedure of 1860 and 1861 respectively, and with the development of varied provincial policing systems where British gendarmerie and state civilian models were adapted and superimposed on local village watchmen (Benton, 2002: 127–52; Kolff, 1992; Robb, 1991; Arnold, 1986: ch. 1). How far then did the British adopt and transform pre-existing Indian law? Jane Buckingham assesses the debate with reference to the British control in the early nineteenth century of *sati* and *samadh* – Hindu practices of suicide by widows and leprosy sufferers. She concludes that the British relied on Brahmanic and local royal precedent as the basis for their intervention, as well as pragmatism in balancing their control over life and death with the need to maintain their hold on power.

Evolving ideas about Indian society further shaped the nature of criminal law and policing as the British sought to establish tighter control over the countryside, and especially in the 'frontier' areas of north India. In this context Mark Brown examines the developing concept of hereditary criminal communities and policies for their containment and control which were codified in the Criminal Tribes Act 1871. Here the ambit of colonial state law moved beyond that of the metropolitan centre in criminalising *groups* and extending criminal responsibility and punishment beyond individuals. More broadly, Brown considers how the criminal tribes policy contributes to an understanding of current developments in penal theory and the nature of colonial governance.

Ultimately the criminal tribes policy demonstrated a fundamental ambiguity of the British rule of law in the colonial context, with some groups being viewed as simultaneously 'outside' the law and yet subject to coercion (including lethal violence) justified by it. There are parallels with the position of Aborigines (especially when construed as 'savage tribes') on the expanding frontiers of the British settlement in Australia. Seeing violence against Aborigines as part of the process of their dispossession, Mark Finnane critiques the historiographical assumptions underpinning claims in a recent controversial account by Keith Windschuttle (2002) that such violence has been exaggerated and misinterpreted by historians. Using South Australia as her case study, Julie Evans discusses how the introduction of the rule of law in white settler colonies depended upon its abrogation in favour of 'martial law' and summary justice where necessary to secure the effective assertion of state authority. Accordingly, as Evans comments, Aborigines (and, we can add, Indian and Maori 'tribes') could be construed as both enemies (or 'rebels') and criminals, subject to both warfare and punishment, and to the 'murky legality' of martial law.

In New Zealand from 1840, Maori looked to maintain their *rangatiratanga* (autonomy) in the face of rapid Pakeha (European) colonisation and the advent of a colonial state. Richard Hill discusses the ongoing quest for *rangatiratanga* and the variety of strategies adopted by Maori which are revealed by their involvement in, or resistance to, various systems of state policing – ranging from gendarmeries to co-opted Maori institutions. Indeed the nature and degree of Maori involvement in mid-nineteenth-century colonial policing stands in contrast to that of Aborigines in Australia (Finnane, 1994: ch. 4). From the outset of the New Zealand colonial state, an official policy of racial 'amalgamation' was pursued with varying degrees of intensity. There were few concessions to the practices and oral traditions of Maori customary law which the British saw as uncivilised by comparison with the written texts of Hindu and Muslim law. Nonetheless, the limited coercive power of the early colonial state meant that a weak legal pluralism persisted in Maori-dominated areas until the 1880s. The ending of any state concessions to Maori viewpoints in judicial practices and policing was apparent by the 1890s when Maori assessors lost the right to assist the Pakeha (European) magistrates, and there were no longer any Maori as full members of the state civilian police force (Ward, 1995: ch. 21).

Codification of criminal law in the Australasian colonial states during the 1890s epitomised the formal erasure of legal pluralism; it also reflected the developing independence of colonial legal regimes. Jeremy Finn examines the varied parliamentary histories of the process which ranged from failed attempts to the rapid enactment of Criminal Codes, especially where there were influential lawyers, strong parliamentary leadership and self-consciously progressive governments willing to act in advance of England. In so doing, the Australasian codifiers looked not just to their counterparts in England, but also elsewhere in the empire and beyond.

A similar pattern of emulation among adjacent colonies occurred in Australasian variants of British models of policing. There were common nineteenth-century developments in each state: from local police directed by magistrates to one government-controlled force; from gendarmeries to state civilian police; and with the co-option of Aborigines and Maori to fight in racial conflicts being followed by their elimination from state policing once the frontiers had been pacified (Finnane, 1991, 1994; Hill, 1991). Between 1858 and 1899, however, Tasmania was an exception to these trends. In his essay, Stefan Petrow examines the state's reversion from a centralised gendarmerie to a decentralised English model of municipal civilian forces, and then its return to the antipodean norm by the 1890s of a state civilian force. From the beginning of the twentieth century, an enthusiasm for technical innovations – notably fingerprinting and motorised wireless patrols – revealed another pattern of emulation. Focusing in his chapter on the early adoption of new technologies in Melbourne, Dean Wilson sees a fundamental shift in the symbolic dimension of policing in Australasia as well as the United States and Canada during the early twentieth century: the hitherto defining image of the beat constable was surpassed by new symbols of techno-scientific policing.

Albeit belatedly and in a piecemeal fashion during the first two decades of the twentieth century, Australian and New Zealand prison systems followed European and North American developments in penology (Finnane, 1997: ch. 3; Pratt, 1992: ch. 5). In particular, separate prisons for women were established in Victoria (1894), New South Wales (1908) and New Zealand (1913), with the proponents of the last two institutions looking to adopt the regime of the Massachusetts Reformatory Prison for Women opened in 1877. Here, Anna McKenzie examines the thinking of New Zealand's Minister of Justice in proposing a women's reformatory, and the gap between his aspirations and the outcomes for female inmates. In effect, the separate institution did not represent a significant advance from the earlier separate divisions for women in prisons created for men.

The South African War between Britain and the Boer Republics led to a very different confinement of Boer women and children in concentration camps. These were meant to control and regulate rather than punish a population displaced by British military policy. However, Boer women's testimonies present traumatic experiences of hardship and death as the product of a British genocidal policy. In reassessing these testimonies, Helen Dampier argues that they ignore the 'everyday life' of the camps and misrepresent British intentions for nationalist political purposes. In this instance, those subjugated by imperial power constructed narratives which would dominate the subsequent historiography.

Overall, the criminal justice systems that developed in the British settler colonies during the nineteenth century broadly mimicked the English system in ideology and practice. The degree of institutional convergence suggests that the colonial experience of crime and crime control can be compared with that in England. Recent analyses have noted, for example, a parallel late nineteenth-century decline in national rates of recorded violence in Australasia and England (Godfrey, 2003; Dunstall, 2004). Looking to make more wide-ranging subnational comparisons, Barry Godfrey and Graeme Dunstall report their preliminary findings on trends for violence, drunkenness and offences against property in two rapidly developing new towns in England and New Zealand.

In her chapter, Catharine Coleborne considers the potential of post-colonial theory and methodology to provide different 'ways of seeing' and 'doing' transnational legal historical scholarship in the Australia-Pacific region. She considers that the post-colonial framework enables a sharper focus on: racial distinctions and exclusions, on the gendering of criminality and its regulation, and on the nature of the colonial archives – their biases and omissions in presenting a record for reconstructing the complex sets of relations between the colonised and the colonisers.

Ultimately, the post-colonial approach suggests the need for multiple histories in the comparative study of crime and criminal justice within the context of empire. That remains to be done.

Note

1. This phrase is borrowed from Lauren Benton whose interpretation of 'global legal regimes' informs this discussion (Benton, 2002).

References

Arnold, D. *Police Power and Colonial Rule: Madras 1859–1947*. Oxford University Press, 1986.

Benton, L. *Law and Colonial Cultures*. Cambridge University Press, 2002.

Dunstall, G. 'Frontier and/or cultural fragment? Interpretations of violence in colonial New Zealand', *Social History*, 29, 1, 2004, pp. 59–83.

Emsley, C. 'A typology of nineteenth-century police', *Crime, histoire & sociétés/ Crime, History and Societies*, 3, 1, 1999, pp. 29–44.

Finnane, M. 'The varieties of policing: colonial Queensland, 1860–1900' in Anderson, D. M. and Killingray, D. (eds), *Policing the Empire: Government, Authority and Control, 1830–1940*. Manchester University Press, 1991.

Finnane, M. *Police and Government: Histories of Policing in Australia*. Oxford University Press, 1994.

Finnane, M. *Punishment in Australian Society*. Oxford University Press, 1997.

Godfrey, B. 'Counting and accounting for the decline in non-lethal violence in England, Australia and New Zealand', *British Journal of Criminology*, 43, 2003, pp. 340–53

Hill, R. 'The policing of colonial New Zealand: from informal to formal control, 1840–1907', in Anderson, D. M. and Killingray, D. (eds), *Policing the Empire: Government, Authority and Control, 1830–1940*. Manchester University Press, 1991.

Kelsey, J. 'Legal imperialism and the colonisation of Aotearoa', in Spoonley, P., Macpherson, C., Pearson, D. and Sedgwick, C. (eds), *Tauiwi*. Dunmore Press, 1984.

Kolff, D. H. A. 'The Indian and British law machines: some remarks on law and society in British India', in Mommsen, W. J. and De Moor, J. A. (eds), *European Expansion and Law*. Berg, 1992.

Mann, K. and Roberts, R. (eds), *Law in Colonial Africa*. Heinemann, 1991.

Mommsen, W. J. and De Moor, J. A. (eds), *European Expansion and Law*. Berg, 1992.

Morris, N. and Rothman, D.J. (eds), *The Oxford History of the Prison*. Oxford University Press, 1995.

Philips, D. 'A "Weak" State? The English state, the magistracy and the reform of policing in the 1830s', *English Historical Review*, 119, 2004, pp. 873–91.

Pratt, J. *Punishment in a Perfect Society. The New Zealand Penal System 1840–1939*. Victoria University Press, 1992.

Robb, P. 'The ordering of rural India: the policing of nineteenth-century Bengal and Bihar', in Anderson, D. M. and Killingray, D. (eds), *Policing the Empire: Government, Authority and Control, 1830–1940*. Manchester University Press, 1991.

Ward, A. *A Show of Justice: racial 'amalgamation' in nineteenth century New Zealand*. Auckland University Press, 1995.

Windschuttle, K. *The Fabrication of Aboriginal History*. Macleay Press, 2002.

Chapter 2

The changes in policing and penal policy in nineteenth-century Europe

Clive Emsley

Between the French Revolution and the outbreak of the First World War, what might be termed 'the long nineteenth century', there were enormous changes in the personnel and practices of European criminal justice systems. At the beginning of the twentieth century the victim of a criminal offence could report his or her misfortune to the functionary of a professional, bureaucratic policing institution. The institution then took over the detection, if necessary, and apprehension of the offender, and at no charge to the victim. One hundred years earlier such policing institutions scarcely existed. At the beginning of the twentieth century the perpetrator of a criminal offence was perceived as a 'criminal', and was labelled as such in the press, by a wide range of experts and social commentators, and by the police and the courts. She or more probably he was seen as offending through her own choice or increasingly because of some sort of moral or social defect. One hundred years earlier there was little perception of the 'criminal' as a being from a distinct class or a recognisable social group, and no notion of her or him being mentally or morally defective. At the beginning of the twentieth century, once arrested, an individual accused of an offence was processed through one of the state's courts; there were different levels of court, but there were legal codes that covered entire nation states and the empires of central and eastern Europe. One hundred years earlier even the most centralised state could have a multitude of legal codes. Moreover, at the end of the eighteenth century many offences were resolved within the local community using infra-judicial methods by which decisions or agreements were reached under the direction of a *curé*, a *seigneur's* agent, or some well-respected member of the community. Some form of folkloric vigilantism might resolve other offences, especially those apparently committed by outsiders. At the beginning of the twentieth century the principal punishment available for convicted offenders was generally recognised to be the prison, and while there was often a pendulum effect between punishment and reformation, the prison was also seen as a way to treat and change – to reform – those offenders that were not hardened recidivists. One hundred years earlier there was a range of punishments; many involved shaming the offender, very few aimed directly at reformation.

It is relatively easy to identify shifts and changes in police and policing, in the availability of nationally uniform legal codes, in the perception of the 'criminal' and in the use of prison as punishment. It is rather more difficult to account for them. It used to be assumed that bad, barbaric practices, the vestiges of feudalism and the medieval period, were replaced by rational, humane systems. But if this was the case, and this is something that will be discussed below, this does not explain why the new systems and practices that were established were the ones to be chosen. These new systems and practices were not the only ways in which change could have been managed. What follows is an essay designed to highlight the changes and to raise some of the issues that need to be considered in explaining them. It is organised under three broad and overlapping headings: the pattern of change; cause and effect; and national and international perspectives and interrelationships.

The pattern of change

It is easy to slip into the idea that historical change is linear. But change sometimes goes by fits and starts, and it does not always go in the same direction, especially in what might be called a progressive direction. The changes outlined above were once perceived as moving from the vestiges of a barbaric, 'primitive' medieval system of trial and punishment to a rational and more humane system. There are elements that suit this interpretation. Nineteenth-century legal systems appear more rational and systematic. In the most serious cases they no longer depended on playing a game of mercy that was dispensed by a prince in a way that enhanced the prince's authority and power (Davis, 1987). In the less serious cases they no longer permitted a master or patriarch to beat an offending servant or wife, and no longer allowed a suspect-outsider to be shamed and brutalised, sometimes even killed, by an outraged local community (Emsley, 1997: 168–71). Executions and punishments in general became less spectacular, less physically violent and less public. They gave way to the prison, and where punishment was to be inflicted on an offender's body, this was increasingly done behind the prison walls. Some legal codes, even in countries with particularly violent forms of criminality such as the new nation state of Italy, went so far as to abolish the death penalty. The early nineteenth-century attempt to provide for the religious and moral reform of the prisoner – which in itself arguably was a progressive shift away from leaving those awaiting trial, those serving a sentence and those awaiting execution, male, female, child and adult, all mixed together in the same institution – gave way to rational, scientific explanations of offending and to 'treatment'.

Many penal reformers argued that their ideas were progressive and humanitarian, and that they thus fitted in with the new enlightened, rational and progressive age. Cesare Beccaria, whose acclaimed *Dei Delitti e delle Pene* was first published in 1764, was a man of the Enlightenment. So too were those eighteenth-century reformers who, in many instances, had already come to a similar intellectual standpoint regarding crime and punishment from their own experience and understanding, and who took up his ideas enthusiastically (Porret, 1997, 2003). The early nineteenth-century beliefs about the reformation of convicts were formed by a progressive view of the nature of individual human beings that grew out of Enlightenment thinking. Convicts were to be encouraged to understand their place in a hierarchical society by being given work in prison, and they were to understand their wrongdoing by being given a Bible, silence and solitude in which to reflect on their behaviour. The later nineteenth-century beliefs that science might be used to treat and hence to reform offenders had similar origins but were rooted in a different strand of rationality and new forms of thinking.

At the beginning of the twenty-first century, people are less comfortable with ideas of the 'progress' of western civilisation, and perhaps less comfortable also with Enlightenment rationality. Moreover, modern historians are more inclined to contextualise Enlightenment ideologies and to see them less clearly as progressive ideals shaping a progressive modern world. Beccaria may have argued for more rational punishments and for the abolition of the death penalty, but he also proposed replacing capital punishment with forced labour, in public, for life. Early nineteenth-century penal reformers debated the respective possibilities of work regimes, solitary confinement, complete anonymity through prison uniforms and face masks, and total silence as ways of both punishing and reforming offenders. But compelling prisoners to silence, solitude and a loss of identity prompted some to suicide and drove others mad.

Moreover, compelling prisoners to pointless work so as to teach them the 'virtue' of work and of their social situation reflected a narrow class perception of who was criminal. The early nineteenth-century offender was seen as an individual making rational choices and choosing to reject the values and virtues espoused by respectable society for a life of drink, idleness and luxury. The persistence of criminality, as manifested in the records of the new, bureaucratic nation states, and the offender's failure to conform contributed to a shift in the perception of criminality. Criminal behaviour was seen increasingly less as an offender's choice and more as an offender's physical and mental inheritance (Becker, 2002). The problem was seen more and more as one that needed to be addressed by the burgeoning medical and social sciences; but while such sciences were perceived as progressive, their proposed remedies often appear cruel and stark. Bringing medical science into the treatment of offenders led to some young women being labelled as fit only for life in an institution simply because they had shown themselves morally at fault by giving birth to an illegitimate child. The interaction of medical science with Social Darwinism fostered the new science of eugenics, and this, in turn, led to the extreme 'scientific' proposals for lifetime incarceration or the sterilisation of moral defectives. 'If these *habituées* were confined for life,' declared J. Bruce Thomson, the doctor of Perth Prison and a father figure to the eugenics movement, 'the residue outside would be small, and the propagation of the criminal class prevented' (Rafter, 1997: 82). The experts might have stressed their humanitarianism and their reforming beliefs, but such humanitarianism and beliefs are relative.

The traditional view of police, law and penal reform being progressive and increasingly driven by humanitarianism and rationality slots easily into the Whig interpretation of history. This interpretation was first described by a quintessentially English historian (Butterfield, 1931),[1] but it suits well the more general European perspective of the superiority of European civilisation that developed in the nineteenth century and outlived the trauma of the First World War. In the fields of crime and criminal justice history, as elsewhere, the Whig perspective was never set out formally as an explanation for change. Rather it was assumed by those who wrote about these subjects and the assumption was essentially a narrative of progressive, linear change driven by far-sighted reformers groping towards modern forms. Few would subscribe to this inter-pretation in the contemporary world, and the recent growth of the history of crime and criminal justice has been much more consciously informed by systematic attempts to theorise patterns of change. Interestingly, this use of theory has coincided with a period during which some historians have argued for a new focus on narrative rather than 'coherent scientific explanations of change' (Stone, 1979). But perhaps the history of policing

11

and penal institutions is closer to work in the social sciences than to much traditional history and a range of theories has been used in the new research. Some of the most influential of the first historians working in the area, while not necessarily Marxist, drew on a conceptualisation of history that stressed class conflict rather than consensus.[2] Others have looked to Émile Durkheim's stress on the shift to urban societies with the resulting *anomie* and normlessness, and to his insistence that crime is 'normal' within society and important for establishing and maintaining boundaries.[3] Still others have found value in Norbert Elias's 'civilising process' or Michel Foucault's ideas regarding the structures of power and the growth of surveillance and discipline.[4] All of these concepts and perspectives have been fruitful in stimulating new questions and new research. As ever, danger arises when a concept or theory ceases to be a tool and becomes the guiding principle, but the sensible application of theory enables at least an initial marshalling of evidence and the formulation of questions.

It is impossible to deny the existence of class conflict in nineteenth-century European society and the theorising that situated a criminal class in the lowest depths of the working class replete with all the vices that the respectable middle class condemned – idleness, drunkenness, love of luxury and so forth. But a genuine humanitarianism and a commitment to a new sensibility could motivate even the most class-conscious prison reformer. Equally there were shifting structures of power and a growth in control mechanisms managed by new kinds of expert, all of which were reflected in policing and prison developments. But again there could be genuine humanitarian commitment, and experts were never given blank cheques or carte blanche. Governments always kept some rein on expenditure, notably in prisons, and they also kept an eye on what was acceptable and agreeable at least to the articulate and hence influential public. Nineteenth-century Europeans considered themselves to be more civilised than their predecessors, and this belief was rooted in significant differences in behaviours and sensibilities that impacted upon criminal justice systems. None of these developments is mutually exclusive, which would suggest that an eclectic use of theory to explore changes in policing and penal policy is ultimately more rewarding than becoming a true believer.[5]

Cause and effect

A series of changes have been identified in policing, in the understanding of offenders, in law codes and in prisons. They are interlinked in as much as they are all part of criminal justice systems and structures, but can they all be linked to similar intellectual origins? The Enlightenment with its innate ideas of humanity, progress and rationality might be considered as furnishing these intellectual origins, always providing that the old Whig ideas of a progressive movement in history are treated with the appropriate circumspection. But finding intellectual origins does not help in explaining a multitude of specific changes across many different countries.

The history of criminal justice, like much other history, tends to be written with a focus on a single country. It also tends to be researched and written with a focus on a single issue or institution. Thus the change in the structure of policing in nineteenth-century England has been attributed to far-sighted reformers seeking to control an increase in crime and disorder. More recently the same changes have been interpreted as issuing from a perceived need to domesticate the new workforce called into being by changes in the economic and urban structure. These are mirror images that are based, respectively, on consensual and conflictual views of society. Moreover the former tends to take at face value the arguments presented by police reformers that crime was rising, while the latter can imply that urban worthies and new industrialists had few reservations about financing a new system of control. Crime statistics are notoriously un-reliable for proving a rise in crime, though they may contribute to contemporary fears about such a rise. It seems possible that the collection and publication of national crime statistics for the first time in the early nineteenth century made people much more aware of crime as a national 'problem'. The statistics showed increases, though what these increases actually meant remains the subject of heated debate (Taylor, 1998a, 1998b, 1999; Morris, 2001). Proving a rise in disorder is equally difficult, though the violence of the Gordon Riots and of Luddism and the reports of the *journées* of the French Revolution generated new concerns about the potential threat from protesting crowds. There is plenty of evidence to show that many London vestries resented the cost of the new police because they were required to pay an increased rate for a force over which, unlike the old watch, they had no control (Emsley, 1996: 26–7). Moreover, in the West Riding of Yorkshire it appears that industrialists in the worsted industry preferred their private police to any county or borough institutions; these men controlled the factory, but had little interest in working-class behaviour beyond the workplace (Godfrey, 2002). A history of English policing in the nineteenth century has to take account of these problems and complexities. Does it need also to take account of the significant changes in policing that were taking place simultaneously across much of the continent of Europe?

Shifting the focus to continental Europe shows some parallels with the English experience, but also many differences. It may be a statement of the blindingly obvious but it remains worth stressing that processes of change in different countries and regions do not start from the same point and do not carry the same baggage in the sense of traditions, understandings and practices. On continental Europe the activities of revolutionary crowds also generated anxieties. The term the 'dangerous classes' was coined by a French police bureaucrat working in Paris in the 1830s and 1840s. Similar books by other police officials elsewhere in Europe contributed to a growing perception of a dangerous, criminal class that was distinct from the rest of society, preferred idleness to honest labour and lived, when possible, by the proceeds of crime (Frégier, 1840; Avé-Lallement, 1858–62). There were collections and analyses of national crime statistics for the first time which, as in England, fostered concerns of crime constituting a national problem.[6] But the states of continental Europe had different traditions of policing, law and legal processes. Most of them also had a different experience with the physical presence of French soldiers and French administrators on their territories at the end of the eighteenth and beginning of the nineteenth centuries.

The French Revolution and the Revolutionary and Napoleonic wars swept aside much of the old order. They also provided an example of a centralised, relatively effective criminal justice system to those territories incorporated into France and the French empire, to those temporarily bound to it as satellites and allies, and also to those who spent most of the time confronting it. Legal thinking in restoration Germany was commonly based on Enlightenment ideas mediated through the Code Napoléon and Kantian perspectives of using the law both to deter and to carry out retribution. The penal code promulgated for Bavaria in 1813 was the earliest and the most influential of the new codes drawing on these ideas. The creation or maintenance of military gendarmeries across Europe had similar origins to the new legal codes. The gendarmeries' tasks were to show the flag and to establish a new system of reciprocity in which the citizens yielded regular taxes and conscripts and the state provided its citizens with a degree of protection from criminal offenders and assistance in case of natural disasters (Emsley, 1999a). The new approaches to law and the new gendarmeries also enhanced the power and authority of the prince and his government. This was a different enhancement from the old lottery of pardon and mercy. The law was formally written, it claimed to be based on rationality, and often it claimed some legitimacy from its citizens. It also enabled the prince and his government to reduce further the power and authority of rivals in the shape of some municipalities, the church, and the nobility and gentry. Landowners, as in Prussia up until the end of the

First World War for example, might still have some jurisdiction over their labourers, but overwhelmingly the law was seen as emanating from the central state. Enlightenment ideas, the French example and self-interest all contributed to the central state's determination to push ahead with many of the changes in policing and penal policy on continental Europe. But even authoritarian or apparently successful monarchies could not press change unchallenged in nineteenth-century Europe.

The Congress of Vienna settled the Rhenish provinces of Napoleon's empire on the Kingdom of Prussia. But in preference to the Prussian *Allgemeines Landrecht* of 1794 the Rhinelanders wanted their new masters to let them keep the progressive French code under which they had prospered and seen banditry significantly repressed. There was also the problem that most of the lawyers and judges in the region had been trained in French law and were insufficiently familiar with the Prussian forms. The government in Berlin reluctantly agreed that their new western provinces should be allowed to keep the Napoleonic Code until a revision of the two codes could be made. The King of Prussia was surprised when his law commissioners concluded that the legal principles of the French system were superior, and the eventual revision was not what the victors of 1814 and 1815 had in mind. In 1849 Louis Simons, a Rhenish born lawyer, became minister of justice in Berlin. The revised legal code of the Prussian monarchy that was promulgated in 1851 had several roots. It drew on Enlightenment ideas set out by Beccaria and on the philosophical thinking of Kant; both of these had influenced Paul Anselm von Feuerbach in drafting the Bavarian Code of 1813. But, through the influence of Simons and jurists like him, the new Prussian Code also drew heavily on the Napoleonic model and the legal structure that the Rhinelanders had held out for in the wake of the French defeat. Twenty years after it was established for Prussia this code became the basis of the code for the new German Empire – *Reichsstrafgesetzbuch* (Engelbrecht, 1999; Wetzell, 2000: 74).

The unification of Italy brought a unified criminal code much sooner for the new state than was the situation in Germany. It seems possible that local pride may have had an impact on the way local magistrates responded to the imposition of the Piedmontese code in Italy. In Tuscany, where there was a long, proud tradition of legal liberalism that went back to the reforms of Grand Duke Leopold in the 1780s, the liberal criminal code was allowed to continue after unification. This could create tensions in the courts as, for example, at the celebrated trial of Castillo Grandi for child murder in the 1870s. Grandi's judges combined Tuscans from the old liberal tradition with a Roman schooled in the fearsome criminal code of Pope Gregory XVI (Guarnieri, 1993). When a new and specifically Italian code was promulgated in 1889 the death penalty was rejected in deference to Tuscan liberalism.

The death penalty was virtually re-established in Prussia and then in Imperial Germany as a result of pressure exerted by Bismarck. For the sake of a united Germany the parliamentary Liberals withdrew their opposition to Bismarck's insistence that capital punishment be inserted in the new criminal code. States in the new empire that had previously renounced the death penalty were now compelled to bring it back (Evans, 1996: 329–47). But setting the German experience of capital punishment alongside other forms of punishment and the experience of other countries also warns against reductive assumptions that only authoritarian states have violent, punitive laws. Corporal punishment was abolished in most German states during the liberal ascendancy in 1848. There was an attempt to revive it in the restored authoritarianism of Prussia during the 1850s. But this failed and while Bismarck and his ministers pressed for the death penalty in 1871, their new penal code abolished corporal punishment (Evans, 1998: 105–14). Nineteenth-century Britain prided itself on its constitution, its liberalism and its lack of revolution; in 1914 it went to war against 'Prussian militarism'. Yet nineteenth-century Britain maintained a harsh penal code. Abolitionists were virtually silent after the end of public executions in 1868. The punishment of flogging was resuscitated in the 1860s as a means of dealing with violent offenders following a scare about street robbery. Flogging remained an option available to the courts until 1948, and to prison authorities until 1967. Moreover the British army that went to war in 1914 functioned under a military code that, in terms of the range of offences punishable by death and the lack of any form of appeal, was harsher than either the code of its principal ally – the French Third Republic – or that of its principal opponent – Imperial Germany (Oram, 2001: 93–110).

National and international perspectives and interrelationships

Much academic history is written from a national perspective. There are several reasons for this. Some are relatively trivial, like the unfortunate English tendency to remain proudly monoglot. Probably much more significant is the fact that serious academic history began with the emergence of the nation state during the nineteenth century and took politics and international affairs as its main focus. Even when the focus shifted towards economic or social developments, the national element has remained significant. Crime and criminal justice history emerged as a branch of social history, but they also require an awareness of law and legal structure. Some laws and legal structures can be rooted in the medieval period, and some of the early professional historians of the nineteenth century spent considerable time seeking out such origins. But the major changes in policing and penal policy during the nineteenth century occurred across Europe. Indeed, they occurred *across* what might be termed the European world, that is countries with a dominant European culture: the United States, Australia, Canada, New Zealand, much of Latin America. Thus any study that focuses entirely on one national experience must be missing something.

The rational ideology of the Enlightenment as an important element feeding in to the understanding of the 'criminal' has already been stressed, as have the scientific assumptions of Social Darwinism of later generations. Similarly the statistical element of the embryonic social sciences, popular novels and the writings of police bureaucrats and journalists who categorised the criminal and dangerous classes, exposed their *argot* and described their haunts had a cumulative effect on the understanding of the expanding reading public. It is also worth stressing the role of the new nation state and the new relationship between state and those increasingly seen as citizens. The law codes of the new nation states were the sole legal authority and they promised the fair administration of justice for all. In central Europe especially the concept of the *Rechtsstaat* was developed. This was a state governed by law, whose functionaries could not act arbitrarily but were under and answerable to the law. The Russian Empire may in general be a poor example, nevertheless one reason for the development of the Corps of Gendarmes within the notorious Third Section was to check corruption and arbitrary behaviour by members of the imperial bureaucracy. Occasionally, even in notoriously militaristic Prussia, poor, private individuals took state functionaries, including gendarmes, to court for various abuses (Emsley, 1999a: 219, 240).

There were regions and communities that largely rejected the state, its laws and its functionaries. Southern Europe is commonly singled out here as having regions – notably Corsica, Sicily, parts of Greece and the Balkan states – where concepts of honour and vendetta thrived. Local men of power and influence, rather than representatives of the state and its law, continued to be the first resort of people who had suffered personal injury or wrong. In Sicily these local entrepreneurs of power included a cross section of post-unification society ranging from bandits and cattle rustlers, up through estate wardens and managers, farmers and lawyers. These men were not the romantic upholders of family honour and community norms, but entrepreneurs in what one nineteenth-century investigator, Leopoldo Franchetti, labelled 'the violence industry'. They stepped into the vacuum left by the end of the Bourbon monarchy and its variant of feudalism to establish protection rackets that extorted money from local businesses (Dickie, 2004: ch. 1).[7] In all of these regions individuals might be murdered in broad daylight in crowded places, but no witnesses saw anything or were prepared to give evidence to state investigators. In other instances the victor in a plebeian knife fight was happy to have his day in court. The state might punish him with a fine or a prison sentence, but a court appearance gave the accused the opportunity to rehearse the assertion of his honour and prowess, and the humiliation of his opponent (Gallant, 2000; Blok, 1988; Wilson, 1988). Nineteenth-century jurists and police agents condemned this as barbaric, primitive behaviour. Italian jurists and administrators from the north of the peninsula, with their ideas reinforced by the work of Cesare Lombroso and his acolytes, saw their fellow countrymen from the *Mezzogiorno* and the islands as at a different and lower level of civilisation. This, they feared, had been aggravated by the infusion of Arab blood centuries earlier. Even those who rejected such ideas tended to situate Sicily's problems in economic and social backwardness (Pick, 1989: 114–15; Dickie, 2004: 87–91). The biggest problem, however, and one which makes the relationship between the Italian mainland and Sicily stand out, was the inclination of Italian politicians to strike bargains with Sicily's violent entrepreneurs and hence to allow the system to become infused into the body politic of the newly united nation.

In some instances the new agent of the state appears very gradually to have assumed some of the attributes of the traditional, well-respected community leader who had dispensed infra-judicial resolutions. The American anthropologist Sydel Silverman found a *mareschiallo* of the Carabinieri occasionally acting in such a manner in Umbria during the 1960s, though again, this may have been villagers using the state's representative to rehearse their success in a particular community contest (Silverman, 1975: 141, 242 n.7). A new agent of the state might also bring change to a community, not directly as central government may have intended, but through enforcing the law to the benefit of those who had little voice within the community. Geoffroy Le Clercq, for example, has shown how in rural Belgium the state gendarme could be the man to help the victim of a rape when the dominant members of the male community were prepared to resolve the matter without recourse to law (Le Clercq, 1999). These examples also serve to illustrate a classic chicken and egg problem. Did the new functionaries usurp and abolish the old infra-judical practices, or did they move into a vacuum left by other social changes? In particular areas of France, for example, it appears that the old practices were already disintegrating as the new legal code and its agents moved in. Fewer and fewer men of authority appear to have been prepared to fulfil the old extra-judicial role of arbitrator. Agreements that had once been made before *curés*, seigneurial agents and magistrates were now made before men such as innkeepers who could never carry the same sort of authority even among the consenting parties (Ploux, 1992). But here, too, it is important to be aware of regional and national contrasts and peculiarities. In Sicily it was the entrepreneurs of violence who stepped into the vacuum left by the end of the old order. Those agents of the new state who sought to enforce the state's laws often found themselves undermined by their superiors' preparedness to do deals with what was to become a state within the state – mafia.

The decline of infra-judicial practices involved shifting social relationships within countries as well as action by the state and it was something that happened broadly *across* Europe. It is easier to identify and compare the actions of different states than the shifts in social relationships that can take place over a very long period with no clearly identifiable beginning. The states' aspirations can be seen in legislation, ordinances, the physical situation of police and legal officers, their offices and their courts across the country. Shifting social relationships between the members of local communities during the nineteenth century probably drew little on the observations of what was happening elsewhere, though those men from the social group that made up mayors probably did observe their neighbours and may have made the decisions to back away from infra-judicial resolutions as a result of this. In France at least, the mayor was increasingly a man of the state rather than just a man of the local community. Reformers and individuals at the centre of government or government institutions, however, commonly looked at what was happening elsewhere, sought to learn from it and mould the developments of success in one country into change within their own country. This happened with reference to police, laws and penal sanctions.

The way in which the French gendarmerie system was adopted elsewhere in Europe has already been mentioned. There was also considerable interest in the civilian-style metropolitan police established in London in 1829. Napoleon III required that several of its characteristics be adopted in Paris in the 1850s. Cities as far apart as Bologna and Hamburg wrote to Scotland Yard for information about different aspects of the force. The parliament of the newly unified Italy debated the positive merits of *il bobby inglesi* during the 1860s, but decided that the population that Cavour had determined to turn into Italians was not yet ready for the unarmed, English-style Bobby (Emsley, 1999b). But whereas there were exchanges between national and municipal police authorities about best practice, police cooperation tended to founder on the rocks of national pride and separateness. Only the violent behaviour of anarchists and anxieties about white slave traffic brought delegates together at the turn of the century to discuss international policing measures (Deflem, 2002: ch. 1). Penal reformers, in contrast, had long exchanged ideas and met in international congresses.

Prison reformers were exchanging ideas across frontiers from at least the last third of the eighteenth century. In particular, a significant network corresponded and transmitted pamphlet material across the Atlantic. This began as exchanges between individuals, but by the beginning of the nineteenth century there were organised groups such as the Philadelphia Society for Alleviating the Miseries of Public Prisons and the British Society for Diffusing Information upon the Punishment of Death. The Philadelphia society acknowledged the English penal reformer John Howard as its inspiration, but by the end of the Napoleonic wars British reformers were arguing that Britain could learn from the progressive penal experiments that were being tried in the infant United States (Burgoyne, 1997). Official and semi-official delegations crossed the Atlantic from both Britain and France to investigate the American prisons of Auburn, in New York State, and Cherry Hill, in Philadelphia, with their varying systems of solitude and labour. The French looked also to develop the British use of transportation for their own incorrigibles. The British, and others, looked to the French experiments in the reformation of juvenile male offenders in the school established at Mettray, near Tours in 1838 (O'Brien, 1982: 23, 263–4; Wright, 1983: 72–7, 95, 140, 145; Ignatieff, 1978: 194–7; Radzinowicz and Hood, 1990: 158–61).

By the mid-1840s international meetings were being organised formally for government functionaries to exchange ideas and make recommendations on penal matters. The first two International Penitentiary Congresses, for example, held at Frankfurt-am-Main in 1846 and Brussels in 1847, recommended the use of the separate system. But within twenty years, across the continent, the consensus saw this practice falling from favour as the cure-all for criminal behaviour. The growth of national statistics and of scientific information about offenders – photographs, fingerprints, Bertillonage and so forth – highlighted the extent of recidivism. This, in turn, fostered the more concentrated focus by doctors, legal experts and social scientists on the criminal as an individual. The official international prison congresses met with greater regularity: London (1872), Stockholm (1878), Rome (1885), St Petersburg (1890), Paris (1895), Brussels (1900), Budapest (1905), Washington, DC (1910). They were paralleled by meetings of the International Criminal Anthropology Congress – Rome (1885), Paris (1889), Brussels (1892), Geneva (1896), Amsterdam (1901), Turin (1906), Cologne (1911). The first of these was convened by the disciples of the Italian criminologist Cesare Lombroso but, from the outset, there were fierce debates between experts over the origins and cause of criminality. In 1889 some of the reformers who participated in these congresses came together in the *Internationale Kriminalistische Vereinigung*. This international union of criminal law was driven by a young, Viennese-born professor of Criminal Law, Franz von List, who had established his own criminological institute at the University of Halle and was shortly to move to Berlin. List and his collaborators were keen to explore issues comparatively and to campaign for what they perceived as progressive changes in penal institutions and systems.[8] They developed the concept of *psychopathische Minderwertigkeiten* (psychopathic defects) that, before 1914, was virtually interchangeable with the idea of criminality being the result of degeneracy but, subsequently, took its own, separate path. The union's successes in changing legal codes and procedures to ensure that the offender was 'treated' rather than simply 'punished' were relatively limited before the First World War. Nevertheless, it played an important role in formulating the idea of criminology as a body of knowledge based on scientific pretensions (Wetzell, 2000: 33, 38, 40–2, 83–90; Nye, 1984: 97).

There are no startling conclusions here. This has been designed as an introductory and explanatory essay to indicate the scale of the changes and developments in policing and penal policies over the long nineteenth century. By implication it has suggested the value of cross-cultural and cross-national comparisons, something that many historians and criminologists have often appeared reluctant to attempt, but the importance of which has been urged elsewhere in a collection ranging widely over the European world (Godfrey, Emsley and Dunstall, 2003). With its stress on the extent of the changes, the way that they impacted across all areas of society and involved both top-down and bottom-up pressures, the chapter has argued also the need for theory but for an eclectic use of theory to probe the issues. Finally, it has urged the historian of policing and penal change to develop awareness of international developments, and of developments beyond what are often the usual local frontiers of historical research.

Notes

1. The numerous subsequent editions testify to the persistence of the interpretation.
2. Marx himself wrote remarkably little on the subject of crime and the criminal justice system. His best known article on the subject appeared in the *Rheinische Zeitung* in 1842 and discussed the debates about the law of wood theft. See Lascombes and Zander (1984).

3. The writings of Durkheim most often cited by historians of crime and criminal justice would appear to be *Le suicide*, 1897 (numerous translations) and *De la division du travail social: Étude sur l'organisation des sociétés supérieurs*, 1893 (numerous translations as *The Division of Labour in Society*).

4. The key texts here are Elias, 1939 (translated as *The Civilising Process*, Oxford University Press, 1978 and 1982) and Michel Foucault, *Surveiller et punir: Naissance de la prison*, Éditions Gallimard, 1975 (translated as *Discipline and Punish: The Birth of the Prison*, Allen Lane, 1977). The English translation of Elias's title loses some of the subtlety of the original. *Prozess* in German can mean 'trial' as well as 'process'. Elias does not suggest that societies can be judged as either civilised or uncivilised in any final sense and as the Whig historians often appear to have done; rather, he was interested in the shifting balance and the understanding of 'civilising' processes.

5. For an attempt to explore the theories of Marx, Foucault and Durkheim with reference to changing attitudes to punishment see Garland (1991). For an interesting attempt to combine the work of Elias and Durkheim in theorising the pattern of violence see Thome (2001).

6. For an introduction see the special edition of *Déviance et société*, 22, 2, 1998, *La statistique judiciaire: son histoire et ses usages scientifiques*.

7. For Franchetti's analysis following his explorations with Sidney Sonnino in 1876 see Dickie (2004: 47–54).

8. They sponsored, for example, a study of the policing systems of England. Budding (1908) made comparisons between the English and German policing systems and recommended a move towards the English practices of greater reliance on the discretion of individual officers and less form filling and report writing. The Home Office was flattered and impressed: see PRO HO 45/103/148769.

References

Avé-Lallement, F. C. B. *Das deutsche Gaunerthum in seiner social-politischen, literarischen und linguistischen Ausbildung zu seinem heutigen Bestände*, 4 vols. Leipzig, 1858–62.

Becker, P. *Verderbnis und Entartung: Eine Geschicte der Kriminologie des 19. Jahrhunderts als Diskurs und Praxis*. Vandenhoeck & Ruprecht, 2002.

Blok, A. *The Mafia of a Sicilian Village, 1860–1960: A Study of Violent Peasant Entrepreneurs*, 2nd edn. Polity Press, 1988.

Budding, C. *Die Polizie in Stadt und Land in Großbritannien*. Guttentag, 1908.

Burgoyne, C. C. '"Imprisonment the Best Punishment": The Transatlantic Exchange and Communication of Ideas in the Field of Penology, 1750–1820'. Unpublished PhD, University of Sunderland, 1997.

Butterfield, H. *The Whig Interpretation of History*. G. Bell & Sons, 1931.

Davis, N. Z. *Fiction in the Archives: Pardon Tales and their Tellers in Sixteenth-Century France*. Polity Press, 1987.

Deflem, M. *Policing World Society: Historical Foundations of International Police Cooperation*. Oxford University Press, 2002.

Dickie, J. *Cosa Nostra: A History of the Sicilian Mafia*. Hodder & Stoughton, 2004.

Elias, N. *The Civilising Process*. Oxford University Press, 1978 and 1982.

Emsley, C. *The English Police: A Political and Social History*, 2nd edn. Longman, 1996.

Emsley, C. 'The nation state, the law and the peasant in nineteenth-century Europe', in Lévy, R. and Rousseaux, X. (eds), *Le pénal dans tous ses États: Justice, États et sociétés en Europe (XIIe–XXe siècles)*. Publications des Facultés Universitaires Saint-Louis, 1997.

Emsley, C. *Gendarmes and the State in Nineteenth-Century Europe*. Oxford University Press, 1999a.

Emsley, C. 'A typology of nineteenth-century police', *Crime, histoire et sociétés/ Crime, History and Societies*, 3, 1, 1999b, pp. 29–44.

Engelbrecht, J. 'The French model and German society: the impact of the *Code pénal* on the Rhineland', in Rousseaux, X., Dupont-Bouchat, M. and Vael, C. (eds), *Révolutuions et justice pénal en Europe: Modèles français et traditions nationales (1780–1830)*. L'Harmattan, 1999.

Evans, R. J. *Rituals of Retribution: Capital Punishment in Germany 1600–1987*. Oxford University Press, 1996.

Evans, R. J. *Tales from the German Underworld*. Yale University Press, 1998.

Foucault, M. *Discipline and Punish: The Birth of the Prison*. Allen Lane, 1977.

Frégier, H.A. *Des classes dangereuses de la population dans les grandes villes et des moyens de les rendre meilleures*, 2 vols. Paris, 1840.

Gallant, T. W. 'Honor, masculinity, and ritual knife fighting in nineteenth-century Greece', *American Historical Review*, 105, 2, 2000, pp. 359–82.

Garland, D. *Punishment and Modern Society: A Study in Social Theory*. Clarendon Press, 1991.

Godfrey, B. 'Private policing and the workplace: the Worsted Committee and the policing of labor in Northern England, 1840–1880', in Knafla, L. A. (ed.), *Policing and War in Europe: Criminal Justice History*, 16. Greenwood, 2002, pp. 87–106.

Godfrey, B., Emsley, C. and Dunstall, G. (eds), *Comparative Histories of Crime*. Willan, 2003.

Guarnieri, P. *A Case of Child Murder: Law and Science in Nineteenth-Century Tuscany*. Polity Press, 1993.

Ignatieff, M. *A Just Measure of Pain: The Penitentiary in the Industrial Revolution*. Macmillan, 1978.

Lascombes, P. and Zander, H. *Marx: du 'vol de bois' à la critique du droit*. Presses Universitaires de France, 1984.

Le Clercq, G. 'Violences sexuelles, scandale et ordre public. Le regard du législateur, de la justice et des autres acteurs sociaux au 19 siècle', *Belgisch Tijdschrift voor Nieuwste Geschiedenis/Revue Belge d'histoire contemporaine*, 28, 1–2, 1999, pp. 5–53.

Morris, R. M. '"Lies, damned lies and criminal statistics": Reinterpreting the criminal statistics in England and Wales', *Crime, histoire et sociétés/Crime, History and Societies*, 5, 1, 2001, pp. 111–27.

Nye, R. A. *Crime, Madness and Politics in Modern France: The Medical Concept of National Decline*. Princeton University Press, 1984.

O'Brien, P. *The Promise of Punishment: Prisons in Nineteenth-Century France*. Princeton University Press, 1982.

Oram, G. '"The administration of discipline by the English is very rigid": British military law and the death penalty (1868–1918)', *Crime, histoire et sociétés/Crime, History and Societies*, 5, 1, 2001, pp. 93–110.

Pick, P. *Faces of Degeneration: A European Disorder, c.1848–c.1918*. Cambridge University Press, 1989.

Ploux, F. 'L'"arrangement" dans les campagnes du Haut-Quercy (1815–1850)', *Histoire de la Justice*, 5, 1992, pp. 95–115.

Porret, M. (ed.), *Beccaria et la culture juridique des lumières*. Librairie Droz, 1997.

Porret, M. *Beccaria: Le Droit de punir*. Éditions Michalon, 2003.

Radzinowicz, L. and Hood, R. *The Emergence of Penal Policy in Victorian and Edwardian England*. Clarendon Press, 1990.

Rafter, N. H. *Creating Born Criminals*. University of Illinois Press, 1997.

Silverman, S. *Three Bells of Civilization: The Life of an Italian Hill Town*. Columbia University Press, 1975.

Stone, L. 'The revival of narrative: reflections on a new old history', *Past and Present*, 85, 1979, pp. 3–24.

Taylor, H. 'The politics of the rising crime statistics in England and Wales, 1914–1960', *Crime, histoire et sociétés/Crime, History and Societies*, 2, 1, 1998a, pp. 5–28.

Taylor, H. 'Rationing crime: the political economy of the criminal statistics since the 1850s', *Economic History Review*, 51, 3, 1998b, pp. 569–90.

Taylor, H. 'Forging the job', *British Journal of Criminology*, 39, 1999, pp. 113–35.

Thome, H. 'Explaining long term trends in violent crime', *Crime, histoire et sociétés/Crime, History and Societies*, 5, 2, 2001, pp. 69–86.

Wetzell, R. F. *Inventing the Criminal: A History of German Criminology 1880–1945*. University of North Carolina Press, 2000.

Wilson, S. *Feuding, Conflict and Banditry in Nineteenth-Century Corsica*. Cambridge University Press, 1988.

Wright, G. *Between the Guillotine and Liberty: Two Centuries of the Crime Problem in France*. Oxford University Press, 1983.

Chapter 3

Explaining the history of punishment

John Pratt

After inviting me to give a seminar on my work to a local criminology society meeting, a colleague later introduced me to the audience as 'an armchair academic'. In their mind, because I had been engaged in historical research, it was as if what I was doing was some sort of esoteric but largely irrelevant luxury. Happily, I am certain that this depressing view of the parameters and possibilities of criminological research is idiosyncratic to that person rather than normative of the discipline as a whole. Indeed, as I show in this chapter, the history of punishment has demonstrated an exhilarating expansion and fortitude over the last three decades or so. Not that it was always like this, though. There had been a dearth of historical scholarship before then. Why this might have been so, how and in what ways the history of punishment has become such a dynamic subject since that point, and how our understanding of the purposes and nature of historical inquiry have changed will be the main themes of this chapter.

The contribution of Radzinowicz

Sir Leon Radzinowicz (1948: ix) began the preface to what ultimately became his monumental five volumed *History of English Criminal Law* with the statement that:

Lord Macauley's generalisation that the history of England is the history of progress is as true of the criminal law of this country as of the other social institutions of which it is a part. Child of the Common Law, nourished and moulded by statute, the criminal law of England has always been sensitive to the needs and aspirations of the English people, and it has continually changed under the impact of the predominant opinion of the day.

In his foreword to this first volume, Lord Macmillan[1] (1948: v) noted that:

Hitherto the history of our criminal law has been expounded mainly from the juristic standpoint of statutes, decided cases and text-writers ... the dominant purpose of the present treatise is to set out the results of the investigations which Dr Radzinowicz has undertaken in this largely unexplored field, in order to display the gradual growth of public opinion which has led to the reforms brought about by modern criminal legislation.

These two extracts highlight both the *originality* of Radzinowicz's project (which ultimately became something more like a history of the origins and development of modern penal arrangements in England, finishing with the Report of the Gladstone Committee (1895)) and its *intellectual* parameters. Prior to Radzinowicz's remarkable work which ultimately spanned five decades (Volume 5 being completed with Roger Hood (Radzinowicz and Hood, 1986)) there was virtually no history of criminal law and punishment (at least in the English-speaking world) which tried to trace the social contours of any such developments. As Radzinowicz (1944: 181) noted in a precursive article to the first volume:

the writers on the subject as a rule make use of the general mass of relatively modern juristic literature, of the work of the ancient authorities such as Coke and Hale, and of the decisions of the Courts ... and so it may occur that an important connection or interdependence between an institution of criminal justice and other institutions of social life cannot be explained or sometimes even ascertained.

At that point, what history there was in these areas, other than the litanies of statutes and cases that Radzinowicz referred to, consisted almost wholly of the memoirs of 'great men', such as judges and Prison Commissioners (see, for example, Du Cane, 1885; Ruggles-Brise, 1921). In contrast, Radzinowicz (1944: 184) drew attention to what was then the originality of the sources he would be using in his research. These consisted of 'two masses of information: one derived from the State Papers, and divided into three sections (Commissions of Inquiry, Accounts and Papers, Annual Reports), the other from the Parliamentary Debates'. Favourably mentioning Webb and Webb's (1922) *English Prisons under Local Government*, the only other English study which had made use of these sources – which are known today as the 'official discourse' of the subject – it is clear that what Radzinowicz ultimately had in mind then[2] is something akin to Dicey's (1906) work[3] on the relationship between changes in legal form and social structure in Britain from the end of the eighteenth century to the beginning of the twentieth (for the acknowledgement he makes to Dicey, see Radzinowicz, 1944: 193).

In terms of intellectual parameters, what Radzinowicz produced now tends to be characterised (often disparagingly) as a history of progress, or 'Whig history'. That is to say, with the advance of rationality, humanitarian sentiment and social scientific research, modern society would leave in the past penal brutalities and excesses (such as the English 'Bloody Code' of the late eighteenth and early nineteenth century which is the focus of Radzinowicz's first volume) and move steadily down a long, unending path of penal reform, culminating, of course, in the postwar emphasis on the scientific treatment and rehabilitation of criminals. In this way, the past and the present seemed to mutually confirm the inexorable course of history towards a planned, rational and humane penal system. At the same time, the intellectual climate in which Radzinowicz's work was situated and of which it was a product perhaps also indicates why the history of punishment was for so long seen as having little more than antiquarian or curiosity value: it was an exploration of the past purely for the sake of looking into the past, or else it traced a unilinear line of progress to the present day. Thus Lord Macmillan (1948: v) in his preface to the first volume:

> the result is much more than a law book for lawyers; it is a full and comprehensive study of the phenomena of a great social evolution, at once technically accurate and humanly interesting. The light thus shed on the process of the awakening of the public conscience is as novel as it is illuminating.

But again, once it could be established that the public conscience had indeed been awakened then the need for any further *explanatory* historical inquiry (as opposed to that of purely esoteric interest) was questionable: the history of modern punishment could be taken for granted as being attributable to this post-Enlightenment awakening. Radzinowicz's history provided a magisterial and sufficient backcloth to contemporary debates and issues.

The view that historical research in this field served no particular purpose other than to uncover the past had informed Webb and Webb (1922). Here, they comment that:

> we make no attempt to pass judgement upon the English prison system at any stage of its development. As regards the past, any deliberate assessment of the character and effects of the prisons of any particular period would not only be, perforce, wanting in accuracy, but would, moreover, now serve no useful purpose.

This self-deprecation at the end of their study seems all the more remarkable given that they then go on to raise valuable insights (largely ignored for many decades by scholars and penal officials alike) from their history of the shift in the control of English prisons from local to central government. That is, that centralisation brought with it a problematic invisibility and opacity to prison administration, with attendant consequences in terms of accountability and public detachment. Nonetheless, they also saw, in conjunction with the political Zeitgeist of the period in which they were writing, the shift from local to central governance of prisons as both inevitable and ultimately desirable (Webb and Webb, 1922: 232–4).

Sociological inquiries: the legacy of Rusche and Kirchheimer (1939, 1978)

A very different kind of history had been written in the period between the work of the Webbs and Radzinowicz – Rusche and Kirchheimer's *Punishment and Social Structure* – but which was almost completely ignored in the English-speaking world (Radzinowicz (1944) himself makes no reference to it in his overview of the existing field of study[4]). In this text, penal arrangements so described were not simply demonstrative of the brutality, chaos and inhumanity associated with the premodern era on the one hand or the order, rationality and sensitivity associated with the modern on the other. Instead, in charting the history of punishment from the Middle Ages to the early twentieth century, they argue that:

> Punishment is neither a simple consequence of crime, nor the reverse side of crime, nor a mere means which is determined by the end to be achieved. Punishment must be understood as a social phenomenon

freed from both its juristic concept and its social ends. We do not deny that punishment has specific ends, but we do deny that that it can be understood from its ends alone. (Rusche and Kirchheimer, 1939, 1968: 5)

Not only did they argue that there was no simplistic relationship between crime and punishment but, in addition, whatever the stated aims of penal development – reform, rehabilitation and so on – there were inevitably much broader social influences and determinants on the form that punishment would take in a given historical period. As Garland (1990: 91) writes of their work, 'penal policy is taken to be one element within a wider strategy of controlling the poor, in which factories, workhouses, the poor law, and, of course, the labour market, all play corresponding parts'. What they were providing, then, was a materialist analysis of penal change, wherein the main object of their work was to relate the rise of imprisonment to the ascendancy of the capitalist mode of production. Thus Georg Rusche (Rusche, 1933, 1978: 6), the main author of the text, argued in the original research proposal that 'in the 17th century confinement takes over the role of corporal punishment and death sentences, "humanitarianism" replaces cruelty; wherever there used to be gallows, now prisons stand'. After describing how prisoners then became a useful source of cheap labour in the mercantile period, he adds that:

This 'humanitarian' system of punishment lost its utility when the Industrial Revolution, the replacement of the worker by the machine at the turn of the 18th century, removed the scarcity of workers, and the industrial reserve army came into existence. The lower classes sank into misery, underbid each other on the labour market … Prisons were no longer profitable. When wages were high, they had brought high gains; but when workers voluntarily offered their labour for a minimum existence, it was no longer worth it to come up with the cost for confinement and supervision.

Here, he adopts the reverse position of what has subsequently become an orthodoxy of critical criminology: that unemployment is associated with the growth of imprisonment (see Box, 1987). For Rusche, instead, the supply of cheap labour in periods of high unemployment meant that imprisonment was an unnecessary sanction in terms of instilling work discipline: the market itself could provide this.

There are some well known flaws in both the historical detail and the economic determinism that runs through this work (see Garland, 1990) which do not need any further elaboration here. The most important aspect of *Punishment and Social Structure* for the purposes of this chapter is that it provided a different way of explaining the history of punishment: as such, the historical facts did not simply speak for themselves but had to be situated within a sociological framework of inquiry if their significance was to be properly understood. As it was, for several decades their work stood on its own, amid the minimal intellectual interest in the subject. However, around 1970, we find the emergence of an embryonic revisionist history of punishment, even though the first two books of this genre owe more to the critical criminology and anti-psychiatry intellectual interests then gaining momentum rather than any latent influence of Rusche and Kirchheimer. In these respects, Tony Platt's (1969) *The Child Savers* was a pathbreaking book, arguing that the late nineteenth-century child-saving movement in the United States, far from demonstrating humanitarian reform, was an exercise in the disciplining and control of poor children. Similarly, David Rothman's *The Discovery of the Asylum* (1971), although much more influenced by Weber than Marx, argued that the benevolent and humane intentions of penal and mental health reformers around the beginning of the nineteenth century ultimately led to the horrors of confinement in mental institutions. Michael Ignatieff's (1978) work on the origins of Pentonville model prison followed a similar theme to Rothman.

In addition, in Britain, the work of historians such as E. P. Thompson (1975) and Douglas Hay *et al.* (1976) drew attention to the specific class interests underlying the criminalisation of many activities of the poor during the eighteenth century. They did this by interpreting history from below, from the point of view of 'humble foresters', as in the case of Thompson, rather than accepting the terms of debate set by the official discourse of the period. It was thus argued that the authority and majesty of criminal procedure served the purpose (crudely, for the sake of brevity here) of reaffirming ruling class power and subjugating an increasingly fractious and rebellious poor. Far from penal reform being the product of consensus and 'public opinion', it was now seen as a reflection of ruling-class interests. Douglas Hay concludes his essay 'Property, Authority and the Criminal Law' (1976: 62–3) as follows:

> A ruling class organizes its power in the state. The sanction of the state is force, but it is force that is legitimized, however imperfectly, and therefore the state deals also in ideologies. Loyalties do not grow simply in complex societies: they are twisted, invoked and often consciously created. Eighteenth century England was not a free market of patronage relations. It was a society with a bloody penal code, *an astute ruling class who manipulated it to their advantage,* and a people schooled in the lessons of Justice, Terror and Mercy. (my italics)

Here, the 'Bloody Code' was not some kind of pre-Enlightenment accident of history which the ensuing rationality and humanitarianism of the post-Enlightenment period resolved; instead, it was an integral feature of the way in which the ruling class had exercised their power at that time. And that it did change was due to class struggle and resistance on the one hand, and the need for penal strategies more suited to the labour demands of industrial capitalism on the other (although these interpretations of eighteenth- and early nineteenth-century history have since been disputed by King (1984) and Beattie (1986)).

By this juncture, the work of Rusche and Kirchheimer had been resurrected and was influential on a number of historical analyses of penal trends and developments that drew on Marxist concepts and ideas (see Melossi and Pavarini, 1981), as well as being at last celebrated and recognised in its own right (see Melossi, 1978, 1980). Indeed, the historical analysis of punishment began to have an increasingly important place within the field of critical criminology: the purpose being to show the underlying material conditions that were responsible for penal change. Scull (1978), for example, argued that the shift towards decarceration then under way in relation to penal and mental institutions was more to do with the fiscal crisis of welfare capitalism than the good intentions of social reformers. He set out his argument by means of an historical analysis of the relationship between the development of modern capitalist society and its 'apparatuses' of social control, and then linked contemporary changes to the harnessing of drug technology to the economic imperatives of fiscal restraint by the state.[5]

Foucault and histories of the present

If, by now, interest in the history of punishment had been prompted by this revisionism, it is difficult to overstate the impact of Michel Foucault's (1978) *Discipline and Punish* (subtitled *The Birth of the Prison*) both on historical and more contemporary penological scholarship. The central argument running through the book is that the shift from corporeal to carceral punishment at the beginning of the nineteenth century did not after all mark the triumph of Enlightenment humanitarianism over pre-modern barbarism. Rather than look to any qualitative reduction in the modalities of suffering that we might otherwise associate with the development of modern punishment, we must look instead to the way in which the power/knowledge interplay of modern society made possible a new economy of penal suffering. Hence the opening of the book with the spectacular execution of the regicide Damien in 1757, which is then contrasted with an early nineteenth-century reformatory timetable – the point being to demonstrate the distinct 'systems of thought' which made the two episodes possible and non-interchangeable. His explanation for this contrast is that it marked a shift from the sporadic, brutal, ostentatious penal arrangements of the premodern world to a new set which were more carefully regulated and finely tuned, but were also more secretive, extensive and systematic. From being a means to destroy an unlucky few in the premodern era, punishment in modern society becomes a strategy designed to control entire populations:

> The 'carceral' with its many diffuse or compact forms, its institutions of supervision or constraint, of discreet surveillance and insistent coercion, assured the communication of punishments according to quality and quantity; it connected in series or disposed according to subtle divisions the minor and the serious penalties, the mild and the strict forms of treatment, bad marks and light sentences. 'You will end up in the convict ship, the slightest indiscipline seems to say; and the harshest of prisons says to the prisoners condemned to life: I shall note the slightest irregularity in your conduct'. (Foucault, 1978: 299)

To enable him to make these claims, Foucault argues that the origins of modern punishment begin with Jeremy Bentham's late eighteenth-century blueprint for a model prison – the panopticon. Its characteristics of indefinite discipline and surveillance initially colonised the penal system and were then diffused right across modern society, ultimately providing it with a 'carceral texture', creating a 'carceral archipelago' and so on: a relentless, efficient progression again – but now not of humanitarian reform but of more impermeable, enmeshing social control. Foucault's work thus contains the more general message that the very essence of what we understand today as Western freedom which (at the time he was writing at least) allowed us to differentiate ourselves from Eastern bloc totalitarianism and repression, is in itself rooted in the disciplinary programmes and surveillance procedures of early nineteenth-century penal arrangements taken from the panopticon model. That it was only ever put into the most limited effect and that there was a range of other architectural influences on the prisons of that period was no deterrent to Foucault's argument.

One of the reasons for the book's importance is not simply that it rewrites our understanding of penal history. In addition, it shows how the past sets the 'conditions of possibility' for the way in which we know and understand the present. This stems from his 'genealogical' method of historical research. For Foucault, there were no essential meanings, values and virtues. Instead, when such claims were made, genealogical history in the genre he established seeks to explore the conditions of possibility for the discursive formation that such claims represent: for example, the idea that the 'birth of the prison' was the product of humanitarian reform. Foucault-influenced scholars, then, want to show, through historical inquiry, what it is that makes the present possible. David Garland's (2001) most recent book – *The Culture of Control* – a more contemporary history of the sharp changes that have taken place in crime control and penal policy in Britain and America from the 1970s onwards – provides one such 'history of the present'. It seeks

> to understand the historical conditions of existence upon which contemporary practices depend, particularly those that seem most puzzling and unsettling. Historical inquiry … is employed here as a means to discover how these phenomena came to acquire their current characteristics. The history that I propose is motivated not by a historical concern to understand the past but by a critical concern to come to terms with the present. It is a genealogical account that aims to trace the forces that gave birth to our present day practices and to identify the historical and social conditions upon which they still depend. The point is not to think historically about the past but rather to use that history to rethink the present. (Garland, 2001: 2)

Foucault has been influential on some wonderful penological scholarship, some of which revolves exclusively around historical inquiry, and some of which provides an historical backcloth to analysis of more contemporary developments. There is Cohen's (1985) *Visions of Social Control* where, in Foucault style, penal arrangements are seen as belonging to broad but decisive and exclusive 'epistemes' or 'systems of thought'. Pre-nineteenth-century corporeal penality (another Foucault neologism) was followed by the carceral arrangements of the nineteenth and much of the twentieth centuries; and then (or so it seemed in 1985) the emergence of a new set of arrangements: a penality rooted in the community as much as the prison (indeed, Cohen claimed it was becoming increasingly difficult to disentangle the two sectors), and where the apparent benevolence of those seeking to extend the unquestionably more humane community punishments in opposition to the prison was to be questioned and mistrusted. What such benevolence really represented was the onset of a new, more discreet and pervasive system of social control.

As a second example, Garland (1985) used Foucault's ideas to illustrate that the foundations of the English penal system lay not just in the reform processes which began to have effect at the end of the nineteenth-century, but were related to broader social structures: in particular, the emergence of welfare state political and ideological forces which then produced new modalities of governing the poor and irresponsible. The Report of the Gladstone Committee (1895), as with Radzinowicz and Hood (1986) earlier, is seen as a pivotal moment in this respect: but now because it paved the way for new forms of penal control – 'the welfare sanction', as Garland puts the matter – which, in Foucaultian fashion, is seen as encouraging the development of more extensive and intrusive forms of penal control rather than reform. In a rather grudging acknowledgement of this new history, Radzinowicz and Hood (1986: 776) note that 'some penal historians have made much of the widespread use of "mass imprisonment", of the spreading tentacles of the "carceral archipelago" in the nineteenth century'. Though, by contrast, they go on to insist that at the end of the nineteenth century 'what we witness is rather a mass movement away from reliance on incarceration … This set the pattern for the very optimistic approach towards crime and its control which [then] flourished … The penal policy of England seemed to be entering on a phase of new hopes and large expectations.'

Elias and the civilising process

While due recognition is paid to the way in which Foucault galvanised the history of punishment it has become clear in the last few years that the central themes he saw in modern penal arrangements – power, domination and control exercised through the state's penal authorities – do not seem sufficient to describe current trends. What had been critical to his work on the development of modern penality was the way in which this presented a mirror image to the humanitarian intent characteristic of official penal policy. There was indeed a rationality to modern punishment – in so far as it was used by the state's penal authorities to transform criminals into 'docile bodies' thereby enabling them to make a positive contribution to the functioning of society rather than acting as a drain on its resources. However, one of the most significant *motifs* of penal development in the last two decades has been the very clear change in the cultural forces underpinning it: a tolerance of prison populations that would have been unthinkable at the time when *Discipline and Punish* was being written; a growing division between prison and community sanctions, rather than a seamless interweaving of them; a growing use of expressive language to describe penal intent ('three strikes', 'zero tolerance', 'life means life' and so on); the development of a new expressive penal symbolism – such as the renaissance of public shaming penalties (Pratt, 2000); and above all, perhaps, the way in which 'populist punitiveness' (Bottoms, 1995) has become one of the driving forces of current penal development, with the penal authorities reduced on some occasions to the role of bewildered and helpless onlookers (Zimring, 1996). As such, just as Foucault (1970: 261–2) had declared Marx to be trapped within a nineteenth-century class-based episteme and thereby inappropriate for use in social analysis of the twentieth century, it may be the case that Foucault himself, at least as regards the characteristics of penality today, belongs to an episteme specific to a particular phase of modern development which has now passed. Whatever purchase his ideas may have had in relation to the history of modern punishment, the new configurations of penal power in evidence today would seem to make problematic many of the conceptual assumptions stemming from *Discipline and Punish*.

As a result, more recent scholarship has characterised modern penal development as the product of a history of collective emotions as its driving force (Pratt, 2002)[6] and the way in which these have been channelled into prevailing sensibilities, tolerances and values. The work of Norbert Elias (1939, 1984), one of the most important sociologists of culture, has been very influential on this new historical scholarship. For him, the ebb and flow of human emotion and sensibilities were central components of what he saw as the civilising process characteristic of Western societies: 'civilising' though was used as a theoretical construct rather than as a commonsensical term, and it was not the case that what we understand as the civilised world today is the product of some natural progression. Instead, Elias saw its development as the contingent outcome of long-term socio-cultural and psychic change. From the Middle Ages onwards, the development of the civilising process brought with it two major consequences. First, the modern state itself gradually began to assume much more centralised authority and control over the lives of its subjects, to the point where it came to have a monopoly regarding the use of force, the raising of taxes and the imposition of legal sanctions to address disputes. Second, citizens in modern societies came to internalise restraints, controls and inhibitions on their conduct, as their values reflected an increased sensibility to the suffering of others and a desire for the privatisation of disturbing events (Garland, 1990). In these respects, while Elias himself used changing attitudes to bodily functions and violence to demonstrate these claims, it also seems clear that one of the most important consequences of the gradual spread of these sentiments was, as Pieter Spierenburg (1984) has illustrated (see also Masur, 1989; Strange, 1996), a decline and tempering of corporal and capital punishments. As such, at the onset of modernity, the public performance of such punishments had all but disappeared and their administration in private was increasingly subject to regulations and official scrutiny. Studies in this genre (see, for example, McGowan, 1994, 2000) do more than challenge the explanation put forward by Foucault for these changes. They also raise significant questions about the grander historical claims he makes. Instead of the sharp transition from one modality of suffering to another in Foucault's work, for Spierenburg, the transition from corporeal to carceral penality was much more lengthy, and the change more subtle and gradual. By 1757 the brutality of the execution of Damien had already become most untypical of that period: it was only that he was a regicide because there was such an intensity of violence inflicted on him. More generally, by this time in Europe, executions had not only declined in numbers, but in addition the spectacular nature of the proceedings was diminishing. Therefore, the dramatic contrast between the public execution and the timetable which opens *Discipline and Punish* is misleading and, by extension, calls into question the validity of some of the more fundamental premises of the book.

Pratt (2002) applies – and of necessity extends – the work of Elias to his history of punishment in the main English-speaking societies in the late nineteenth and twentieth centuries. This is because the historical detail of Elias's work ends around the mid-nineteenth century. As such, it does not really capture the significance of the way in which central state monopolistic control then led to the bureaucratisation of wide-ranging aspects of everyday life. In these respects, the features of penal development that the civilising process is seen as leading to – the disappearance of prison from public view, improvements in the physical conditions of confinement, the sanitisation of penal language and the concomitant exclusion of the general public from any significant involvement in penal affairs as the authority of the penal bureaucracies became more solidified – ultimately became the signifiers of punishment in the civilised world. This did not mean, though, that the end product would of necessity be 'civilised'. What it could turn into was a set of penal arrangements that were largely anonymous, remote (which the Webbs had earlier expressed concerns about), and which the growing power of these bureaucratic forces was able to shape, define and make understandable. Precisely because of this framework, brutalities and privations could go largely unchecked or unheeded by a public that preferred not to become involved in the distasteful matter that the infliction of punishment had now become (Pratt, 2002). In this way, Elias's work is conjoined with that of Bauman (1989). That is, under particular circumstances, the qualities we associate with the civilised world – technology, efficiency, rationality on the one hand and moral indifference from the general public on the other – can have harmful, even catastrophic consequences. The values of the civilised world are not only no guarantors against such outcomes (Christie, 1993) – they may even facilitate them.

At the same time, though, Elias was not putting forward some unilinear model of social development. The civilising process itself can be interrupted by phenomena such as war, catastrophe, dramatic social change and the like at any time. In such situations, 'the armour of civilized conduct crumbles very rapidly', with a concomitant fragmentation of centralised governmental authority and a decline in human capacity for rational action (see Elias, 1994; Fletcher, 1997: 82). This would cause the civilising process to be 'put into reverse' and 'decivilising' would occur, bringing with it the re-emergence of conduct and values more appropriate to previous eras. Although the extent and degree of such a reversal is left somewhat open ended and undeveloped by Elias, later commentators have further elucidated this concept (see Mennell, 1990; Fletcher, 1997). Thus, in his explanation of the causes and consequences of the new penal trends today, Pratt (2002) surmises that, in modern societies, the very bureaucratisation brought about by the civilising process is in fact likely to have its own built-in defences against the impact of decivilising forces. Rather than some wholesale reversal taking place when decivilising occurs, the civilising process and decivilising tendencies are likely to run in tandem with each other, with the latter having the potential to push the former out of its familiar orbit and into unfamiliar new regions. Hence the 'new punitiveness' is seen as a fusion of the cultural influences representative of decivilising trends and the existing bureaucratic arrangements of the civilising process that mediates them and then provides them with an effectivity (Pratt, 2002).

New directions and historiographies

It is clear, then, that as a field of study, the history of punishment has undergone a remarkable intellectual transformation since the 1970s. It has become a dynamic and developing subject; rather than having the sole purpose of exploring the past, it has come to be seen as increasingly important in understanding the parameters, limits and boundaries of the present. Having said this, it remains the case that it is a subject dominated by inquiries into punishments to men. The history of the punishment of women has received much less attention, although there has been important new scholarship in this area as well. Zedner (1991), for example, illustrates the way in which, with the decline of women's criminality from around 1880 to 1920, they became, as it were, a bureaucratic inconvenience and nuisance within a prison system preoccupied almost exclusively with its predominantly male inmate population. From a post-Foucault perspective, Howe (1994) relates this decline in women's criminality and prominence in the penal system to the growth of more extensive domestic regulation. Ballinger's (2000) work on executed women in Britain confounds the usual thinking that women are treated more leniently in the courts than men by showing how women who had murdered adults (from 1900 to 1955) had less hope of a reprieve from the death penalty than men. Sim (1990) provides one of the few studies which shows the differential effects of prison strategies on both men and women prisoners: in this case the medicalisation of prison regimes and the growing use of drug control within the prisons.

It also has to be said that much of the English-language history of punishment is still centred around England and the United States, and there has been little that attempts to incorporate and theorise colonial dynamics in the development of penal affairs in countries such as Australia, Canada and New Zealand. Analysis of Australian penal history, despite its incredibly rich (and largely untapped heritage) is still focused primarily on the experience of transportation (see Hughes, 1987, for example). Little is known of later nineteenth- and twentieth-century history, although Finnane (1991, 1998) has made significant contributions to the development of such scholarship. Pratt's (1992) work on the history of the New Zealand penal system (virtually the only sociological inquiry into it) has Durkheimian influences, in that the development (and extensive use) of an English-based penal system – at a distance of 12,000 miles from Britain – was a way of drawing together a diverse, fragmented and scattered British migrant population. Amazingly, so it would seem, the first public building to be built in Wellington was a replica of Pentonville prison in 1843 (that only the first wing was ever completed because of lack of resources, not to say need, is another dimension and prominent theme of colonial penal history). Yet what this also demonstrates is the symbolic power of such penal institutions to unite the settler population against the perceived social dangers to the 'New Britain' that they were attempting to build in the South Pacific, as well as the way in which institutions of law and punishment provided 'badges of identity' in the absence of any others that were then thought appropriate – something legislators would do well to remember in such societies amid ongoing discussion of indigenous legal values and justice practices today.

As the nature of historical inquiry has changed – from charting the official discourse of punishment to more critical interrogations of it – so too has its historiography. In his remarkably detailed study of the decline of public executions in Britain, Gattrell (1994) draws on (in addition to official documents) letters, diaries, ballads, broadsides and contemporary prints and illustrations. There has also been important work on the symbolism of prison architecture (Evans, 1984; Bender, 1987; Brodie *et al.*, 1999). Pratt (2002) uses prisoner memoirs[7] as a counterpoint to official penal discourse. He also attempted to conceptualise (in Pratt, 1992) the dismantling and denial of Maori justice practices in New Zealand as a 'history of silence'. It is still possible to shed fresh light on the official historical documents of penal policy. McConville (1995) in his Weberian studies of Radzinowiczian dimensions achieves this in relation to the development of prison bureaucracy in England. Indeed, he finishes at the same point as Radzinowicz's final volume: the importance of the Gladstone Committee. While for Radzinowicz and Hood (and also Garland from a different point of view) the report is seen as marking a new departure for penal development, for McConville it cemented the trend towards the supremacy and authority of the penal bureaucracy in England which had been accelerating during the nineteenth century and firmly set it in place for much of the twentieth. It thus set the seal on existing trends rather than marked a point of departure for new ones.

Clearly, then, to return to Lord Macmillan's preface to Radzinowicz's first volume, it is not only the 'awakening of public conscience' that now explains the history of punishment. But whatever mode of explanation is now chosen, there has certainly been a much greater 'illumination of the subject' in the intervening period.

Notes

1. Radzinowicz clearly moved in different circles from most other academics. In addition to Lord Macmillan's preface to the book, he also mentions, in his acknowledgements, Viscount Maugham, Lord Wright, Lord Simonds and Sir Arnold D. McNair (Radzinowicz, 1948: x).
2. It is clear from both Radzinowicz (1944) and Macmillan (1948) that what was then envisaged was a history finishing at the present day rather than the end of the nineteenth century.
3. See Wiener (1994) for an extensive study of the relationship between changes in criminal law and penal practice and changing values and norms in Victorian and Edwardian society.
4. As opposed to Rusche and Kirchheimer (1939) being unknown and overlooked as a result of wartime exigencies, Sellin (1943) makes favourable reference to it. However, given that Sellin was writing in the United States, it may be that the book was more readily available there than in Britain because of the former country's later entry in to the war.
5. In fact, his work was published on the eve of the largest expansion of the prison population in American history (O'Malley, 2000). Scull (1984) acknowl-

edges the weaknesses of his earlier argument and recognises the cultural and economic differentiation of the penal and mental health realms.
6. The importance of cultural values on the history of punishment had been a prominent feature in the scholarship on the Deep South of the United States (see Ayers, 1984).
7. See also Priestley (1985, 1989).

References

Ayers, E. *Vengeance and Justice*. Oxford University Press, 1984.

Ballinger, A. *Dead Woman Walking*. Ashgate, 2000.

Bauman, Z. *Modernity and the Holocaust*. Polity Press, 1989.

Beattie, J. *Crime and the Courts in England 1660–1800*. Princeton University Press, 1986.

Bender, J. *Imagining the Penitentiary*. Chicago University Press, 1987.

Bottoms, A. E. 'The politics and philosophy of sentencing', in Clarkson, C. and. Morgan, R. (eds), *The Politics of Sentencing*. Clarendon Press, 1995, pp.170–90.

Box, S. *Recession, Crime and Punishment*. Macmillan, 1987.

Brodie, A., Croom, J. and Davies, J. *The Prison Experience*. English Heritage, 1999.

Christie, N. *Crime Control as Industry*. Martin Robertson, 1993.

Cohen, S. *Visions of Social Control*. Polity Press, 1985.

Dicey, A. *Law and Public Opinion in England during the Nineteenth Century*. Macmillan, 1906.

Du Cane, E. *The Punishment and Prevention of Crime*. Macmillan, 1885.

Elias, N. *The Civilizing Process*. Blackwell, 1939, 1984.

Elias, N. *Reflections on a Life*. Polity Press, 1994.

Evans, R. *The Fabrication of Virtue*. Cambridge University Press, 1984.

Finnane, M. 'After the convicts: towards a history of imprisonment in Australia', *Australian and New Zealand Journal of Criminology*, 24, 1991, pp. 105–17.

Finnane, M. *Punishment in Australian Society*. Oxford University Press, 1998.

Fletcher, J. *Violence and Civilization*. Polity Press, 1997.

Foucault, M. *The Order of Things*. Tavistock, 1970.

Foucault, M. *Discipline and Punish*. Allen Lane, 1978.

Garland, D. *Punishment and Welfare*. Heinemann, 1985.

Garland, D. *Punishment and Modern Society*. Oxford University Press, 1990.

Garland, D. *The Culture of Control*. Oxford University Press, 2001.

Gatrell, V. *The Hanging Tree*. Oxford University Press, 1994.

Hay, D., Linebaugh, P., Rule, J., Thompson, E. P. and Winslow, C. *Albion's Fatal Tree*. Penguin Books, 1976.

Howe, A. *Punish and Critique*. Routledge, 1994.

Hughes, R. *The Fatal Shore*. Alfred Knopf, 1987.

Ignatieff, M. *A Just Measure of Pain*. Macmillan, 1978.

King, P. 'Decision-makers and decision-making in the English criminal law 1750–1800', *Historical Journal*, 27, 1984, pp. 25–58.

Macmillan, Lord, 'Foreword', in Radzinowicz, L., *A History of English Criminal Law, Vol. 1*. Stevens, 1948, pp. v–viii.

Masur, L. *Rites of Execution*. Oxford University Press, 1989.

McConville, S. *English Local Prisons 1860–1900*. Routledge, 1995.

McGowen, R. 'Civilizing punishment: the end of the public execution in England', *Journal of British Studies*, 33, 1994, pp. 257–82.

McGowen, R. 'Revisiting *The Hanging Tree*: Gatrell on emotion and history', *British Journal of Criminology*, 40, 2000, pp. 1–13.

Mennell, S. 'Decivilizing processes: theoretical significance and some lines of research', *International Sociology*, 5, 1990, pp. 205–13.

Melossi, D. 'Georg Rusche and Otto Kirchheimer: *Punishment and Social Structure*', *Crime and Social Justice*, 9, 1978, pp. 73–85.

Melossi, D. 'Georg Rusche: a biographical essay', *Crime and Social Justice*, 14, 1980, pp. 51–64.

Melossi, D. and Pavarini, M. *The Prison and The Factory*. Macmillan, 1981.

O'Malley, P. 'Criminologies of catastrophe? Understanding criminal justice on the edge of the new millennium', *Australian and New Zealand Journal of Criminology*, 33, 2000, pp. 153–67.

Platt, A. *The Child Savers: The Invention of Delinquency*. University of Chicago Press, 1969

Pratt, J. *Punishment in a Perfect Society*. Victoria University Press, 1992.

Pratt, J. 'The return of the Wheelbarrow Men? Or, the arrival of postmodern penality?', *British Journal of Criminology*, 40, 2000, pp. 127–45.

Pratt, J. *Punishment and Civilization*. Sage, 2002.

Priestley, P. *Victorian Prison Lives*. Methuen, 1985.

Priestley, P. *Jail Journeys*. Routledge, 1989.

Radzinowicz, L. 'Some sources of modern English criminal legislation', *Cambridge Law Journal*, 8, 1944, pp. 181–94.

Radzinowicz, L. *A History of English Criminal Law, Vol. 1*. Stevens, 1948.

Radzinowicz, L. and Hood, R. *A History of English Criminal Law, Vol 5*. Butterworths, 1986.

Report of the Gladstone Committee, London: PP LVII, 1895.

Rothman, D. *The Discovery of the Asylum*. Little Brown, 1971.

Ruggles-Brise, E. *The English Prison System*. Macmillan, 1921.

Rusche, G. 'Labour market and penal sanction: thoughts on the sociology of criminal justice', *Crime and social justice*, 10, 1978, pp. 2–8.

Rusche, G. and Kirchheimer, O. *Punishment and Social Structure*. Russell & Russell, 1939, 1978.

Scull, A. *Decarceration*. Prentice Hall, 1978.

Scull, A. *Decarceration*, 2nd edn. Polity Press, 1984.

Sellin, T. *Pioneering in Penology: The Amsterdam Houses of Correction in the Sixteenth and Seventeenth Centuries*. University of Pennsylvania Press, 1943.

Sim, J. *Medical Power in Prisons: The Prison Medical Service in England 1774–1988*. Open University Press, 1990.

Spierenburg, P. *The Spectacle of Suffering*. Cambridge University Press, 1984.

Strange, C. (ed.), *Qualities of Mercy: Justice, Punishment and Discretion*. University of British Columbia Press, 1996.

Thompson, E. P. *Whigs and Hunters*. Allen Lane, 1975.

Webb, B. and Webb, S. *English Prisons under Local Government*. Longmans, 1922.

Wiener, M. *Reconstructing the Criminal*. Cambridge University Press, 1994.

Zedner, L. *Women, Crime and Custody in Victorian England*. Clarendon Press, 1991.

Zimring, F. 'Populism, democratic government and the decline of expert authority', *Pacific Law Journal*, 28, 1996, pp. 243–56.

Chapter 4

Crimes of violence, crimes of empire?

Mark Finnane

After a long period of post-colonial revisionism in which histories of colonial violence were recovered, Australian historians have recently been challenged by a counter-revisionism. In this account, stories of violence and massacres are reputed to be greatly exaggerated, even fabricated. In place of the violent British Empire of the nineteenth century we are presented with a vision of a generally benign imperial settlement of large areas of the globe that were awaiting their moment of civilisation. At the very least, in this account, even when settlers were violent, their cause was justified by the needs of self-defence; and if Indigenous peoples suffered then their descendants are informed that things would have been worse under other masters (Windschuttle, 2000, 2002).

The chronological distance between the settlement of Botany Bay and these contemporary debates over the violence of Australian frontiers is no greater than that which lay between Columbus landing in America and John Locke articulating the most powerful modern theory of property to justify the claims of empire. When historians debate the truths of Australian frontier histories they do so in a context that ties their accounts to contesting views of the legitimacy of Australian settlement. In challenging what he sees as the comfortable, leftist-inspired, orthodoxies of contemporary Australian historiography Keith Windschuttle's *The Fabrication of Aboriginal History* (2002) has appealed especially to long-standing distinctions between criminal acts and those arising out of defensible wars. Insisting rhetorically, without comparative evidence, that Australian frontiers were, in his own words, 'the least violent of European encounters with the New Worlds of the Americas and the Pacific', Windschuttle constructs Indigenous response to settlement not as criminal-like, but as criminal. The volume focuses on Van Diemen's Land (Tasmania) – other volumes are promised on the mainland Australian colonies.

This is not a story of mere parochial interest. As Windschuttle himself reminds us, the Tasmanian example has been long taken as an instance of the general extermination of an Indigenous people. It is so treated in widely-read contemporary world histories, as discussed by Windschuttle (2002: 13–14), most recently by Niall Ferguson, who characterises the events in Tasmania as one of the worst chapters of British imperial history, 'an event which truly merits the now overused term "genocide" ', and who does not seek to deny what he calls the 'ethnic cleansing' of indigenous peoples in the history of the Empire generally (Ferguson, 2004: 108–9, 366). The thinness of the research base of many of these macro-historical works when they reach a case as specific as that of Tasmania helps to sustain Windschuttle's construction of the historiography, though he is on much weaker ground when it comes to describing what he regards as the orthodox Australian historiography.

In the debates that have followed Windschuttle's interventions only limited attention has been paid to his quite specific constructions of the Australian story as part of a larger British imperial enterprise of benign settlement. In what follows I want to explore some of the implications of this recovery of a language that criminalises the actions of those who responded with violence to the incursions of strangers in the Americas and the Pacific. Was the empire so benign and were the colonised so criminal? It goes without saying that an adequate answer to such a question would require a sustained comparative history of a kind that has not yet been attempted. The discussion here will be limited to examining the robustness of Windschuttle's view of the British Empire, its links to ideological justifications for dispossession of the Indigenous peoples, the development of a case for the variety of imperial encounters and finally the consideration of the boundaries between criminality and war.

Windschuttle constructs a rhetorical case which relies on the conflation into a single view of what in truth is a wide variety of perspectives on Australian history. Much debate about the book has centred on the vehemence of his attack on other people's footnotes. In response, as specialists in Tasmanian history pick away at this hastily constructed edifice purporting to be an alternative history of the early colony, there is a sense that in the end little will be left standing (Manne, 2003). Some have noted and condemned the evidence in his writing of elements of racial vilification, and of an incapacity to empathise with those on the other side of imperial frontiers. Others have explored the ethical dimensions of this attack on so-called orthodoxy. In particular a number of people have picked up a challenge embodied in Windschuttle's observation that 'the debate over Aboriginal history goes far beyond its ostensible subject: it is about the character of the nation and, ultimately, the calibre of the civilization Britain brought to these shores in 1788' (Windschuttle, 2002: 3). Those who have done so have highlighted the articulation between Windschuttle's preferred version of Australian history and constructions of national identity – especially those developed in the later nineteenth century and made concrete in the formation of the federation and the consolidation of White Australia, a vision of a British utopia in a hostile world. Finally there have been valuable responses that have looked at the Windschuttle-provoked debates as an opportunity to review major issues in Australian historiography (Foster and Attwood, 2003; Macintyre and Clark 2003; Manne, 2001, 2003).

Generally the debate has proceeded in strictly local (i.e. Australian) terms – although Krygier and van Krieken (2003) have cogently queried the way in which 'civilisation' and 'rule of law' operate in Windschuttle's arguments, eliding the historical conditions that underlie these concepts; while Moses (2003), in a valuable comparative account of the phenomenon of revisionism and counter-revisionism in various national settings (Ireland, Japan, Germany, but the list could go on), has sought to address how this debate might look like if viewed from some place other than the Mitchell Library in Sydney.

Accustomed as they generally are to dealing with Australian history in isolation from other histories, there has been little attention paid by participants in this debate to the portentous vision of the history of the British Empire which grounds Windschuttle's views. Windschuttle's reference to the civilisation brought by Britain to these shores is no idle comment. The case set out in *The Fabrication of Aboriginal History* rests on the view that what Britain brought to Australia were the virtues of the rule of law, Evangelical ethics and Enlightenment thought. These distinct themes overlap in Windschuttle's construction of what he calls 'the legitimization of colonial rule'. Legitimisation was centred in the establishment of a rule-of-law state in which Aborigines as subjects of the Crown were entitled to as much protection as the settlers. By the early nineteenth century evidently, in the words of Windschuttle, 'it was this rule of law that made every British colony in its own eyes, and in truth, a domain of civilization' (Windschuttle, 2002: 186).

This account rests on an account of the British Empire advanced earlier in the book as both explanation and justification of the history which will unfold. The origins of Windschuttle's view of the British Empire are found in his own construction of a straw historiography, in which unnamed historians 'still like to show how closely the British version resembled the Spanish'. A highly selective account of the recent historiography of the British Empire is then used to delineate the ways in which British imperialism shaped its enterprise in opposition to the derided example of alleged Spanish atrocities and failures in the New World. Acknowledging that the stories of Spanish atrocities may themselves have been exaggerated for rhetorical effect (Windschuttle, 2002: 37–40), Windschuttle nevertheless carries their legacy with him into his evaluation of the character of the British imperial enterprise compared with others. In this context Windschuttle draws comfort from a selective reading of the revisionism of the recent *Oxford History of the British Empire*, the principal source of his enlightenment about the character of British colonisation, although he makes no use of this rich and varied source in his book. Elsewhere he has characterised the achievement of these volumes in terms of his growing sense of the Empire's greatness. As the conclusion to his extended review of the *Oxford History* puts it:

> For all their faults, most British colonial officials delivered good government – or at least better government than any of the likely alternatives. The lives of millions of ordinary people in these countries would have been much happier had the British stayed longer, that is, until a more satisfactory path to independence and a more sensible map of territorial boundaries had been drawn up. Indeed, the uncivilized conditions in which many people in the old imperial realm now live is evidence that the world would be a better place today if some parts of it were still ruled by the British Empire. (Windschuttle, 2000)

These more general perspectives about the kind of civilisation brought to the antipodes by the Empire are complemented in *The Fabrication of Aboriginal History* by a misleading treatment of the ideological histories of the Spanish and British empires.

Windschuttle's account of the way in which Britain shaped its empire in opposition to Spanish failures is chiefly dependent on the accounts of a leading historian of European imperialism, Anthony Pagden. Krygier and van Krieken have highlighted Windschuttle's selective use of Pagden, whose book *Lords of All the World* surveys the development of modern (i.e. post-Columbian) ideologies of empire, examining their roots in Roman imperialism and their mutations as Britain, Spain and France essayed across the Atlantic and into Africa. The effect of Windschuttle's misreading of Pagden is a glossing of the distinction between ideological (i.e. legitimising) accounts of British interests and dispositions and the historical character of the New World settlements whose treatment of Indigenous peoples was so often barbarous. As Krygier and van Krieken conclude:

> What *Fabrication* presents as a detached description of the inner nature of British colonisation and its actual consistency with humanitarian values, is in Pagden's book an analysis of the rhetorical strategies pursued by the British (and the French) to legitimise colonisation so as to render it consistent with those humanitarian values. (Krygier and van Krieken, 2003: 94)

Seeking to legitimise the terms of Australian settlement, Windschuttle looks back to this ideological distinction between Spanish conquest and British possession by virtue of the doctrine of *res nullius*. Spanish grants to colonials in the New World he says were feudal titles to labour, giving the colonists rights over the Indian peoples. In contrast he claims, again relying on his account of Pagden, 'British culture legitimated the owner-ship of things, not people' (Windschuttle, 2002: 31). In *Lords of the All the World*, however, Pagden makes a crucial and extended qualification to this contrast of legitimising arguments between Spanish concern with rights over people and British with rights over property, especially land. As he goes on:

> This is not to say that property rights – the dominion exercised over things – was of a lesser kind than the rights exercised over people. Both for the Roman jurists and subsequently for Locke, property was more than the right to possession, since for them it constituted one of the fundamental bases for the development of civil society. (Pagden, 1995: 78)

Indeed we need to recognise that in the famous *Second Treatise on Government* 'property' has a broad as well as narrow meaning. It is not merely the things that one might possess by application of one's labour – but the 'lives, liberties and estates' for the preservation of which men unite under governments (Locke and Laslett,1965: 395, para. 123; see also p. 115 for Laslett's commentary on the meaning of property). Moreover, when Windschuttle adopts this contrast between Spanish and British dis-positions in the ideological sphere as a signal of their attitudes to the treatment of Indigenous peoples, he has to ignore the weighty history of the British investment in slavery in the Americas. In this context Locke's own role in the service of a colonisation company in a country which became the greatest slave trader of the eighteenth century is a striking reminder of the breadth of the notion of property in this 'British culture' (Arneil, 1996). Such a culture was readily able to define Africans as non-people, suitable subjects for slavery and therefore the property of others.

So did British culture legitimate 'the ownership of things not people'? The exclusion of people can only hold if we forget the history of slavery and of British culture's responsibility for it in the Atlantic trade and in the English colonies of North America. When it suited them to expand the category of slaves to include American Indians, the British colonisers of the Americas did so assiduously (Gallay, 2002). But we do not even have to drift too far from London in any case to see the consequences of a focus on property acquired through settlement when linked to a racialised characterisation of those who should be subjected. For in Ireland and the Highlands of Scotland the way was paved in the sixteenth and seventeenth centuries for the colonial experiments of the New World. One of the editors of the *Oxford History of the British Empire* has been among those who have traced the impact of the colonisation and dispossession of the 'savage' Irish in the Elizabethan conquest of Ireland (Canny, 1976: 160; Armitage, 2000: 50–8; Louis *et al.*, 1998: vol. 1: 6–7, 146). In the case of Ireland, as later of the American Indians or even later of the Australian Aborigines, customary owners of the land would be displaced by settlement enforced where necessary by sword or gun. As Nicholas Canny puts it, the colonists in Virginia used the same pretexts for the extermination of the Indians as their counterparts had previously used in Ireland in the 1560s and 1570s:

> Every adventurer claimed that his primary purpose was to reform the Irish … It is evident, however, that no determined effort was ever made to reform the Irish, but rather, at the least pretext – generally resistance to the English – they were dismissed as a 'wicked and faythless peopoll' and put to the sword. This formula was repeated in the treatment of the Indians in the New World. (Canny, 1976: 160)

The confounding case of Ireland is never mentioned in Windschuttle's appraisal of the first or second empires (Windschuttle, 2000).

Windschuttle's misreading of Pagden is compounded by other imaginative, not to say anachronistic, reconstructions. A passage of

Pagden explaining the difficulties of the argument from conquest 'in a political culture such as Britain which, because it had itself been the creation of the Norman Conquest of 1066, was committed to the "continuity theory" of constitutional law' is bowdlerised by Windschuttle in these terms: 'Since 1066, British political culture had been committed to the "continuity theory" of constitutional law' (Pagden, 1995: 77; Windschuttle, 2002: 31). Perhaps a future book will demonstrate that William the Conqueror was the first great political theorist!

On the basis of this parody of a sophisticated and historically grounded account of the development of European imperialist justifications for dispossession, Windschuttle proceeds to construct a vision of Australian colonisation as standing in the line of a civilising British Empire. By the end of the eighteenth century, he says, reviewing the standards of inter-national law of the time, 'the principal fact that legitimized their [British] colonization was that the land was not cultivated and was thus open to annexation' (Windschuttle, 2002: 185). By improving the land, the colonists would establish their Lockean right of possession: 'they were not dispossessing the natives' in this view, but bringing civilisation, and of course the rule of law – for 'a British declaration of sovereignty over a territory meant that all individuals within it, native and colonist, were subject to English law' (Windschuttle, 2002: 186).

Windschuttle's description of the *res nullius* arguments is unexceptional as an account of colonial possessory justifications – familiar stuff to those who have read through the debates over the law of the land in Australia that have been influential and widespread since the 1980s. Yet, in the context of the extended consideration of the modern theories of property and their implications for the standing of colonised peoples that has taken place in recent decades, it is partial and simplistic. It conveys nothing of the advanced understanding of the conditions under which Lockean theory developed as an authoritative and – in its implications for Indigenous peoples – discriminatory underpinning of British colonisation (Ivison *et al.*, 2000; Tully, 1995; Buchan, 2001).

Citing Locke on the unacceptability of conquest as a basis for govern-ment of the colonised, as Windschuttle does (Windschuttle, 2002: 31), cannot save his account from being embedded in the large assumptions and implications of Locke's sustained arguments in favour of dis-possession, if necessary by war. Predictably, Windschuttle does not move from a consideration of the theory of property rights established by the application of labour and use of product to Locke's associated argument for defending settler rights to land in contested territory. In Pagden's words, developing an argument from Tully's major consideration of these questions:

> By the terms of Locke's argument, if once a settlement had been established the natives attempted to regain the lands they were in violation of nature's laws and might, as Locke phrased it, 'be destroyed as a lion or tiger, one of those savage wild beasts'. (Pagden, 1995: 77)

'This violent doctrine', as Tully describes it, 'provided a major justification for the imperial wars against the Aboriginal peoples of North America' (Tully, 1995: 73). The pertinence of these comments for the Australian context as well as for those of other British colonisations is transparent.

In overlooking all the other dimensions of Lockean thought and British attachment to a particular, if profoundly influential, definition of property rights, Windschuttle's account operates as a renewed legitimisation of a historical dispossession. In spite of all the talk of rule of law, the postulated equality of Aboriginal subjects of the Crown in early Australia can only be established through surrendering their status as autonomous subjects of a quite different culture. Not only did Lockean theory contemplate the justness of wars waged against the dispossessed, it crucially provided an authority for dispossession without consent, against all the traditions of constitutionalism, as Tully and Pagden further contend. In this respect Pagden argues (again in a passage that Windschuttle ignores) that the Spanish and British both sought to justify the absence of consent. The Spanish did so by arguing that Papal authority justified possession in the absence of consent and that Native Americans would in time recognise their proper interest in the gifts of Christianity and civil order. The British justified that same absence of consent 'on the grounds that those who could not develop the land God had given them could not be said to be capable of exercising consent at all, at least in those areas where property were concerned' (Pagden, 1995: 78).

The argument so far has suggested the instability of Windschuttle's contrast of Spanish and British imperial ideologies and their implications for the interpretation of subsequent colonial adventures. The particular case of the Australian (including Tasmanian) colonisation took place, of course, somewhat later than the early modern contests of Spain and Britain and France over the possession of the Americas. Windschuttle's British Empire is a latter-day construction of a 'second Empire' in which rule of law and evangelical ethic combined with modern science and technology to spread civilisation. Replicating the ideological contrast between English and continental imperialisms that he seeks at one level to use as a means of explaining the appeal of a particular genre of allegations against the harms of the new empire, Windschuttle overlooks the ways in which the new British Empire of the nineteenth century saw its mission in a longer historical trajectory, one which was part of European imperialism. In this longer trajectory, the contrast of civilised and savage societies was consistently deployed in articulating the policy as well as tactical decisions when settlement faced resistance. Moreover, the notion of a 'second Empire' cannot be used without acknowledging the important changes in imperial context as the nineteenth century proceeded. However much we acknowledge the relevance of the evangelical as well as Enlightenment values represented in the first decades of Australian colonisation, the reality is that later nineteenth-century colonisations proceeded in an ideological context marked by evolutionary and racist thought of a very radical kind. The transformations were so profound that they can be read even in the biography of a single imperial official, such as Edward John Eyre, enlightened in his Australasian service in the 1830s and 1840s, and then the agent of racialising and brutal domination in the West Indies after 1857 (Hall, 1996; but see also Evans, 2002, for the limits of Eyre's enlightenment in his Australian career).

Windschuttle's reading of British imperial history conflates the successive phases and locations of this history in misleading ways, and certainly does so in the Australian context. In my remaining comments I want to consider how this becomes evident in considering the reflections on colonial policy that took place in the despatches of somebody like Queensland's Governor Bowen at the very outset of that colony's self-government, but postdating the events of the Van Diemen's Land's 'Black War' by some three decades.

Queensland was separated from New South Wales in December 1859. It was established as a self-governing colony, but almost all its institutions had to be built from the ground up. What we see in the first years of the colony is a place in which debates about the conditions of settlement, and the threats to successful colonisation still posed by the Aboriginal inhabitants, are alive with all the vigour of those that had already taken place in the other colonies of Australasia, and with all the moral confusion and political self-interest that one sees in seventeenth- and eighteenth-century North America. Into this place in the very month of separation came Governor George Bowen, with his experience as a servant of the Empire in the Ionian Islands during the 1850s – perhaps not one of the hardship posts. After seven years in his Queensland post, he would move on to New Zealand, Victoria, Mauritius, Hong Kong and Malta.

In dealing with his important career in Queensland, Bowen's lengthy entry in the *Australian Dictionary of Biography* concentrates on his encouragement to legislation on land, immigration and education, as well as his political skills in the fractious climate of a small but rapidly growing and geographically vast colony (*Australian Dictionary of Biography*, vol. 3:

203). Not a word is mentioned about his role in the administration of Aboriginal affairs. Yet, through the Executive Council and in his role as the conduit for communications between Brisbane and the Colonial Office, he was familiar with the challenges of this area as well. His despatches from his early months convey a sense of being on a grand mission, one in which the Empire as a reality looms large (Bowen and Lane-Poole, 1889).[1]

The colony governed by Bowen was exposed, he believed, to two security threats – an external one from the French base in New Caledonia, and an internal one 'from the native tribes, which are far more numerous and more formidable in Queensland than in any other portions of Australia'. Writing to the Duke of Newcastle, the Secretary of State for Colonies, only five months into his term, Bowen described a colonial context which appears a far cry from the visions of a rule-of-law empire:

> The life of the pioneers of colonization in the distant prairies of the interior of this colony, presents several distinct phases, when viewed in connection with the Aborigines. The first sight of the horse and his rider appears to strike a tribe of blacks, as yet ignorant of the white man's existence, with supernatural terror, similar to the awe with which the American Indians contemplated the comrades of Columbus and of Cortez. But superstitious fear is soon succeeded by bitter hostility. Mutual provocations between the races lead to mutual reprisals. The fiercer spirits among the native warriors fall before the superior arms and skill of the European, or are driven still further backwards into the unexplored wilderness. The milder nature sink ere long into the well-fed dependents of the colonists, and in the course of a few years no danger remains to be apprehended from them beyond some isolated acts of robbery or revenge. (Bowen and Lane-Poole, 1889: 204–5)

Bowen's account collapsed a historical process of far-reaching consequence into a paragraph that nevertheless tells us a great deal about the mechanisms of empire and dispossession. Most significantly, in my view, he sees this Australian, or indeed Queensland, phase of the empire's history as one that mimics the days of Columbus and Cortez. Spain is not so much the example to avoid here as the historical account that helps provide an understanding of first contact. It does not matter for this governor that he is the latest in a series of governors who have had the challenge of dealing with Indigenous peoples in Australia since 1788. Queensland must go through the same process all over again – one in which civilisation must learn how to deal with the uncivilised. There are lessons from the history of empires in Bowen's despatches, but they are more likely at this early stage of his career to come from other places than the Australian colonies, of which he had no direct knowledge. Hence, when he goes on to outline the management of 'the blacks', his references include South Africa and British Columbia:

> In the early days of the occupation of each district, the colonists are frequently obliged to associate together, for self-defence against the blacks, in a somewhat irregular manner, and after a fashion, as I am informed, of the old Dutch Commandos in South Africa. For many obvious reasons, it seems highly desirable that this border warfare, when absolutely unavoidable, should be carried on under some control on the part of the Govt. The establishment of the NP [Native Police] has contributed much towards this end; and I am inclined to believe that the enrolment of the principal settlers and their servants in several Corps of Yeomanry, or rather of Mounted Rifles, would contribute still more. (Bowan and Lane-Poole, 1889: 204–5)

This was an adventurous proposition to advance in Australia, where colonial government, before and after the self-government granted to most colonies in the 1850s, was more inclined to strict governmental responsibility for armed force, rather than some notion of volunteer force as implied here. But the critical point in any case is the rolling out of imperial examples. As Bowen continued his musings, he considered Australian problems in imperial contexts:

> Sir E Bulwer Lytton [one-time Colonial Secretary] wrote to the Lt-Gov of British Columbia, that 'in a settlement which is surrounded by savage tribes, while sound policy will dictate every effort to conciliate the goodwill and confidence of such uncivilised neighbours, and while humanity will shrink from the application of armed force against the aborigines wherever it can be avoided, yet some military strength and disciplined organisation are essential preservatives to the settlers, and indeed will be attended with far less loss of life, with actions far less sanguinary, than when the white man is left to defend himself against the black [here Bowen replaced Bulwer-Lytton's 'red', alluding to Red Indians of North America] without that decided superiority which is conferred by military skill over savages. In such conflicts the want of discipline is the want of mercy.' (Bowen and Lane-Poole, 1889: 204–5)[2]

In such contexts, the Indigenous inhabitants were not yet subjects of the Crown, but 'savages', and colonies had to secure themselves against 'savage tribes'. Whether in the words of Bowen or Bulwer-Lytton, the object of a security policy for new colonies was a disciplined disposession. A year later the Queensland government was to describe for the benefit of its Colonial Office audience the security arrangements critical to its future as a colony. Again the context is expansively imperial. The idea of a local militia was rejected in the considerations of Governor Bowen's Executive Council. But they contemplated an exception in respect of

> such local forces composed mainly of Natives of the various dependencies, as reasons of climate and economy, or other special circumstances, may render desirable. To the latter class belong such local forces as the Sepoy Regiments in India, the Hottentot Corps at the Cape, the Malay Regiment at Ceylon and the Native Police Corps of Qld – a Border Force which this Govt maintains for the protection of the frontier settlers. This Force costs this Colony about 17,000 Pounds annually [about 6% of total government expenditure in the colony at this time]; and may fairly be said to be (like the Frontier Police at the Cape) a contribution towards the general defence of the Empire, since the inland boundary of Qld is the boundary also of the Empire, which it is necessary to protect from the numerous and hostile savages of this portion of Australia. (Executive Council minute, 7 Jan. 1861, EXE/E3/61/1, QSA)

Wars like these in defence of empires are not made any the more respectable by retrospective legitimation – though it adds immeasurably to our understanding of colonial contexts to recover the contexts in which institutions like the Native Police were formed, authorised and deployed (Finnane and Richards, 2004).

The reality of imperial expansion during the second British Empire was the continuity of forceful expropriation. As Julie Evans argues elsewhere in this volume, this violent process constituted the critical moment in the very establishment of a rule-of-law state in which Indigenous peoples would be subject to 'the racialising and criminalising force of domestic law' (p. 70 below).

When an author concludes that 'In those countries where British culture and legal systems already held sway, such as the United States, Canada, and Australia, modernization was a comparatively painless process' (Windschuttle, 2000), such a judgement can only be sustained in a spirit of indifference to the historical experience of those who had occupied the lands so dispossessed. Such conclusions are also indifferent to imperial realities, as the contemporary reflections and policy-reasoning of imperial administrators like Bowen show us. In a case like Queensland, still in the

1860s imagined as at the frontline of the Empire, the language of warfare and the fear of savages still held sway.

The contemporary debates over the conditions of settlement of Australia are scarcely surprising, coming as they do just two centuries after the original dispossession, and within a lifetime of its completion in central and northern Australia. The criminalisation of the colonised, by law or by historical argument, remains a tactic in legitimising that dispossession. Acknowledging that there was an increase in black violence in Van Diemen's Land during the 1820s, Windschuttle contends that this was not a symptom of resistance or 'resentment' but rather a response to increased opportunity and temptation for the Aborigines to 'engage in robbery and murder, two customs they had come to relish' (Windschuttle, 2002: 129). This amateur criminology is mapped onto a historical account which conflates distinctions of culture, time and place and treats selectively the historiography of empires. The fact that such arguments can still generate such popular appeal, however questionable their standing in the relevant scholarly fields, highlights the importance of more sustained historical examination of the patterns and incidence of violence in the imperial contexts of inter-cultural conflict. Such a project awaits its historians.

Notes

1. My thanks to Jonathan Richards for this important reference, some of the implications of which we have explored elsewhere (Finnane and Richards, 2004).
2. The original of the despatch is Bowen to Newcastle, 10 April 1860, GOV/22, no. 33, Queensland State Archives.

References

Armitage, D. *The Ideological Origins of the British Empire*. Cambridge University Press, 2000.

Arneil, B. *John Locke and America: The Defence of English Colonialism*. Clarendon Press, 1996.

Bowen, G. F. and Lane-Poole, S. *Thirty Years of Colonial Government: A Selection from … [his] Despatches and Letters*. Longmans Green, 1889.

Buchan, B. 'Subjecting the natives: Aborigines, property and possession under early colonial rule', *Social Analysis*, 45, 2, 2001, pp. 143–62.

Canny, N. P. *The Elizabethan conquest of Ireland: A Pattern Established, 1565–76*. Harvester Press, 1976.

Evans, J. 'Re-reading Edward Eyre: race, resistance and repression in Australia and the Caribbean', *Australian Historical Studies*, 118, 2002, pp. 175–98.

Ferguson, N. *Empire: How Britain Made the Modern World*. Penguin, 2001.

Finnane, M. and Richards, J. ' "You'll get nothing out of it": the inquest, police and Aboriginal deaths in colonial Queensland', *Australian Historical Studies*, 123, 2004, pp. 84–105.

Foster, S. G. and Attwood, B. M. (eds) *Frontier Conflict: The Australian Experience*. National Museum of Australia, 2003.

Gallay, A. *The Indian Slave Trade: The Rise of the English Empire in the American South, 1670–1717*. Yale University Press, 2002.

Hall, C. 'Imperial man: Edward Eyre in Australasia and the West Indies, 1833–66', in Schwarz, B. (ed.), *The Expansion of England: Race, Ethnicity, and Cultural History*. Routledge, 1996.

Ivison, D., Patton, P. and Sanders, W. *Political Theory and the Rights of Indigenous Peoples*. Cambridge University Press, 2000.

Krygier, M. and van Krieken, R. 'The character of the nation', in Manne, R. (ed.), *Whitewash: On Keith Windschuttle's Fabrication of Aboriginal History*. Black Inc. Agenda, 2003.

Locke, J. and Laslett, P. *Two treatises of government*, rev. edn. New American Library, 1965.

Louis, W. R., Low, A. M., Canny, N. P. and Marshall, P. J. *The Oxford History of the British Empire*. Oxford University Press, 1998.

Macintyre, S. and Clark, A. *The History Wars*. Melbourne University Press, 2003.

Manne, R. *In Denial: The Stolen Generations and the Right*. Schwartz Publishing, 2001.

Manne, R. (ed.) *Whitewash: On Keith Windschuttle's Fabrication of Aboriginal History*. Black Inc. Agenda, 2003.

Moses, A. D. 'Revisionism and denial', in Manne, R. (ed.), *Whitewash: On Keith Windschuttle's Fabrication of Aboriginal History*. Black Inc. Agenda, 2003.

Pagden, A. *Lords of All the World: Ideologies of Empire in Spain, Britain and France c. 1500–c. 1800*. Yale University Press, 1995.

Tully, J. *Strange Multiplicity: Constitutionalism in an Age of Diversity*. Cambridge University Press, 1995.

Windschuttle, K. 'Rewriting the history of the British Empire', *The New Criterion*, May 2000 (accessed at http://www.newcriterion.com/archive/18/may00/keith.htm).

Windschuttle, K. *The Fabrication of Aboriginal History*. Macleay Press, 2002.

Chapter 5

Colonialism and the rule of law: the case of South Australia

Julie Evans

In 1841, Herman Merivale, Professor of Political Economy at Oxford University and soon to become a senior Colonial Office bureaucrat, lectured his students on 'the uncontrolled violence of individuals, if not of colonial authorities' that characterised British settlements throughout the Empire.[2] In lamenting that 'our practice may yet be far short of our principles', Merivale went on to advocate a more systematic and orderly approach to colonial governance. He observed that the first purpose for which native peoples 'in their uninstructed state' should be brought within the pale of criminal justice was that of 'deterring them from attacks on the persons and property of colonists'. This protection of colonial interests, he continued, could be best achieved 'by placing them, in the first instance, under a species of martial or summary law …' (Merivale, 1967: 490–8).

While purporting to pre-empt jury bias and regulate widespread violence in the settlements, Merivale's ameliorative proposal signalled something more akin to the exercise of naked power that he had previously deplored than to the principles of the rule of law, whose disinterested reign was seen to sanction Britain's colonising mission and distinguish it from those of its less scrupulous European rivals. As the historical record throughout the Empire would demonstrate (Havemann, 1999; Chanock, 2001; Reynolds, 1992; Evans *et al.*, 2003; Belich, 1996), being within rather than beyond the pale of English law would by no means accord Britain's (supposedly equal) Indigenous subjects the protection from coercion that their settler counterparts enjoyed. In the following analysis I discuss such a campaign to legalise the use of force in the colonies and outline a theoretical and conceptual framework to account for this apparent contradiction within the rule of law.

The rule of law

The rule of law is the opposite of the rule of men, a legal counter to tyranny and the arbitrary use of force. The idea of the rule of law in both its procedural and rhetorical forms is to prevent and redress injustice. But its complex ancestry, including how its representation in practice has been made possible by the very actions it abhors as well as by the principles and values it defends, belies the innocence or simplicity of its authority.

Perceived as a quintessentially English notion, the rule of law encapsulates the long struggle against tyranny from the time of the Magna Carta and its confirmations, through to the Petition of Right, the Habeas Corpus Acts, the Bill of Rights and the Act of Settlement. Brian Simpson claims that the idea permeated Blackstone's *Commentaries on the Laws of England* a century before it was formally expressed as a unified doctrine by Dicey in 1885 (Simpson, 2001: 25–7; Blackstone, 1765–9; Dicey, 1952). Certainly by the nineteenth century the concept of the rule of law had become one of the principal ideological justifications of the British Empire (Simpson, 2001: 22–37). Its extension to the dominions, in particular, has been seen as one of the great achievements of British colonialism as all of the Crown's subjects, whether coloniser or colonised, were theoretically equally amenable to its force and protection.

Although the rule of law has become the jurisprudential standard for assessing the success or desirability of general theories of law (Collins, 1982: 14), the historical record unsettles the apparent neutrality of the doctrine. Looking closely at the rule of law in the early stages of colonial rule helps identify its particularistic and racial underpinnings as certain sections of the population, despite being equal subjects, were deemed to fall outside its full protection. Significantly, these initial exclusions in the colonies would not be confined to their immediate time and place but would set the pattern for discriminatory policies and practices that continued throughout the nineteenth century and beyond (Evans *et al.*, 2003). In becoming embedded in the constitutions and the founding legislation of the new nations that would eventually emerge, such structural discrimination demonstrates how the rule of law represents the interests of a demographically narrow group of people posited universally. I therefore understand the rule of law to be not simply an abstract ideal but, like the law itself, actively constitutive of the nation state it presupposes, both at home and abroad (Fitzpatrick, 1995, 2001; Guha, 1994).

I discuss the rule of law here in its early formulation in the Australian colonies, in times and places when it was most susceptible to breaking down. In outlining these developments, the argument highlights the unsuitability of the rule of law to certain colonial conditions and seeks to lay bare what the rule of law needs to secure before it can come into its own: exclusive sovereignty, private property and a market economy.

The rule of law in colonies of settlement

Given the accelerated push for democracy in British settlements, certain settlers in the colonies could enjoy rights and privileges that even surpassed their metropolitan contemporaries (Grimshaw *et al.*, 2001; Kercher, 1995; Neal, 1991). But the rule of law was massively attenuated when viewed in relation to colonised populations. Such discrimination is often understood as *contravening* the rule of law (Krygier, 2002; McLaren, 2002; Borrows, 1999). On the other hand, the internal critique adopted here, in outlining the economic imperatives of the settler-colonial formation that supported discriminatory practices, seeks to sublimate the rhetorical power of the rule of law as a stable legitimising force susceptible only to unlawful contravention. Rather, it understands such discrimination as actually *producing* the rule of law it simultaneously abrogates. Accordingly, the argument suggests that the installation of the rule of law in developing settler-states was contingent upon its abrogation in relation to Indigenous peoples whose dispossession had to be secured before 'normal times' could prevail.

I focus attention here on Merivale's 'first instance', that is, on the formative stage of colonial rule when persistent reports of settlers 'taking the law into their own hands' brought colonial law's relation to Indigenous peoples more clearly to the fore. In seeking to stem 'unlawful' violence arising from both sides of the frontier, local and imperial authorities claimed to impose the rule of law. But though the rule of law appealed rhetorically to impartial justice and equality, its material interests were comprehensively colonial. When Europeans were outnumbered or where significant infrastructure had yet to be established, legal assertions of sovereignty over the lands of others could mean little in practical terms. While settlers would be warned of the risk of prosecution for unlawful violence, in this critical interstitial period between a formal determination of sovereignty under international law and its practical transformation, dispossession remained paramount if state-building were to succeed. Already non-sovereigns in international law (Williams, 1990; Anghie, 1999a, 1999b), Indigenous peoples would face further exclusions when brought within domestic legal systems. Bringing Indigenous peoples more fully within the protective pale of English law (and thereby helping realise the sovereignty Britain already claimed to possess) simply mediated different modes of coercion, effectively rendering them prey to force in another guise as their lands were being transferred.[3]

I present below a case study of how, in the light of widespread concern, local and imperial authorities sought to regularise, if not to regulate, frontier violence by attempting to bring it within the rule of law. The study is situated at the very point of inclusion/exclusion in the developing 'normal order' when colonial law's relation to Indigenous peoples was at its most unstable, where its intersections with the lawful force of international law and the unlawful force of the frontier were brought into stark relief. It examines the resort to martial or summary procedures against Indigenous peoples in support of British sovereignty, invested and made manifest in the persons and property of colonists. The context outlined here is the settler colony of South Australia although the analysis has broader application to colonies of settlement more generally as Indigenous peoples shifted from being beyond to being within the pale of English law.

Settler colonialism

It is important to elaborate the characteristics of South Australia as representative of a very particular colonial formation, that of settler colonialism. As distinct from franchise colonies, like India, or the slave colonies of the Caribbean where resource value was maximised through extracting the surplus value of the *labour* of the colonised, economic interest in settler colonies was vested primarily in the *land*. Although their labour was certainly called upon in certain times and places, in purely structural terms, Indigenous peoples were superfluous to colonial interests and in fact stood in the way of the primary objective of securing permanent control of the land and converting it to alienable private property. Unlike in colonies of exploitation, the settlers had come to stay, literally *replacing* the Indigenous inhabitants on the land by segregating onto reserves those who survived the initial onslaught and then attempting to assimilate out of separate existence those who still remained (Wolfe, 1994).

It is hardly surprising, then, that indigeneity assumed, and continues to assume, a heightened significance in colonies of settlement as native peoples' alternative claims to the land threatened, and continue to threaten, the colonisers' assertions of exclusive sovereignty.[4] So it is in this very particular context, that of settler colonialism, that the discussion investigates the rule of law in the colonial encounter – that is, in terms of its meaning and manifestation *in the lands of others*. The focus in this instance is the violence associated with the initial onslaught.

The case of South Australia

Initial plans for the settlement of South Australia reflected the high moral hopes and the canny pecuniary expectations of a generation of British colonisers who questioned what they regarded as the haphazard colonising ways of the past. Herman Merivale was among those who promoted such 'systematic' colonisation schemes (Pares, 1961: 62). In the decade heralding the abolition of slavery, South Australia was settled according to new, notionally humane guidelines that were intended to attract investment capital, provide for the interests of free settlers and ensure that Indigenous peoples' lands and laws would be respected. The Letters Patent outlined the rights of Aborigines to the occupation and enjoyment of their lands and recommended the appointment of a Protector. On Governor Hindmarsh's arrival in December 1836, half of his Proclamation concerned Aborigines and the need for according them the rights and protection of British subjects.[5] But despite this apparent concern, the Foundation Act, which had established South Australia as a province in 1834, had made no mention of Aborigines or of their rights. Crucially, all land in South Australia was declared 'waste and unoccupied' (a powerful discursive construction rooted more broadly in colonialism) and available for settlement.

While treaties were conceded elsewhere in empire where Britain recognised prior title, in South Australia, like the other Australian colonies, Indigenous peoples were deemed to have no proprietorial interest in the land.[6] Despite Britain's claims to sovereignty, however, its jurisdictional and territorial limits were still to be tested where settlements were few and far between and in the vastness of the remote desert regions. As pastoralists ventured beyond the fledgling settlements that hugged the coastline of colonial South Australia or travelled overland from the eastern seaboard, the central significance of the quest to secure the land in the face of resistance would become apparent.

Early reports of 'friendly intercourse' with Aborigines were increasingly interspersed with stories of frontier conflict – particularly along the overland routes travelled by settlers seeking pastureland for cattle and sheep. These overlanders added their reports of 'affrays' with Aborigines, accused of 'stealing' stock or otherwise interfering with their progress, to those of isolated station-owners who told of huts being raided and shepherds and stock attacked. It is during these first few years of the colony's expansion that we encounter circumstances informing Merivale's claim that the first purpose of bringing Indigenous peoples within the pale of English law was to protect the persons and property of colonists, through the use of martial or summary law.

While proclamations of martial law elsewhere in empire were usually associated with chronic or acute civil disturbances involving riotous attacks on courthouses, officials or other symbols of state authority (Simpson, 2001: 54–90), in the Australian colonies extraordinary measures were generally considered in relation to episodic conflicts in sparsely populated rural areas. It is difficult to see any of these actions as constituting a threat to state authority unless this was represented in individual settlers attempting to make manifest the state's exclusive sovereignty in their assertions of claims to private property in the lands of others. Given the structural characteristics of settler colonialism, it is perhaps not surprising that we should encounter calls to suspend the rule of law as the land was being transferred. It was certainly during this period of pastoral expansion in each of these colonies that demands for extraordinary procedures to deal with Aborigines appeared (Evans, 2005).

I will establish this correlation through an analysis of events surrounding the wreck of the brig *Maria* along the Coorong coast in July 1840 and the subsequent discovery of the bloodied bodies of survivors interred in shallow graves in the lands of the Milmenrura people. Although some Aborigines had already been brought before courts in South Australia, reports of these 'murders' precipitated anxious deliberation in Adelaide about the law's relation to Indigenous peoples, the implementation of summary justice according to the principles of martial law, shootings and hangings in the field – and a colonial governor and his commissioner of police judged legally guilty of murder.[7]

I will elaborate the significance of events surrounding the *Maria* incident for understanding the meaning of the rule of law in the lands of others. Against the background of the Governor's 1836 Proclamation guaranteeing legal equality for Aborigines, 'who are as much under the safeguard of the law as the colonists themselves, and equally entitled to the privileges of British subjects',[8] the analysis tests the limits of the rule of law. Suspensions of the rule of law are always controversial, revealing, as they do, the partiality of its interests. Events on this remote Australian coast would test faith in the rule of law by the staunchest of its proponents who strove, nevertheless, to abide by and remain committed to its precepts which so patently failed to transcend the political actuality of the settler-colonial encounter. The way through this quagmire is to ask the simple question: why didn't the ordinary procedures of the law prevail?

The *Maria* incident

In 1840 Aborigines were the subject of much discussion in South Australia. From July the Assistant Land Commissioner Charles Sturt had been engaged in correspondence with certain settlers over 'whether the aboriginal inhabitants or the European preliminary purchasers' had the first right of selection from waste lands.[9] Both Sturt and the Governor, George Gawler, defended the rights of Aborigines against the protests of the settlers and, furthermore, objected strongly to any thought of selecting land for Aborigines outside districts familiar to them as 'extremely harsh towards men who, by their general conduct, merit a very different treatment'.[10] While colonial interests had even then been to the fore, these protestations about Aboriginal conduct would soon be called upon to advance colonial interests even further. For by the end of that month, reports were coming in of murder by Aborigines 'within thirty miles of … surveyed and located territory' along the coast near Encounter Bay. These Aborigines, Gawler informed his superiors in London, had been 'remarkable for their ferocity from the first discovery of the Province'.[11] He would soon employ their difference from those he had just defended to justify the abrogation of their rights under the rule of law.

Marine surveyor W. J. S. Pullen had been sent out to find the bodies of the Europeans. His report published in the *South Australian Gazette* on 13th August stated that at the end of July he had uncovered remains in various sites along the coast where the survivors of the shipwreck had presumably wandered. He later observed Aborigines wearing items of clothing and blankets, which, together with their 'silence … when questioned respecting the murder', made him confident he was among the guilty parties. Moreover, 'if looks were a sufficient condemnation', he added, 'there were two who were certainly possessed of such, for, without exception, they were the most villainous looking characters I ever saw.' It was 11th August before he returned to Adelaide and finalised his report for the government.[12]

The governor immediately convened a special meeting of Council for the 12th to decide the course of action against 'the tribes in that neighbourhood'. Gawler argued that since his arrival in Adelaide he had 'strenuously required from Europeans forbearance in their conduct towards the Natives' and was bound to 'do justice to Europeans, when any of their number become the victims of unprovoked ferocity among the opposite class.'[13] He requested an opinion from Justice Charles Cooper as to whether the law could be brought to take effect in the case.[14] Cooper replied that the crimes in question were beyond the reach of law. It was impossible to try according to the forms of English law 'people of a wild and savage tribe whose country, although within the limits of the Province of South Australia, has never been occupied by settlers, who have never submitted themselves to our dominion, and between whom and the colonists there has been no social intercourse'.[15] Cooper's denial of jurisdiction fortified the government's intention. Gawler had already decided that, as Aborigines were not valid witnesses, convictions could not be secured under the ordinary law as no evidence of perpetration 'commonly recognised as legal' could be procured.[16]

The Council decided to declare the district of the Milmenrura people in a disturbed state and proceed on the principles of martial law.[17] Gawler instructed the Commissioner of Police Major O'Halloran to proceed to the area with a detachment of 30, including three or four Aborigines from the neighbouring Encounter Bay people. He was to capture all of those Milmenrura congregated with the murderers, establish the actual murderers with the assistance of the 'Encounter Bay Blacks' and bring no more than three of them to summary justice.[18] In the event, although bloodshed was to be avoided unless absolutely necessary, two Aborigines identified by Pullen as 'the actual murderers' were shot while fleeing their captors.[19] Two other prisoners were then tried 'in the most formal and deliberate manner ... found guilty on the universal evidence or to the declared conviction of all the other natives present' and to the formally declared conviction of Major O'Halloran and the other Europeans of the party. They were hanged in an exemplary execution at the gravesites of the victims with their fellows as witnesses. O'Halloran then scoured the territory of the Milmenrura 'proving to them that he possessed full power to punish future atrocities'.[20]

Gawler wrote his first report of these proceedings to the Colonial Office from the expedition's depot where he had ridden out to meet O'Halloran. He was anxious for official approval of the extraordinary measures he had set in train – no one was more desirous than he to show justice and humanity to the Aborigines by keeping within the strict limits of British laws. On this occasion, however, where ordinary law could not reach them he thought it wiser not to suffer 'a band of most ferocious, insidious, unprovoked and inveterate murderers and robbers to continue in their crimes with impunity'.[21]

The British government did not approve. But long before the official despatch expressing its objections arrived in Adelaide, the South Australian government had to answer local protests asserting the rights of Aborigines as British subjects to be tried in a court of law.[22] Gawler's Attorney-General Smillie referred to international law to authorise the distinction he observed between those 'friendly', acquiescent Aborigines whose territories had been occupied by settlers and therefore were entitled to rights as British subjects and the Milmenrura people who were not. Calling on Vattel, Smillie aligned the Milmenrura with those who failed to cultivate their lands and who, in choosing to live by plunder, *'deserve[d] to be extirpated as savage and pernicious beasts'*. In the case in question, the 'unprovoked massacre' of innocent shipwreck victims reflected the *'character of the tribe'* and therefore had to be dealt with 'on very different grounds from the solitary or occasional *offence of an individual against the Municipal Law'*. This, rather, was *'the crime of the nation'* which demanded severe summary measures 'to terrify the whole tribe by a sense of our power and determination to punish':[23]

> The crime therefore was to be regarded, not as that of *individual British Subjects*, but of a whole hostile tribe, that is of a *nation at enmity with Her Majesty's Subjects* ... [T]his view is strictly in accordance with the law of nations ...[24]

Although, Smillie went on, international law would have authorised an 'indiscriminate slaughter', in this case the government had decided on a middle road in abandoning ordinary forms which were inadequate to the emergency and taking on more ample powers 'for the welfare of the state and the peace of society'.[25]

George Stevenson, editor of the *Register* and the man who had drafted the 1836 Proclamation protecting the rights of Aborigines, was not persuaded by the arguments of the Attorney-General. He challenged Smillie's attempt to draw a legal distinction between Aborigines and vehemently denied the Executive's right to exceed the ordinary law:[26]

> The natives have been condemned and executed, not merely by an unauthorised, illegal, and unconstitutional tribunal, but upon evidence, which in a court either civil or military would not be sufficient to hang a dog ... Vague assumptions and loose conjectures there are in abundance – some suspicious circumstances, which might have been possibly explained ... the hearsay assertions of another tribe in avowed and inveterate hostility to that implicated ... Beyond this there is nothing ...[27]

A 'Colonist of 1836' wrote to the *Register* in 'the interests of justice and humanity'. Why had the Protector of Aborigines not been heard from? How could the Milmenrura be declared 'cruel and remorseless savages' if so little of 'their number, character and disposition' was positively known? If the Milmenrura had indeed become less than friendly the Governor and the Attorney-General should look to the overlanders and not the 'nature' of the Aborigines for provocation. Seldom did new settlers arrive without some tale 'of boasting and butchering the natives on the way'. Moreover, the Milmenrura had helped the survivors of the shipwrecked *Fanny* two years previously 'for no less a period than forty days' feeding them and guiding them to the borders of their territory.[28] The *Fanny's* captain, Captain Gill, had publicly stated that in their seven-week stay with the Milmenrura 'they at all times evinced the greatest friendship. They are decidedly the most inoffensive race I ever met.'[29] The whole history of the murders, the colonist went on, was 'one upon which there is no evidence beyond hearsay; and the bodies and clothes of the passengers'. It was a case 'of supposition from beginning to end'.

The Colonial Office was no more persuaded by Gawler's arguments. 'It did not follow', Permanent Under-Secretary James Stephen minuted when he first received news of Gawler's intentions in February of the following year, 'that because he could not try he might slay them.'[30] While Gawler's correspondence requesting approbation arrived in London long after Commissioner O'Halloran had headed out along the coastland to determine the executions, the despatch expressing the Secretary of State's disapproval would not even be written until December, following months of legal deliberation from the law officers. It was eventually received in Adelaide in 1842 not by Gawler but by his replacement who was himself facing yet another round of frontier 'affrays' along the overland routes.[31] The time lapse is critically significant and of more than historical interest. In the absence of even telegraphic communication technology, the ultimate authority of Britain, assumed and sought by anxious colonial governors, was meaningless in distant colonies.

It was Governor Grey who received the confidential despatch stating that the British government 'must strongly object' to the course pursued by his predecessor. The law officers rejected Cooper's denial of juris- diction, asserting that the Aborigines should have been brought before an ordinary legal tribunal and that the summary execution of the supposed murderers 'was contrary to Law; and that the legal character of the act [executed by O'Halloran and assisted by Gawler] was murder'.[32] This political and legal condemnation was sparse in the style of such govern- ment pronouncements. It was tellingly elaborated, however, by James Stephen, who had overseen the progress of the whole correspondence concerning the *Maria* incident through official channels in London. While conceding there might be some injustice in trying 'savages' under a code of which they were ignorant and to which they had not submitted, he had little time for Cooper's opinion. It was incomparably more just, he considered, 'to try these men with all these seeming and real incongruities, than to try them by an armed police, exasperated by popular prejudice and excited by a long and toilsome pursuit'.[33]

Stephen's opinion was informed not just by events in South Australia but by the multiple reports of frontier violence he received from the colonies. By October 1841 he would claim that every such report added to his conviction that Aboriginal peoples throughout the empire were 'doomed to an early and an entire extermination'. The sympathies of the White race were all against them, apparently humane men were 'borne away by the current' while even the Protectors become 'apologists for the doers of the wrong instead of advocates for these who suffer by it'. Maddened 'by oppression, and every kind of misery' brought upon them by the colonists, Aborigines were forced to become revengeful 'and then are hung or shot in a summary way as murderers'. Stephen advised his political superiors that the situation was 'an evil which we have hitherto only deplored without knowing where or how to find an effectual remedy'.[34]

Stephen's faith in the rule of law in the colonies had perhaps reached its limits. In responding to Governor Grey's attempts to abide more closely by ordinary procedures in South Australia – or, at least, to abrogate them less spectacularly than his predecessor – Stephen doubted the wisdom or humanity of leniency in the administration of justice in relation to Aborigines involved in frontier violence:

> The theory might be quite sound if society will but so regard it. But it is not a sound theory if the effect on the passions and the conduct of the European herdsmen be left out of account. It is easy in these matters to spin a thread too fine for use.[35]

At certain points on the road to nationhood, the rule of law – and the sovereignty it both presupposed and produced – simply could not transcend its social origins. In applying or not applying it to Indigenous peoples, the rule of law would do them few favours.

The resort to martial or summary law – understanding the exception

In light of contradictory viewpoints concerning Gawler's actions, it is perhaps best to return to the simple question, why didn't the ordinary law prevail? If we understand the *Maria* incident as *contravening* the rule of law we might begin to seek explanation in a chief justice inordinately concerned with the technical forms of law, a governor overly zealous in his demonstration of colonial force to quell settler fears, an attorney-general desperate for legal precedents to justify its use.[36] Within this model, we might understand such extraordinary actions primarily in procedural terms, or, despite their ubiquity throughout the empire, as (a series of) aberrations, reducible, perhaps, to individual personality, the sociological make-up of particular colonies or simply the misguided racism of the past. On the other hand, if we seek to understand the incident as *constitutive* of the rule of law we need to cast our net more broadly to find an explanation that relates not just to the local colonial context but to that of settler colonialism more generally. Such an approach promotes certain observations, too, about the nature of the rule of law – and about the nature of the authority vested in the decision to suspend its operations – both at home and abroad, in the past and in the present.

It is helpful in this regard to consider Carl Schmitt's critique of the liberal state, particularly in terms of the broader conceptual problem outlined more recently by Italian philosopher Giorgio Agamben – the paradoxical capacity of the law to authorise its own suspension (Schmitt, 1988; Agamben, 1998). This analytical model challenges accepted juridico-political definitions of sovereignty.[37] In contrast, the very essence of sovereignty is expressed in the legal power to suspend the validity of the law, that is, in the sovereign legally placing himself outside the law. It is at this point, that is, at the time and place of the decision to suspend the law, that the limits of juridical order can be perceived and we get closer to 'the original – if concealed – nucleus of sovereign power' (Agamben, 1998: 6). Schmitt's notion of the exception – wherein exceptions to the rule are regarded as intimately related to, rather than separate from, its regular form – elaborates this critical juncture where 'authority proves itself not to need law to create law' (in Agamben, 1998: 16). For Schmitt, the exception 'does not only confirm the rule; the rule as such lives off the exception alone':

> There is no rule that is applicable to chaos. Order must be established for juridical order to make sense. A regular situation must be created, and sovereign is he who definitely decides if this situation is actually effective. (In Agamben, 1998: 16)

As Agamben paraphrases Schmitt, the law 'must first of all create the space for its own reference in real life and *make that reference regular*' (Agamben, 1998: 26, italics in original):

The relation of exception thus simply expresses the originary formal structure of the juridical relation. In this sense, the sovereign decision on the exception is the originary juridico-political structure on the basis of which what is included in the juridical order and what is excluded from it acquire their meaning. In its archetypal form, the state of exception is therefore the principle of every juridical localization, since only the state of exception opens the space in which the determination of a certain juridical order and a particular territory first becomes possible.

What is at issue in the exception, then, is 'the creation and definition of the very space in which the juridico-political order can have validity' (Agamben, 1998: 19).

Both Schmitt and Agamben assume a European origin impossible to localise in specific temporal or spatial terms, a 'time immemorial'. But in the colonies, in the critical formative stages of establishing state power through the transformation of sovereignty, we encounter native society as the origin that has to be suppressed – through the constitution of the law that at once presupposes and authorises its suppression.

Conclusion

As observed at the outset, in the formative years of colonial rule the universal ideals of the rule of law could not prevail where the very particular conditions of its operation had yet to be established. The *Maria* incident allows us a point of entry into this puzzling paradox by signifying a point of origin – the creation of a new juridico-political order from the disorder and chaos of the frontier – rather than a point of contravention of an established legal regime.

While this theoretical trajectory helps us relate a seemingly extra-ordinary experience in far-off South Australia to similar events throughout the empire – and to the formulation of state power more generally – the empirical actuality was, of course, far from cut and dried. As the various stakeholders strove to anchor their interests in stable ground, they drew on both international law and municipal contexts in their attempts to regularise within a legal framework the specifically colonial violence which would secure the transfer of the land. Accordingly, in a supposedly sovereign domestic jurisdiction, we see Aborigines drawn as both enemies and criminals, susceptible both to warfare and punishment, and to something powerful in between – the martial law whose murky legality precipitated and reflected the anxiety of colonial governors everywhere.

Such ambivalence also helps us understand the broader context of the transformation of sovereignty that was taking place in the lands of the Milmenrura people. For frontiers were not untethered autochthonous zones but were the potent residues of international law whose declarations of sovereignty over the lands of others could only ever be fully realised on the ground, together with the assistance of domestic (colonial) law and the violence it could additionally condone. Within this model, conceiving frontiers simply as places of arbitrary violence does not adequately signify their lawlessness. Frontiers can perhaps more accurately be understood as zones that were produced between – and had yet to be caught within – two jurisdictional orders, where the monopoly on violence still could fall outside the hands of the state.[38]

Demands for extraordinary procedures in the Australian colonies correlated with conflicts over dispossession. Such suspensions created a space in which the 'normal order' could develop – where exclusive sovereignty could be secured, individual property could be defended and the broader liberal political, social and economic order could be fully installed. This broader context helps resolve the paradox of the violent terms Merivale had outlined for bringing Indigenous peoples in British settlements within the pale of English law. And the idea of the rule of law, providing universal equality for those not excluded from its particular domain – that of the nation – could be seen less problematically to prevail.

In reviewing the *Maria* incident in light of this conceptual framework, we see the essence of European sovereignty in the legal capacity to suppress alternative claims through the resort to force otherwise condemned in law. This state of exception was, of course, not only expressed in Gawler's actions on this occasion in South Australia but had long been prefigured in Europe whose nation states had in turn been created through a history of conquest, coercion and colonialism. It would be repeated elsewhere and in other forms throughout the empire as colonised peoples (Simpson, 2001: 54–90)[39] were cast 'both within the reach of the law and yet outside its protection' (Anghie, 1999b: 103). But whether through outright martial law, summary justice legislation, the banning of testimony, exemplary punishments or the suspension of habeas corpus, to name just some of its modes, the state of exception would simply *inaugurate* Indigenous peoples' collective subjection to the racialising and criminalising force of domestic law.

Notes

1. This research has been supported by the Australian Research Council. The chapter draws on and develops the conceptual framework outlined in an earlier essay published as 'The rule of law in the colonial encounter: the case of Western Australia', in *Adventures of the Law: Proceedings of the 16th British Legal History Conference, Dublin, 2003* (Four Courts Press, 2005). I thank Patrick Wolfe for his critical reading.
2. Merivale succeeded Sir James Stephen in 1847.
3. Although individual settler violence was more clearly unlawful, the difficulty of securing convictions given the limits of the law, let alone within the grim politics of the settler-colonial encounter, undermined putative safeguards.
4. For recent controversial discussion in the Australian context see Windschuttle (2002) and responses in Manne (2003) and Attwood and Foster (2003). See also Mark Finnane's chapter in this collection where he explains the critical importance of bringing a more comprehensive legal and historical perspective to bear on analyses of colonial violence in local contexts.
5. This concentration on the welfare of Aborigines in South Australia drew on a much broader awareness of the shocking impact of settlement on Indigenous peoples across Britain's empire. Throughout the 1830s, in particular, British and colonial officials, some with connections to the then powerful humanitarian lobby, voiced their concerns about the common right of Indigenous peoples in the colonies of settlement to the equal justice and protection of the law. By 1835, the House of Commons appointed a Select Committee to consider the best means of protecting the rights of Aboriginal people, in Australia as elsewhere. See *Report from the Select Committee on Aborigines* (1837, reprinted 1968), p. 3.
6. Acknowledged as a legal fiction in *Mabo* v. *Queensland* (No. 2) (1992) 175 CLR 1.
7. These reports intensified earlier settler fears arising from the deaths of two shepherds in 1839. Pope suggests that in the 1839 cases, speedy arrests and subsequent trials of the accused Aborigines prevented settlers taking the law in to their own hands. See Pope (1998: 48–51).
8. *The South Australian Register*, 19 September, 1840.
9. Sturt to McLaren *et al.*, 17 July, 1840, in *The South Australian Gazette*, 23 July 1840, encl. in Gawler to S/S, no. 8, 1 August 1840, CO 13/16.
10. Sturt to McLaren *et al.*, 17 July 1840, in *SA Gazette*, 23 July 1840, encl. in Gawler to S/S, no. 8, 1 August 1840, CO 13/16.
11. Gawler to S/S, no. 12, 15 August 1840, CO 13/16.
12. *SA Gazette*, 13 August 1840, encl. in Gawler to S/S, no. 12, 15 August 1840, CO 13/16. Pullen had been accompanied by Aborigines from the neighbouring Encounter Bay group.
13. Gawler to S/S, no. 12, 15 August 1840, CO 13/16.
14. Gawler to Cooper, no. 5, 12 August 1840 encl. in Gawler to S/S, no. 12, 15 August 1840, CO 13/16.

15. Cooper to Gawler, no. 6, 12 August 1840, encl. in Gawler to S/S, no. 12, 15 August 1840, CO 13/16.
16. Council Proceedings, 15 September 1840, in *SA Register*, 15 September 1840. See also Pope (1998) and Wright (2001).
17. Wary of the adverse publicity an actual proclamation would have upon the colony, the Council decided against an actual proclamation but otherwise proceeded 'on strict principles of martial justice'. Council Proceedings, 15 September 1840, in *SA Register*, 15 September 1840.
18. Gawler to S/S, no. 12, 15 August 1840, CO 13/16. The number would have been increased had Gawler known the full extent of the alleged murders. See Council proceedings, 15 September 1840, in *SA Register*, 15 September 1840.
19. Gawler to S/S, no. 13, 5 September 1840, CO 13/16. The detailed instructions to O'Halloran stated that if temperate measures failed, O'Halloran would not be held blameable if he had to resort to 'extreme force against the whole tribe'. See Gawler to O'Halloran, 14 August 1840, in *SA Register*, 15 September 1840.
20. Gawler to S/S, no. 13, 5 September 1840, CO 13/16.
21. Gawler to S/S, no. 13, 5 September 1840, CO 13/16.
22. As discussed in note 7, some Aborigines had already been brought before courts in Adelaide. See *SA Register*, 19 September 1840 and Bennett (2002. Ch. 5).
23. Council proceedings, Attorney-General Smillie, 15 September 1840 in *SA Register*, 15 September 1840.
24. *SA Register*, 15 September 1840. While elaboration is not possible here, it is important to note such a declaration confounded the claim that Aborigines were not sovereigns.
25. *SA Register*, 15 September 1840. Major O'Halloran's official character was also of a mixed nature 'not exclusively that of a civil or judicial functionary, acting in the exercise of ordinary and defined duties, but partly that of a military officer, commissioned to execute a particular service'.
26. Editorial, 'Summary execution of the natives', in *SA Register*, 19 September 1840.
27. *SA Register*, 19 September 1840.
28. 'The Natives', *SA Register*, 3 October 1840.
29. Captain Gill's statement, *SA Register*, 3 October 1840. According to contemporary descendants, a group of Milmenrura people rescued 26 survivors from the *Maria* at Lacepede Bay, providing them with food and water and escorting them through their territory towards the settlement at Encounter Bay. They had already experienced violence from whalers, sealers and overlanders who abducted their women so when *Maria* sailors began interfering with their women the Milmenrura men attacked to protect their families. In 1934 Milerum, 'one of the last of the *narumbe* or Ngarinyeri initiates', gave this Ngarinyeri explanation to anthropologist N. B. Tindale. See Mattingley and Hampton (1992: 37).
30. Stephen's minute, 19 February 1841, Gawler to S/S, no. 12, 15 August 1840, CO 13/16.

31. Gawler had been recalled due to perceived financial mismanagement of the colony.
32. S/S to Grey, 'Confidential', 14 December 1841, CO 396/2. The question of indemnity would be addressed if prosecutions were brought against Gawler and O'Halloran.
33. Stephen to Hope, 14 October 1841, attached to Gawler to S/S, 30 April 1841, CO 13/20.
34. Stephen to Hope, 14 October 1841, attached to Gawler to S/S, 30 April 1841, CO 13/20. Stephen refers specifically here to Protector Moorhouse who was later involved in retributive violence in the year following the *Maria* incident.
35. Stephen's minute, Grey to S/S, no. 15, 5 July 1841, CO 13/20.
36. For a detailed account of the legal questions in the *Maria* incident see Lendrum (1977: 26–43).
37. For a study of colonial India which adopts a related approach see Hussain (2003).
38. While my broader research 'Beyond the pale: law, sovereignty and Indigenous peoples' considers the nature and scope of this threshold space and its more orderly legal precedents, I consider here the beginning of its aftermath, as Indigenous peoples were brought within the pale of domestic law.
39. Simpson demonstrates that official mechanisms of repression were authorised all over the British Empire as well as domestically and most of them under the rule of law (although some were certainly more controversial than others and caused politicians and bureaucrats in London to scramble for justifications).

References

Agamben, G. *Homo Sacer: Sovereign Power and Bare Life.* Stanford University Press, 1998.
Anghie, A. 'Finding the peripheries: sovereignty and colonialism in nineteenth-century international law', *Harvard International Law Journal*, 10, 1, 1999a, pp. 1–80.
Anghie, A. 'Francisco de Vitoria and the colonial origins of international law', in Fitzpatrick, P. and Darian-Smith, E. (eds), *Laws of the Postcolonial*. University of Michigan Press, 1999b, pp. 89–107.
Armitage, D. *The Ideological Origins of the British Empire.* Cambridge University Press, 2002.
Arneil, B. *John Locke and America: The Defence of English Colonialism.* Clarendon Press, 1996.
Attwood, B. and Foster, S. G. *Frontier Conflict: The Australian Experience.* National Museum of Australia, 2003.
Belich, J. *Making Peoples: A History of the New Zealanders: From Polynesian Settlement to the End of the Nineteenth Century.* Penguin Press, 1996.

Bennett, J. M. *Sir Charles Cooper: First Chief Justice of South Australia 1856–61.* Federation Press, 2002.

Blackstone, W. *Commentaries on the Laws of England.* Clarendon Press, 1765–9.

Borrows, J. 'Sovereignty's alchemy: an analysis of *Delgamuukw* v. *British Columbia*', *Osgoode Hall Law Journal*, 37, 1999, pp. 537–96, esp. 581–5.

Chanock, M. *The Making of South African Legal Culture, 1902–1936: Fear, Favour, and Prejudice.* Cambridge University Press, 2001.

Collins, H. *Marxism and Law.* Clarendon Press, 1982.

Colonial Office records for South Australia, Public Record Office, London.

Dicey, A. V. *Introduction to the Study of the Law of the Constitution*, 1st edn 1885, 9th edn by E. C. S. Wade. Macmillan, 1952.

Evans, J., Grimshaw, P., Philips, D. and Swain, S. *Equal Subjects, Unequal Rights: Indigenous Peoples in British Settler Colonies, 1830–1910.* Manchester University Press, 2003.

Evans, J. 'The rule of law in the colonial encounter: the case of Western Australia', in *Adventures of the Law: Proceedings of the 16th British Legal History Conference, Dublin, 2003.* Four Courts Press, forthcoming, 2005.

Fitzpatrick, P. 'Introduction', in Fitzpatrick, P. (ed.), *Nationalism, Racism and the Rule of Law.* Dartmouth, 1995.

Fitzpatrick, P. *Modernism and the Grounds of Law.* Cambridge University Press, 2001.

Grimshaw, P., Reynolds, R. and Swain, S. 'The paradox of "ultra-democratic" government: indigenous civil rights in nineteenth-century New Zealand, Canada and Australia', in Kirkby, D. and Coleborne, C. (eds), *Law, History, Colonialism: The Reach of Empire.* Manchester University Press, 2001, pp. 78–90.

Guha, R. 'Dominance without hegemony and its historiography', in Guha, R. (ed.), *Subaltern Studies VI: Writings on South Asian History and Society.* Oxford University Press, 1994, pp. 210–301.

Havemann, P. (ed.), *Indigenous Peoples' Rights: in Australia, Canada and New Zealand.* Oxford University Press, 1999.

Hussain, N. *The Jurisprudence of Emergency: Colonialism and the Rule of Law.* University of Michigan Press, 2003.

Kercher, B. *An Unruly Child: A History of Law in Australia.* Allen & Unwin, 1995.

Krygier, M. 'The grammar of colonial legality: subjects, objects, and the Australian rule of law', in Brennan, G. and Castles, F. G. (eds), *Australia Reshaped: 200 Years of Institutional Transformation.* Cambridge University Press, 2002, pp. 220–60.

Lendrum, S. D. 'The "Coorong Massacre": martial law and the Aborigines at first settlement', *Adelaide Law Review*, 6, 1977, pp. 26–43.

Mabo v. *Queensland (No. 2)* (1992) 175 CLR 1.

Manne, R. (ed.), *Whitewash: On Keith Windschuttle's Fabrication of Aboriginal History.* Black Inc. Agenda, 2003.

Mattingley, C. and Hampton, K. (eds) *Survival In Our Own Land: 'Aboriginal' Experiences in 'South Australia' since 1836*, told by Nungas and others. Sydney: Hodder & Stoughton, 1992.

McLaren, J. 'Reflections on the rule of law: the Georgian colonies of New South Wales and Upper Canada, 1788–1837', in Kirkby, D. and Coleborne, C. (eds),

Law, History, Colonialism: The Reach of Empire. Manchester University Press, 2001, pp. 46–62.

Merivale, H. *Lectures on Colonization and Colonies*, delivered before the University of Oxford in 1839, 1840 and 1841 and reprinted in 1861. Frank Cass, 1967.

Neal, D. *The Rule of Law in a Penal Colony: Law and Power in Early New South Wales*. Cambridge University Press, 1991.

Pares, R.. 'The economic factors in the history of empire', in Humphreys, R. A. and E. (eds), *The Historian's Business and Other Essays*. Clarendon Press, 1961, pp. 49–76.

Pope, A. R. *Aborigines and the Criminal Law in South Australia: The First Twenty-Five Years*, PhD thesis, Deakin University, Victoria, 1998.

Report from the Select Committee on Aborigines (British Settlements) with Minutes of Evidence and Appendices, 1837, British Parliamentary Papers. Irish University Press, 1968.

Reynolds, H. *The Law of the Land*. Penguin, 1992.

Schmitt, C. *Political Theology: Four Chapters on the Concept of Sovereignty* (1st edn 1922). MIT Press, 1988.

Simpson, A. W. B. *Human Rights and the End of Empire: Britain and the Genesis of the European Convention*. Oxford University Press, 2001.

South Australian Gazette, July to August 1840, encl. in CO 13/16, Public Record Office, London.

South Australian Register, July to October, 1840, State Library of Victoria.

Williams, R. *The American Indian in Western Legal Thought*. Oxford University Press, 1990.

Windschuttle, K., *The Fabrication of Aboriginal History*, vol.1, *Van Diemen's Land 1803–47*. Macleay Press, 2002.

Wolfe, P. 'Nation and miscege nation: discursive continuity in the post-Mabo era', *Social Analysis*, 36, 1994, pp. 93–152.

Wright, N. E. 'The problem of Aboriginal evidence in early colonial New South Wales', in Kirkby D. and Coleborne, C. (eds), *Law, History, Colonialism: The Reach of Empire*. Manchester University Press, 2001, pp. 140–55.

Chapter 6

Colonial history and theories of the present: some reflections upon penal history and theory

Mark Brown

The aim of this chapter is to connect colonial history with contemporary penal theory. More specifically, I aim in this chapter to consider how an understanding of justice and social control in late nineteenth-century British India might be able to inform contemporary debates over the meaning and significance of recent 'penal innovations'. These include a variety of strategies designed to incapacitate and limit the rights of offenders, including sexual predator laws, sex offender registration schemes and the phenomenon of mass imprisonment (see Pratt *et al.*, forthcoming). I aim here to address a lacuna within both criminology and social history. On the one hand, the discipline of criminology, only recently shed of its modernist state-sponsored role of penal science, has seldom looked back over its shoulder to the past. Moreover, where it has done so (for example, Garland, 1985; Radzinowicz, 1986; Morris and Rothman, 1995) its vision has been blinkered, tunnelled and largely Anglocentric, defining the past largely in terms of the penal histories of Britain and the United States. On the other hand, social historians, whose gaze has been more wide ranging and whose theoretical historical models far more differentiated (e.g. Arnold, 1986; Ludden, 2001), seldom seem inclined to bring contemporary issues to the centre of their analysis, except perhaps in the most abstract sense, such as in evolving discussions of topics like alterity or sovereignty. This is all a pity, for colonial history is coextensive with that of the metropolitan centres and no understanding of past nor present penal forms is likely to be complete without the sort of interlinking proposed here. Thus this chapter represents an effort to understand how historical understanding of one kind of colonial encounter – British rule in India from the mid-nineteenth century forward – may assist us in understanding current trends in governance and punishment in western societies.

To that end, the chapter will be divided into two parts. The first part will focus upon a unique penal innovation of mid-nineteenth-century colonial practice: a policy providing for the exclusion and social control of certain settled and nomadic tribes in north India. As is so often the case, what is interesting about this addition to the colonial penal apparatus is not just the specific character of the reform itself, but also the conditions, policies and context within which it arose. When viewed in this way the policy, known as the criminal tribes policy, emerges less as a stand-alone 'innovation' than as a concentration and expression of a variety of prevailing views, theories, problem solutions and the like. The first part of the chapter will therefore briefly touch upon the more important of these various strands, showing how they each shaped in crucial ways the final formulation of the policy. Consistent with the comparative theme of this volume and my desire to see connections drawn between past and present, the second part of the chapter will attempt to draw out of this nineteenth-century case study something for today. More specifically, I will describe how an understanding of the criminal tribes policy and the field of colonial governance within which it emerged assists us in making sense of the sorts of recent penal developments just mentioned.

The 'criminal tribes' of north India

In recent years considerable attention has been devoted to the process by which tribes operating on the margins of north Indian society came to be constituted, in colonial parlance, as 'criminal communities' or 'criminal tribes' (e.g. Brown, 2001, 2002a, 2002b, 2003, 2004; Freitag, 1985, 1991, 1998; Gordon, 1985; Major, 1999; Nigam, 1990a, 1990b; Radhakrishna, 2001; Tolen, 1995; Yang, 1985). The roots of this formulation are to be found in a number of relatively disjointed projects and enterprises of law and administration that developed across the Indian colonial sphere from at least the third quarter of the eighteenth century. They came together, however, much in the same way as Foucault (1977) describes the birth of the prison: to form something that was more than the sum of its parts, something in fact that became in many ways an archetypal formation. But before moving to describe the colonial construct of criminal tribes and its embellishment through an apparatus of law and regulation it is worth while briefly tracing the various projects and shifts in thinking that provided for its emergence in the terrain of nineteenth-century colonial power.

One of the more remarkable and enduring of these shaping forces was a peculiar conceptual difficulty that ran through British engagements with Indian people and society. For almost the entire period of their rule, the British struggled to develop a satisfactory understanding of the relationship between the individual and his or her social group. Indeed, it is out of this confusion that the colonial construct of caste emerged (Dirks, 2001). In the field of crime and social control this conceptual difficulty was reduced to a simple question: was criminal conduct best understood in individual or in collective terms? Certainly, English society and English law were grounded upon bedrock assumptions of social and legal individuality. But were such assumptions appropriate for India and, indeed, would they be practicable for government? As early as the 1770s the East India Company had begun to issue laws that extended criminal responsibility and punishment beyond the individual. Governor General Warren Hastings' Article 35 of 1772, for example, provided for the punishment not just of convicted dacoits but of their families also. In the 1850s so called 'Track Laws' meant that if an offender could be tracked to a village, but not located within it, then responsibility for the crime would be borne by the village as a whole. Later, Frontier Regulations in the Punjab would establish such collective responsibility across a wide territory and would regulate not just individual conduct but also a much wider range of tribal activities thought inimical to law and good order.

The special demands of maintaining law and order in India gave rise to a second important precursor to the criminal tribes policy: the development of novel legal arrangements. These had first been developed to counter the problem of thuggee (Brown, 2002b; Singha, 1993). Thugs operated in small bands, waylaying travellers and murdering their victims in remote settings before hiding the body and decamping with whatever valuables might have been in the traveller's possession. The remoteness of the crime, the lack of a body and the lack of witnesses to the event meant that it was almost impossible to obtain a conviction for murder in such cases, or indeed even to allocate responsibility between various parties to the crime. The result was the promulgation of Act XXX of 1836, the Thuggee Act. Among its many innovative features, the Act had two that are important for this discussion. First was the shift of attention from behaviour to association. While the individual cases of murder perpetrated by thugs would continue to be prosecuted under the criminal code, the Thuggee Act sought to curtail thugs' activity through criminalising gang membership itself. Thus it became an offence under the Act to be 'a thug', to be reputed to be a thug or to associate with thugs. Secondly, the Act as amended reduced the normal legal standards for evidence by establishing and privileging a special form of hearsay. Captured thugs who turned crown witness could provide 'approvers testimony' to establish that others were thugs and that they were present and participated in certain crimes. The approvers system solved the problem of witnesses, provided for the discovery of crimes, dealt with the difficulty of extracting confessions and established a new 'practical standard' for evidence in novel forms of crime in India. With its criminalisation of association and group membership and its much relaxed sense of what counted for evidence in these sorts of cases, the Thuggee Act established a legal and administrative structure within which the criminal tribes policy would eventually be placed.

Yet while the Thuggee Act was legally innovative, thuggee itself and other forms of native crime to which the Act eventually applied (including, for instance, poisoning and child stealing) remained only vaguely understood. The development of ideas about criminal communities, about whole tribes that were 'born criminal', awaited later advances in thinking about native criminality. These advances came through two relatively independent lines of thought that eventually converged and coalesced in the 1860s into the idea of hereditary criminal communities (Brown, 2001, 2003). First among these was increasing attention to 'classes' or 'varieties' of native crime and criminal. These nascent criminal taxonomies were, to begin with, only very loosely organised. Reflecting perhaps the undeveloped state of scientific classification at the time, taxonomies mixed and matched the criteria by which individuals were allocated to groups. In some cases criminal 'types' were defined by the location of their activities (e.g. central India), in others by their common religion and in still others by their nomadic or settled status. By the early 1860s this activity had been organised and structured by ethnographic assessments that focused upon socio-cultural indices of 'advancement' and 'civilisation' and by attention to a new organising concept: caste. Thus ideas about caste converged during the 1860s with ideas about crime more generally. This was almost inevitable, since caste as it came to be understood in the 1860s was thought to define both socio-religious status and occupational status. What ethnographers and administrators had by this time discovered about crime was that it appeared to be of two sorts: on the one hand there were the 'ordinary' crimes of ordinary folk, while on the other there were 'special' crimes of communities in which criminal behaviour was both endemic and apparently intergenerational. To British administrators of the 1860s this pointed to crime as a profession and a hereditary activity and, indeed, it was the argument that some kinds of crime *were* hereditary and *were* requirements of caste that provided the strong case for special measures against them.

A fourth precursor to legislation to deal with such supposedly hereditary crime was a sense that its prevalence was increasing at precisely the time when good government should have rendered the need for it obsolete. Various types of crime were from time to time given a political blush and construed as affronts not just to civil society but to government itself. Roy (1996: 125) argues that thuggee was 'addressed (even if not acknowledged) as a peculiarly potent threat to the authority and benevolence of the empire in India'. And Brandstadter (1985: 102) makes similar observations about official British views of human sacrifice as it was practised by the isolated Kond hill tribe of the Madras Presidency. 'Administrators from Madras to London', she writes, 'agreed that Kond defiance of British proscriptions against the performance of human sacrifice constituted not merely a clash of cultures and ethical systems but also an act of rebellion against Government itself.' But increasing rates of apparently hereditary criminal activity in the 1860s were perceived as a more direct threat to safety and civility in the countryside (a key guarantee of British paramountcy) and so to British power itself. Just why such crime appeared to have increased so rapidly did not receive great attention. Partly this was because responsibility for measuring and responding to it was split across the provinces, non-regulation areas and the Government of India, in so far as it monitored criminal activity in the native states. Partly also it was probably felt that no good baseline measure for such criminal activity had been established and so what statistics were at hand were best read as progressively revealing the extent of a previously unknown social phenomenon. Such a view would have been reinforced also by the concentration of supposedly hereditary criminal communities in the relatively newly annexed areas of the Punjab, North West Provinces and Oudh. In fact, it seems that a significant part of the increase was due to the demilitarisation of these areas by the conquering British power and the disestablishment of native states' armies and militias. The resulting flow of ex-soldiers and mercenaries into the open society created considerable poverty, social disruption and crime within whole communities at the lower bounds of the social strata.

Yet not all crime attributed to 'criminal communities' could be put down to the removal of previously valid, if not always predictable or consistent, careers in military service. A final precursor to the criminal tribes policy was the knowledge, well established by the 1860s, that native states, petty princes, large landholders and a variety of other important figures in the countryside were deeply implicated in the crimes undertaken by members of these subordinate classes. Since at least the turn of the century the connivance of large landholders and police in a market in stolen goods had been known (Chattopadhyay, 2000; McLane, 1985). Yet British attitudes toward these higher social strata had always been distinctly ambivalent. On the one hand British policy aimed to develop and secure the loyalty of an aristocratic class similar to that existing in England. On the other, British administrators viewed with some dismay the venality, corruption and incompetence of many who made up this rural elite. Prior to the mutiny-revolt of 1857 policy toward rural elites was therefore less than consistent, governed not by any set principle but by the demands and opportunities of circumstance. After 1857 all this changed, however. Dissatisfaction with the erosion of their traditional perquisites and authority had led many rural elites to side with the rebel cause. In the aftermath of the uprising a shaken British government in India decided that restitution of power to this segment of society was essential to shoring up and maintaining its own power in the countryside. Thus when it came time in the 1860s to deal with the problems of crime endemic in north India and so to improve the safety of native life and property outside the main towns, there was little chance that the rural elites who supported this crime trade would become the main targets of the crime reduction strategy.

Instead, local governments in the Punjab and North West Provinces elected to lobby the government of India for some statutory power to restrict the movement and association of those tribes at the margins of Indian society that were most commonly involved in this criminal enterprise. In fact, both these states had previously experimented with such techniques of control through extraordinary government regulation (Major, 1999; Nigam, 1990a). In the Punjab, in particular, it had long been the approach of government to maintain good relations with rural elites and to concentrate reform efforts at grass-roots level, even when such reforms might have had longer-term goals of modifying or restructuring relations between those at the top and bottom of the native social order (Major, 1986). In 1856 the Punjab government had through executive order established a system for the internment of three tribes reported to be deeply involved in criminal activity within the province – the *Sansis*, *Harnis* and *Baurias* (see Hutchinson, 1866). The logic behind the experiment was that if tribes such as these could be forced to settle they might, as a consequence, also be induced to take up some form of settled agricultural production and to shake off their otherwise strong preference for criminal activity. Perhaps not surprisingly, the tribes resisted this quite remarkable experiment in extra-judicial imprisonment, often refusing to take part in the subsistence agriculture offered to them and rejecting the norms of hygiene, sanitation, dress and comportment that the penal regime attempted to force upon them. They frequently fell sick and many of the reservations in which they were held – known as *kots* – failed to provide sufficient food for the subsistence of their inmates, thus requiring food aid to be provided by the state. Perhaps the experiment would not have lasted so long if the tribes concerned had been nearer to the centre of native society and thus more inclined to bring the matter before the courts. Eventually, in 1867, the Punjab Chief Court did strike down the executive order on the basis that it was unlawful, thus ending rather promptly the restrictions upon these tribes and the experiment in restriction and control of 'criminal tribes' in the Punjab.

It was against this background that the Punjab and North West Provinces went to the Government of India with a request for a proper criminal tribes policy and for proper powers to undertake the restrictions it would require. But it is an important argument of this chapter that their request should not be viewed as arriving upon the desks of the Government of India in Calcutta cold, as it were. Rather, each of the conditions and developments reviewed in this first part of the chapter contributed to the practical and conceptual framework within which this request would be inserted for consideration and debate. From a variety of different quarters the government had been receiving information about the special nature of the crime problem in north India. The Department of Thuggee and Dacoity, in particular, now restricted in its activities to the Native States, had been lobbying furiously for some sort of special measures to deal with criminal communities. The Department had extensive experience in the framing and administration of such rules and its network of intelligence gatherers was one of the primary conduits by which information about these tribes' criminal activities reached government notice. Furthermore, the concept of caste classification was, by the end of the 1860s, rising to something like the status of a settled fact. And, with the passage of time, the relative order that had settled onto the Indian countryside by 1870 made tribes whose habits were nomadic or to one degree or another criminal seem all that much further from the sway and influence of British government and authority. It was in this context then that the Government of India circulated in mid-1870 a draft bill for the 'Registration of Criminal Tribes and Eunuchs'.

The details of its passage through the colonial bureaucracy and Viceroy's Council have been described elsewhere and are not central to the arguments being made here (see Nigam, 1990a). Rather what is of interest is the emergence a year later of Act XXVII of 1871, the Criminal Tribes Act. This Act strengthened, codified and thus put on a proper legal footing a quasi-penal apparatus for the containment and control of so-called criminal communities in the Punjab, Oudh and North West Provinces. Of course, the problem of adequately defining which tribes were criminal, and which might emerge as criminal in the future, was not specified in the Act but instead left to the discretion of the provincial governments. These governments, having gathered sufficient evidence that members of a tribe were 'addicted to non-bailable offences', could petition the Government of India for that tribe to be declared a criminal tribe under the meaning of the Act. Once so notified, a tribe and its members would become subject to a whole range of restrictions and additional punitive measures. These included the registration of members of the tribe, restriction of movement to the vicinity of their village, a daily roll call, nightly curfew and require-ment to apply for a passport to travel out of the area. If the notified tribe was nomadic, it could be settled; if settled and thought to be inappro-priately located it could be moved and resettled elsewhere. Notifications under the Act could not be tested in court, for 'every such notification shall be conclusive proof that it has been issued in accordance with law'. And finally, any further offending by notified members of a tribe would be met with greater penal severity; a second conviction for a scheduled offence would attract a mandatory seven years sentence of imprisonment, while a third would result in transportation for life. Later the Act would be extended to provide for tribes' internment in agricultural, industrial or reformatory settlements and later still provisions would be made for the removal of children from their 'habitually criminal' parents. Though it was initially restricted to the Punjab, Oudh and North West Provinces, the Act would in time be further extended to provide all-India coverage.

The Criminal Tribes Act 1871 grew to become a centrepiece of colonial administrators' efforts to deal with criminal, suspect, marginal, vagrant and otherwise difficult communities. By 1947, when Britain quit India, almost 3.5 million natives were subject to its provisions – almost 1 per cent of the entire population (Major, 1999). Yet well before this time, perhaps even by the turn of the century, the Act had lost its singular focus on 'hereditary' criminal conduct. Vivian's *Handbook of Criminal Tribes of the Punjab* (1912) identifies a number of tribes in that jurisdiction that are remarked to be only marginally criminal, if at all, within the meaning of the Act. One group, for instance, is described as 'not a criminal tribe except in so far as any aboriginal of the tract may be [so] regarded' – the main reason for their registration being that other measures to check their unruly behaviour (including opposition to native colonists moving onto their lands) had not been successful (Vivian, 1912: 123). In a recent study Radhakrishna (2001) details how tribes in south India came to be developed as an important source of cheap labour, let out by the govern-ment to an emerging industrial sector. Yet, whether interned in their own village, shifted to a settlement of one sort or another, or developed as a source of prison labour, once caught within the criminal tribes policy few tribes found themselves able to escape its grip. Such has been the conceptual and practical power of the criminal tribes policy and apparatus that those tribes remaining within its grasp at Independence have since struggled to re-enter Indian society. Now known as de-notified tribes, this highly marginalised sector of Indian society, together with nomadic tribes, numbers as many as 60 million individuals, according to one estimate (Rathod, 2000).

Criminal tribes and comparative penal theory

To what use might this understanding of the development of a criminal tribes policy in nineteenth-century British India be put? Is there a sense in which this knowledge has comparative utility for contemporary penal theory? I will suggest the answer is yes, but there seem to be two ways in which the knowledge might be so used and one way is of more substantive value than the other. The aim of this section of the chapter is to examine these approaches, beginning first with what is in my view the weaker of the two.

The criminal tribes policy as metaphor for exclusion

Nigam's (1990a, 1990b) detailed account of the development of the criminal tribes policy and its application in the North West Province draws upon Said's (1978) notion of Orientalism as a framework within which to interpret not just the policy but also the very notion and image of the criminal tribesman. For Nigam, the criminal tribesman stands as a classic instance of Orientalist thought and the stereotypical images of natives and native society that it generated. In comparative terms, it seems equally possible to take up the trope of alterity, the Saidian theme of the oriental Other and the analytical binaries that underpin it, in order to see what the criminal tribes policy can say for contemporary debates on penality. Said's argument was that the Orient, as a concept, was constructed not only as a polar opposite to the West, the Occident, but also as a largely stereotyped and essentialised amalgam of European preconceptions and prejudices toward the non-western Other. A sense of Said's argument can be gained from the following passage of *Orientalism*:

> We are immediately brought back to the realization that Orientalists, like many other early-nineteenth century thinkers, conceive of humanity either in large collective terms or in abstract generalities.

> Orientalists are neither interested in nor capable of discussing individuals; instead artificial entities, perhaps with their roots in Herderian populism, predominate. There are Orientals, Asiatics, Semites, Muslims, Jews, races, mentalities, nations, and the like … Similarly, the age-old distinction between 'Europe' and 'Asia' or 'Occident' and 'Orient' herds beneath very wide labels every possible variety of human plurality, reducing it in the process to one or two terminal, collective abstractions. (Said, 1978: 154–5)

Much debate within contemporary penal theory is concerned with interpreting trends remarkably similar to what Said describes. Garland (1996), for instance, coins the term 'the criminological other' to describe those offenders whom the state separates from so-called normal citizens and who become subject to a variety of particularly severe penal sanctions. Many of these, like the criminal tribes policy, work directly to exclude the serious or dangerous offender from society through much lengthened prison terms, denial of eligibility for early release on parole and even through indefinite detention and forms of civil commitment. Like the collective abstractions described by Said, these offenders come into public and political discourse not as individuals but as 'sexual psychopaths', 'paedophiles', 'drug traffickers' and, increasingly, as 'illegal immigrants' or 'terror suspects'. Drawing on somewhat different theoretical inspiration, Rose (2000) claims to have identified in contemporary western society what he terms 'circuits of inclusion' and 'circuits of exclusion', the latter being reserved for those offenders whose conduct, like that of the criminal tribesman, fails to conform to the rapidly changing norms of a modernising society. Thus, in this way, the criminal tribes policy assists us to understand seemingly recurrent desires and tendencies within modernity to establish in-group/out-group binaries, to categorise and to exclude. Moreover, it is possible to see historical traces of this tendency not only in colonial crime control, but in policies originating in the metropolitan centre as well (such in the English Habitual Offenders Act 1869 – see Wiener, 1990). Contemporary penal policies that blur boundaries between the penal and civil spheres, and policies that seem to draw penality to the very centre of governance, can, under this metaphorical view, be understood as but one more instance of governance within a criminal tribes type framework. Yet for all the clarity that such comparison provides, seeing contemporary trends solely in this metaphorical mode is ultimately limiting. The criminal tribes policy as metaphor for modernist impulses to distinction, categorisation and exclusion leaves too much unexplained, including the teleological questions of how and why such impulses might be such an enduring feature of modern government.

Criminal tribes and colonial governance

The key to understanding the relevance of the criminal tribes policy to contemporary penality therefore lies, I believe, in paying much greater attention to the broader field of the policy's emergence: the sphere or domain of the colonial. Recent post-colonial scholarship has invested great energy in retrieving the colonial state from theoretical moribundity and establishing it as a key analytic category in its own right. Chatterjee (1993), for example, asks how the colonial state ought to be positioned, theoretically, in relation to the modern state, that product of western Enlightenment reason. His answer, in an Indian context, locates the colonial state as a distinct political formation standing in opposition to the modern state. By way of contrast, Scott (1999) posits the existence of a form of colonial governmentality. In Scott's formulation, modernity itself exerts a force on colonial governance such that the character of the colonial state changes over time. In the context of Indian colonial history he charts a break, from around the middle of the nineteenth century, after which point the colonial state takes on a distinctively modern character and a mode of rule that is distinctly governmental. I have recently elaborated my own view on this theoretical debate (Brown, 2005), suggesting a position somewhere between these two in which colonial state formations developed as distinct political structures, underpinned by unique rationalities that were particular to their colonial context yet also driven in important ways by the impulses of modernity. I have accepted Chatterjee's important claim about a 'rule of colonial difference' that allowed the exclusion of natives from the modern, liberal state developing around them. Yet I differ in arguing that the basis of such a rule was not race, as he claims, but instead a more complex and finely graded concept, that of character. In order to make clear how this aids understanding of the criminal tribes policy's development and the comparative utility of both the policy and its political context for contemporary times, it will be necessary to expand briefly upon this understanding of colonial governance.

Colonial governance and colonial power cannot be discussed as homogeneous or essentialised concepts. Both developed differently in different geographical locations and under the influence of different colonising nations. As the colonial state developed in India from the mid-nineteenth century onward, it took on distinctive features that set it apart from other such state formations (such as, for instance, that developed by the French in Algeria – see Sartre, 2001) and from the modern states developing in the metropolitan West. But perhaps *the* key feature of the British colonial state in India was the relationship established there between state and subject. This was a relationship in which, from at least the mid-nineteenth century onward, subjects' access to civic life and state institutions came to be governed not by a structure of rights (civil, political and social), as was the case in modernising western states, but rather by a new and quite unique alternative structure: that of obligation and its attendant commitment to ideas of virtue and character. Colonial power conceived in this way operated quite differently to political power in the metropolitan West. For a start, the colonial subject was constituted in the first instance not as a *recipient* of liberty rights, a person who could make direct claims upon the state or other subjects, but as an *agent* of obligation (see O'Neill (1996) for the philosophical underpinnings of such a distinction, and Brown (2005) for a more detailed argument). This made possible a whole discourse on the proper virtues required of native subjects in order for them to enter civic life and to participate in state institutions. It also paved the way for the constitution of a whole array of special obligations that could be required of the colonial subject. Such obligations, which O'Neill terms imperfect obligations, are obligations that lack counterpart rights. In the colonial sphere they thus were elaborated as preconditions for entry into a sphere that might best be described as a progressively refashioned civic space: the civil society of a modern India.

The virtues required of Indian subjects in order to enter this space from the mid nineteenth-century onward are reflected precisely in the sorts of grounds upon which the criminal tribes policy was justified. The modern native subject of British colonial power was to be settled, was to be obedient to law, to develop skills of agricultural (and later industrial) production, to subscribe to or at least accept modern norms of sanitation and hygiene, dress and comportment, thrift and prudence, and so on. Thus it was the very ungovernability of the tribes, not just in legal terms but also in their refusal to accept these new British-led norms of Indian society and required forms of individual subjectivity, that led to their exclusion under the criminal tribes policy. The utility of this framework for understanding contemporary penal practices is, I believe, considerable. The notion of a colonial form of power, of distinctly colonial forms of logic and rationality, invites us to examine contemporary political practices for traces of their influence. Furthermore, this conception of colonial power as establishing structures of obligations, with their attendant assessments of virtue and character, as preconditions for political subjects' entry into civic life invites us to ask how such a process might conceivably operate in contemporary society. My suggestion is that a form of colonial rationality is entering the political discourse of some modern western nations. But now, rather than accounting for the ways in which subjects were able to *enter* the modern civic society of a colonial state, it provides a basis for understanding how, why and on what grounds certain individuals, groups and communities may be evaluated for *exclusion from* modern society. Though I disagree with Rose (2000) on the breadth of what he defines as exclusionary practices or mechanisms, his description of the character of those who are excluded makes sense within the framework proposed here:

> These excluded sub-populations have either refused the bonds of civility and self responsibility, or they are unable to assume them for constitutional reasons, or they aspire to them but have not been given the skills, capacities and means. It appears as if, outside the circuits of inclusion – in 'marginalised' spaces, in the decaying council estate, in the chaotic lone parent family, in the shop doorways of inner city streets – exists an array of micro-circuits, micro-cultures of non-citizens, failed citizens, anti-citizens, comprised of those who are unable or unwilling to enterprise their lives or manage their own risk, incapable of exercising responsible self-government, either attached to no moral community or to a community of anti-morality. (Rose, 2000: 331)

It is Rose's suggestion, working as he does within a governmentality framework, that these 'non-citizens', 'failed citizens' or 'anti-citizens' become subject to a mode of rule that shifts them to the periphery of society and ultimately into the hands of the criminal justice process. The latter, he claims, takes on a distinctly exclusionary character as it becomes drawn into the task of maintaining a separation between the 'included' and 'excluded' of society. However, I feel that if we are to take seriously the comparative potential of the criminal tribes policy and idea of colonial forms of governance, then we should tend to emphasise what might best be termed forms of wholesale exclusion, that is removals *from* contemporary society of the same order of magnitude as the criminal tribes policy's restrictions of access *to* then contemporary colonial society. Viewed in this way, the so-called exclusions that make up much of contemporary social policy discourse probably do not qualify. What do qualify are the radical and marked exclusions of the contemporary penal sphere in which punishments or quasi-punitive measures (like civil commitment) work to *remove* a citizen from society on a permanent basis.

Conclusion

This chapter has taken up the theme of comparative history by attempting to link the conditions under which a penal policy was born in nineteenth-century India with contemporary penal developments in western societies. In doing so I have attempted to establish at least two levels of historical analysis. In the first, I hope to have shown how the criminal tribes policy, emerging at the end of the 1860s and codified in the Criminal Tribes Act 1871, was made both thinkable and possible by the confluence of very specific conditions. These were widespread and various, ranging from gradually evolving ideas about native society and social structures to new 'scientific' approaches to classifying native criminals and further to particular problems of governance – animated by concerns for order and the constitution of new forms of native subjectivity – that necessitated attention to lower social orders in order to curtail the unwanted criminal activities of those atop the native social hierarchy. At the second level of analysis I have attempted, albeit briefly, to suggest that these circumstances in their combination established the conditions for a particular form of colonial governance to emerge, one that was peculiar to the Indian colonial context. It is through an understanding of this form of colonial power and the logics and rationalities that underpinned it that we are able to make better sense of the criminal tribes policy. But this second level of analysis has also provided a conceptual frame through which contemporary developments may be viewed in a new light. It is a frame that seems to indicate that practices and forms of power and rationality that might otherwise have been regarded as purely historical in character are in fact finding their way back into the political terrain of some modern western societies.

References

Arnold, D. *Police Power and Colonial Rule, Madras, 1859–1947*. Oxford University Press, 1986.

Brandstadter, E. S. 'Human sacrifice and British–Kond relations, 1759–1862', in Yang. A. A. (ed.), *Crime and Criminality in British India*. University of Arizona Press, 1985.

Brown, M. 'Race, science and the construction of native criminality in colonial India', *Theoretical Criminology*, 5, 2001, pp. 345–68.

Brown, M. 'The politics of penal excess and the echo of colonial penality', *Punishment and Society*, 4, 2002a, pp. 403–23.

Brown, M. 'Crime, governance and the company Raj: the discovery of thuggee', *British Journal of Criminology*, 42, 2002b, pp. 77–95.

Brown, M. 'Ethnology and colonial administration in nineteenth-century British India: the question of native crime and criminality', *British Journal of the History of Science*, 36, 2003, pp. 1–19.

Brown, M. 'Crime, liberalism and empire: governing the *Mina* tribe of northern India', *Social and Legal Studies*, 13, 2004, pp. 191–218.

Brown, M. '"That heavy machine": reprising the colonial apparatus in 21st century crime control', *Social Justice* (forthcoming, 2005).

Chatterjee, P. *The Nation and Its Fragments: Colonial and Postcolonial Histories.* Princeton University Press, 1993.

Chattopadhyay, B. *Crime and Control in Early Colonial Bengal 1770–1860.* K. P. Bagchi & Co., 2000.

Dirks, N. B. *Castes of Mind: Colonialism and the Making of Modern India.* Princeton University Press, 2001.

Foucault, M. *Discipline and Punish: The Birth of the Prison.* Allen Lane, 1977.

Freitag, S. 'Collective crime and authority in North India', in Yang, A. A. (ed.), *Crime and Criminality in British India.* University of Arizona Press, 1985.

Freitag, S. 'Crime in the social order of colonial North India', *Modern Asian Studies,* 25, 1991, pp. 227–61.

Freitag, S. '*Sansiahs* and the state: the changing nature of "crime" and "justice" in nineteenth-century British India', in Anderson, M. R. and Guha, S. (eds), *Changing Concepts of Rights and Justice in South Asia.* Oxford University Press, 1998.

Garland, D. *Punishment and Welfare: A History of Penal Strategies.* Aldershot: Gower, 1985.

Garland, D. 'The limits of the sovereign state: strategies of crime control in contemporary society', *British Journal of Criminology,* 36, 1996, pp. 445–71.

Gordon, S. N. 'Bhils and the idea of a criminal tribe in nineteenth-century India', in Yang, A. A. (ed.), *Crime and Criminality in British India.* University of Arizona Press, 1985.

Hutchinson, Major G. *Reformatory Measures Connected with the Treatment of Criminals in India.* Punjab Printing Co., 1866.

Ludden, D. (ed.), *Reading Subaltern Studies: Critical History, Contested Meaning and the Globalisation of South Asia.* Anthem Press, 2001.

Major, A. *Return to Empire: Punjab under the Sikhs and British in the Mid-Nineteenth Century.* Sterling Publishers, 1986.

Major, A. 'State and criminal tribes in colonial Punjab: surveillance, control and reclamation of the "Dangerous Classes"', *Modern Asian Studies,* 33, 1999, pp. 657–88.

McLane, J. R. 'Bengali bandits, police and landlords after the permanent settlement', in Yang, A. (ed.), *Crime and Criminality in British India.* University of Arizona Press, 1985.

Metcalf, T. R. *Ideologies of the Raj: The New Cambridge History of India, Vol. 3, 4.* Cambridge University Press, 1994.

Morris, N. and Rothman, D. J. (eds) *The Oxford History of the Prison: The Practice of Punishment in Western Society.* Oxford University Press, 1995.

Nigam, S. 'Disciplining and policing the "criminals by birth", Part 1: The making of a colonial stereotype – the criminal tribes and castes of North India', *Indian Economic and Social History Review,* 27, 1990a, pp. 131–64.

Nigam, S. 'Disciplining and policing the "criminals by birth", Part 2: The development of a disciplinary system, 1871–1900', *Indian Economic and Social History Review,* 27, 1990b, pp. 257–87.

O'Neill, O. *Towards Justice and Virtue: A Constructive Account of Practical Reasoning*. Cambridge University Press, 1996.

Pratt, J., Brown, D., Hallsworth, S., Brown, M. and Morrison, W. *The New Punitiveness: Current Trends, Theories, Perspectives*. Willan Publishing (forthcoming).

Radhakrishna, M. *Dishonoured by History: Criminal Tribes and British Colonial Policy*. Orient Longman, 2001.

Radzinowicz, L. *A History of English Criminal Law and Its Administration from 1750*. Stevens and Sons, 1986.

Rathod, M. 'Denotified and nomadic tribes in Maharashtra', *The Denotified and Nomadic Tribes Rights Action Group Newsletter*, November 2000.

Rose, N. 'Government and control', *British Journal of Criminology*, 40, 2000, pp. 321–39.

Roy, P. 'Discovering India, imagining thuggee', *Yale Journal of Criticism*, 9, 1996, pp. 121–45.

Said, E. W. *Orientalism: Western Conceptions of the Orient*. Penguin, 1978.

Sartre, J. P. *Colonialism and Neocolonialism*. Routledge, 2001.

Scott, D. *Refashioning Futures: Criticism after Postcoloniality*. Princeton University Press, 1999.

Sen, S. *Disciplining Punishment: Colonialism and Convict Society in the Andaman Islands*. Oxford University Press, 2000.

Singha, R. '"Providential" circumstances: the thuggee campaign of the 1830s and legal innovation', *Modern Asian Studies*, 27, 1993, pp. 83–156.

Tolen, R. J. 'Colonising and transforming the criminal tribesman: the Salvation Army in British India', in Terry, J. and Urla, J. (eds), *Deviant Bodies: Critical Perspectives on Difference in Science and Popular Culture*. Indiana University Press, 1995.

Vivian, V. T. P. *A Handbook of the Criminal Tribes of the Punjab*. Government of Punjab Press, 1912.

Wiener, M. *Reconstructing the Criminal: Culture, Law and Policy in England, 1830–1914*. Cambridge University Press, 1990.

Yang, A. A. 'Dangerous castes and tribes: the Criminal Tribes Act and the Magahiya Doms of Northeast India', in Yang, A. A. (ed.), *Crime and Criminality in British India*. University of Arizona Press, 1985.

Chapter 7

Crime, the legal archive and postcolonial histories

Catharine Coleborne

Scholars have recently begun to explore the possibilities and meanings of post-colonial theory and methodology for legal-historical research.[1] This chapter suggests that it is possible to use and read sources from the colonial legal archive in order to explore the workings of the law and its effects in the colonial era in Australia, New Zealand and the Pacific.[2] Part of a series of my own preliminary explorations of this field, made within the context of discussing the problem of post-colonial theory and method, the chapter signals that legal history might take up the problems and rewards of such transnational historical studies in order to better understand the importance and potential of postcolonial theory and methodological approaches to law and history scholarship. It also asks why existing histories of crime have not played a more obvious role in reshaping the theoretical directions of legal history. It draws upon a range of published works and signals the imperative for renewed attention to colonial archival sources.

This study emerges from a particular interest in a kind of history that seeks to investigate the interconnections between colonial populations and the meanings of colonialism. Historians have recently begun to investigate 'legal regimes and colonial cultures', to take a phrase from the title of Lauren Benton's new book *Law and Colonial Cultures* (Benton, 2002). One relatively 'new' geographical site for this exploration is nineteenth- and early twentieth-century Australia, New Zealand and the Pacific. Here historians might productively examine the ways in which European communities produced themselves through ideas of colonialism and colonial ideologies including 'race', class and gender during what we could call the 'colonial era' to 1901. Gender(ing), 'race'(ialising) and class(ifying) were pervasive activities; they were always being actively negotiated and renegotiated, forever escaping precise characterisation, and they had (especially by the end of the period) an even more particular and peculiar context and meaning in this world made up of colonial worlds as separate places lurched towards distinct constructions of 'nationality'.[3] This enterprise attempts to move beyond 'national' history narratives, or the problem of exceptionalist histories, and has more recently been referred to as transnational history (Gibbons, 2003: 40–1; Curthoys, 2002: 145–9; Mein-Smith, 2003). How did people's lives and worlds collide, connect and intersect in this region before 1901? And specifically, what can crime and its regulation in different parts of this region tell us about colonialism?

This chapter takes the operations and effects of colonialism in the region, specifically the effects and consequences of the labour trade, as its central example in order to foreground useful methodological and theoretical approaches to examining the problem of crime in the past. As Louis A. Knafla has suggested: ' "Crime" and "Colonialism" are two terms that reflected thinking on gender, race and class in the age of imperialism' (Knafla, 2002: xiv). This study proposes three key strategies for historians interested in colonialism and crime history. First, historians might reinterpret the fields of 'legal history' and 'colonial history' through the theme of crime and criminality in the region defined here, and by placing it within a post-colonial framework; this means returning to some significant published work. Second, within a theoretical approach informed by post-colonial theory, gender might be used here as a productive category of historical analysis in relation to crime and its regulation. And third, historians might further interrogate colonial archives, including legal archives, as sites of knowledge production about crime and colonised peoples, including deploying new reading and writing strategies. Read separately, perhaps none of these propositions is especially startling, but read together, I argue that they constitute a potential new approach to the field.

Before going on to develop each of these three strategies, I offer a brief justification for the regional and theoretical frameworks for this study. In his book *Nature, Culture, History: The 'Knowing' of Oceania* published by the University of Hawai'i Press (Howe, 2000), historian of the Pacific, Kerry Howe, interrogates the field of 'Pacific history'. He acknowledges a range of scholarship about gender and the Pacific as being part of Pacific history as he traces its development over time. Yet despite the depth of scholarship about colonialism, gender, history, culture and peoples in the Asia-Pacific region, to fully appreciate the complexity of this history of the region in the nineteenth century is to acknowledge its relative newness as a site of historical investigation. Collections of essays including the inter-disciplinary collection *Body Trade: Captivity, Cannibalism and Colonialism in the Pacific* (Creed and Hoorn, 2001) only go a little way towards interpreting the entire history of the region, and its central aim is to explore different bodies ('raced', sexed and gendered) in mostly discursive constructions of the Pacific and its peoples.

Another recent work, Donald Denoon and Philippa Mein-Smith's *A History of Australia, New Zealand and the Pacific*, published as part of Blackwell's World History series (Denoon and Mein-Smith, 2001), is more successful as it attempts to draw together the separate colonial and twentieth-century histories of places in this region in relation to one another. However, it is curiously silent on the subjects of crime and law and its textbook style approach means that the exploration of theoretical concepts like gender is performed in only limited ways. To find out more here we need to return to specific published studies – in some cases, micro-studies – explored later in this chapter.

'Legal histories' and 'colonial histories' and post-colonialism

Howe has argued that 'the role of postcolonial history is to be an agent of postcoloniality', because imperial history was and is 'an agent of imperialism' (Howe, 2000: 86). What does the term 'post-colonial' mean to historians? Perhaps it means that we ought to try to reconceive of the past in the present, especially thinking about what drives us to understand the past. Part of this process means questioning or destabilising accepted versions of the past. In order to render its complexities and to find new meanings for the past, we must find a place for the post-colonial, rather than research and write comparative national histories of colonialism in the Pacific. Several years ago, the imperative to write comparative histories of colonialism was suggested by Peter Hempenstall (Hempenstall, 1992: 70).[4] This comparative history was rightly seen as a new type of history in a field where scholars had mostly not yet attempted such work. At the same time, the challenge to write different kinds of history, including taking an ethnographic approach to the source materials, was laid down by Hempenstall. Such readings and comparisons between sites in the Pacific region, he argued, would enable a kind of Pacific 'subaltern studies' (Hempenstall, 1992: 72–4). Hempenstall would agree that the post-colonial historian 'has taken an active role in challenging unequal power relations through [a] process of interrogating and rewriting … canonized' historical narratives (Gallagher, 1999: 951). Thus I also mean to distinguish this work from the 'two worlds' approach, or the 'other side of the frontier' approach, both of which potentially limit our readings of the many different histories of peoples in this region.[5]

In order to reinterpret the fields of 'legal history' and 'colonial history' through the theme of crime and criminality in the region defined here, historians first need to return to some significant published work. In this part of my discussion I briefly explore the two fields of 'colonial history' and 'legal history' and existing published work about crime that utilises the insights of both fields. Law has historically been a 'core institution of colonial control' (Merry, 2000: 8). Within legal history, Bruce Kercher's book *An Unruly Child* shows that certain areas of colonial law developed in Australian colonies from about the 1820s as part of the shift towards 'responsible' government (Kercher, 1995). Legal-historical scholarship in New Zealand tells a similar tale (Spiller, Finn and Boast, 2001). These areas of law were labour legislation (and later, industrial disputes laws), land laws, laws regulating private life and marriage, property laws, immigration legislation, and laws expressly designed to control indigenous populations and other specific social groups including vagrants. The criminal law also played a role in this shift, as shown by other essays in this volume, including the essay by Jeremy Finn.

In Clive Emsley and Lou Knafla's collection *Crime History and Histories of Crime* (Emsley and Knafla, 1996) Australian historian Stephen Garton examined the key themes that have shaped Australian and New Zealand 'crime histories', including convicts and bushranging, aspects of frontier crime, policing and punishment, urban crime and women and crime. He concluded with the observation that the 'best research' will emerge through the 'recognition of the importance of comparative histories of crime' (Garton, 1996: 286). But taking this further involves not just comparison but an awareness of interdisciplinary work. For instance, Peter King's bibliographical essay 'Locating histories of crime' (King, 1999) makes a case for historians understanding the theoretical insights of criminological and/or sociological studies of crime. My concern lies with an understanding of the way colonial knowledges were constructed, and with reading techniques, a point to which I will return.

What we might term 'colonial histories' of labour have also been concerned with 'crime' as a problem. In their study of Melanesian workers and the Queensland criminal justice system in the 1890s Mark Finnane and Clive Moore assert that Melanesian workers experienced the criminal justice system in ways similar to other working-class groups. But their 'vulnerability to attentions of police' was 'offense-specific' (Finnane and Moore, 1992: 148–9) and partly defined through their employment status. They also used the Summons Court to defend their legal rights but were paradoxically more likely to come under the attention of the law as they moved more freely into colonial culture. Recent work by Tracey Banivanua-Mar examines an earlier period in Queensland, the 1870s, and focuses on the violence directed at Pacific Islander workers in the sugar industry, including murders and assaults (Banivanua-Mar, 2002). There are other geographical and cultural sites, and imperial legal jurisdictions, that must be examined for their potential uses to any wider regional study, including Papua and New Guinea, Fiji, the Solomons and the different experiences of colonised Samoa. A little work has appeared about these places (see, for instance, Ralston, 1977; Moore, Leckie and Munro, 1990; Lal, Munro and Beechert, 1993). In Hawai'i, 'contract' or indentured labourers were regarded as people of modest means who would be relatively easy to control through the law (Bjork, 2002: 142–3).[6]

In their study of the peoples in the region of Australia, New Zealand and the Pacific, Denoon and Mein-Smith have argued that '[t]o preserve their identity, the settler polities adopted racial exclusion' (Denoon and Mein-Smith, 2001: 210). However, this process is about the *creation* of a 'new identity', not only the *preservation* of an older one. There was also a wider context: 'Concern with racial purity was not only a factor of settlement and colonial isolation but also an echo of ideas from overseas' (Gibbons, 1992: 310). By 1900 in most parts of this region including Hawai'i, the demographic shift tells a familiar story: the depopulation of indigenous peoples was a cumulative but dramatic process. By the early 1900s there were restrictions on non-whites everywhere too. These included legislative measures to restrict non-white immigration and labour (the latter partly ameliorating conditions of indentured labour but also leading to the expulsion of some Pacific Islander labourers from parts of Australia). At the end of the nineteenth century, defining the borders of new settler nations involved building barriers to the outside world. At the same time some populations of indigenous peoples were further obscured and made invisible, and further dispossessed: for instance, there was 'a constitutional silence' about Aborigines in Australia.

Writing about South-East Asia, Ann Laura Stoler refers to the 'exclusionary politics of the colonial state' (Stoler, 1997: 226). Settler societies in the Australia-Pacific region attempted to apply understandings of 'race' to the demographic mix of peoples in the region in ways that privileged Europeans and characterised parts of the region as 'white' and 'for whites' only; thus one set of peoples created opportunities for society to contain and constrain 'other' peoples. There were limits placed on who could 'belong' to these places as they became 'nations'. 'Whiteness' was, and is, a powerful imaginary construct.

Gender, crime and its regulation

The second strategy described at the outset of this chapter suggested that within a theoretical approach informed by post-colonial theory, gender might be used as a productive category of historical analysis in relation to crime and its regulation. Thinking about the constraints placed on peoples moving around in this region, how did such restrictions and limitations collude to produce specific gendered experiences? In the north of Australia, as historian Clive Moore has argued, non-white women were 'cast as subordinates' and 'rigorously defined' through 'Eurocentric assumptions and male sexual attitudes' (Moore, 1996: 59). Moore shows that social relationships and the lives of women and men in this context had more in common with those in the societies of Port Moresby, Rabaul, Levuka and Apia than southern societies in colonial Australia. These women included Chinese, Japanese and Melanesian workers. Between 1864 and 1904 more than 6,000 Melanesian Pacific islanders took up contracts as indentured labourers in Queensland, mostly in the coastal sugar industry. They came from many islands now part of New Caledonia, Vanuatu, the Solomon Islands, Papua and New Guinea, Kiribati and Tuvalu. Women constituted about 6.5 per cent of the overall total, with most coming in the 1890s (9.6 per cent in 1891). Moore comments on their particular relationships to indenture: women, like men, worked in the fields as labourers, and some worked as domestic servants (illegally from the mid-1880s). Women labourers worked in separate gangs, often taking their children into the cane fields. It was difficult for women and men to maintain specific cultural practices.

After the Pacific Island Labourers' Act 1901 when two-thirds of the Pacific Islanders working in the northern parts of Australia were deported, only very small numbers of married women (in marriages to Europeans, Chinese, Japanese and Aborigines) remained. Melanesian women, like Asian women, were stereotyped as 'easy sexual conquests' and historians have suggested that they were seen as the 'chattels' of both Melanesian and European men, traded between men. They were, therefore, not always the 'active agents of their destinies', despite attempts by contemporaries and some historians, drawing on contemporary evidence, to show how indentured labourers made choices and had 'agency' in their lives.[7]

Historians have shown that female indentured labourers had similar experiences elsewhere. From 1879 to 1920, over 60,000 people were recruited in South Asia and brought to work in Fiji as plantation labourers (Kelly, 1997: 74). In Fiji young Indian women could find themselves working as prostitutes with European or Indian men as overseers, showing that, as reports of 1916 and 1918 indicated, indentured labour practices in Fiji cruelly exploited women in a number of ways: the forced work was conducted in harsh conditions; women were recruited in smaller numbers than men which made them targets of sexual cruelty; and once again their traditional cultural practices were not recognised. Women were subject to the control of both Indian and European men (Knapman, 1986: 173–4). Thus one area of research in this region, already touched on by some historians, might be crimes of sexual violence perpetrated against female workers, and the responses of colonial justice systems. We could broaden this to include violence, gender and sexuality and consider constructions of non-white male labourers as criminal.

Colonial archives, crime and colonised peoples

How historians find out about these aspects of the colonial past is a question that has been examined by historians in the field before now. Yet historians might further interrogate colonial archives, including legal archives, as sites of knowledge production about crime and colonised peoples, including deploying new reading/writing strategies, in order to freshly examine the relationship between crime and colonialism.

Ann Laura Stoler and other scholars have begun to examine the colonial archive as an institution that produced colonial populations and 'identities'. Through its productions, the archive was another 'technology of rule' (Stoler, 2002: 83). Tony Ballantyne connects the work of South Asian colonial archives to later historical productions; he writes that the 'archive itself was the site where the transformative power of colonialism was enacted and contested', and later, 'historians of empire … made sense of the diverse peoples over which the British Empire exercised authority' (Ballantyne, 2003: 102). As Stoler's work about colonial archives argues, the colonial/imperial archive, through its omissions, also embodies 'documents of exclusions' (Stoler, 2002: 89). Stoler is talking about the official archive, but we can broaden our concept of archive to include a range of sources including published sources and visual artifacts and material culture. As Giselle Byrnes has shown so well in her recent book *Boundary Markers* on the subject of colonial surveyors, all forms of colonial writing and representation can and should be analysed for their value to postcolonial histories (Byrnes, 2001). James Mills, who has examined the archives of colonial lunatic asylums in India, agrees: colonial writing 'reflect[s] and reproduce[s] colonial ways of seeing and thinking' (Mills, 2000: 5).

Yet past editors of volumes of writings by Pakeha or Europeans who travelled, lived and worked in the colonies of New Zealand and Victoria, New South Wales, Queensland and beyond in the Pacific, have made stark and sometimes deliberate omissions. In her 1959 edition of a book entitled *Early Travellers in New Zealand*, Nancy M. Taylor lets us in on what now seems to us like an awful, editorial secret in her notes to pages concerning John Turnbull Thompson, the New Zealand land surveyor: 'Six pages are omitted here, mainly hearsay remarks on whalers, mutton birds, local Maoris, and the sounds of the West Coast' (Taylor, 1959: 348). As readers are now too knowing to be shocked by the effects of Taylor's collapsing here of Maori people, mutton birds and soundscapes, whalers (many of whom were Maori) which had little relevance to mid-twentieth-century editors of historical documents for different reasons. Historians and history as a discipline were focused on histories of nation.

Such omissions make our task even more perilous: how are we to tell the multiple stories of the pasts of these places and peoples, with limited, partial textual sources? The disappearing record of many colonists and indigenous peoples and other dispossessed peoples including indentured labourers (whose lives were and are more readily obscured in any case) makes this work very much like the work of early feminist historians seeking to tell the stories of women in the past. Their investigations were marked by reflections on absences and gaps in the record, and by attempts to look for silences and their significance. Other historians have also mostly interpreted the task of writing history through such methodological constraints, always aware of the silences and gaps in texts, and also the absences within the archives to which we have access (Dalley, 2001: 36). Furthermore, the archives are not entirely silent.

Nevertheless, numerous questions remain about how historians can find out about the particular past examined in this chapter: for instance, the experiences of the many thousands of indentured labourers in Queensland, Fiji and Hawai'i to the end of the nineteenth century; their interactions with one another, or with indigenous peoples, or with the Europeans who were their bosses; what we know about their 'culture(s)'; and what we can find out about gender, crime and labour.

Taking up this story, John D. Kelly explores the collision between my themes of crime, gender and the legal archive in instructive ways. In a piece entitled 'Gaze and grasp: plantations, desires, indentured Indians, and colonial law in Fiji', Kelly examines the records of a stipendiary magistrate named Adolph Brewster Joske, who was magistrate at a remote courthouse in Colo North, a hinterland province of the Fijian islands

(Kelly, 1997). Kelly found widespread evidence of sexual violence within the indenture system and plantation life in Fiji, perpetrated by Indian men upon Indian women, and mostly blamed on the 'Indian trait' of 'sexual jealousy' by European officials investigating cases. European men were also responsible for sexual crimes, but not readily punished for these; instead, the Indian women who made rape allegations against European men were cast as 'promiscuous'.

Kelly's use of court records coupled with the memoirs of Fijian colonists emphasises that historians need to take account of the 'materiality' of this history: the 'grasp', not just the 'gaze'. Kelly unpacks the 'gaze' asking 'which gazes had what effects? What was made real … which gazes "inscribed" what, where?' (Kelly, 1997: 75). Using the legal archive in this way to look for the physical encounters between men and women, women's words and responses, men's actions and reactions, Kelly suggests that the difference between colonial histories and post-colonial histories is less a preoccupation with *looking at* the colonised, and more of an engagement with the complex sets of relations existing under colonial rule and beyond. Like Ranajit Guha on India, Kelly suggests that colonial rule never achieved hegemony (Guha, 1997). Importantly, he also notes that the 'colonized world included modes of knowledge and order beyond the ken of the Europeans' as witnessed through efforts to codify customary law (Kelly, 1997: 93).[8]

Like John D. Kelly, Sally Engle Merry finds court records especially useful in a study of the 'colonial process' (Merry, 2000: 8). She trains her gaze on around 60 years of the lower court records of the Hilo District Court, Hawai'i, in the second half of the nineteenth century. Not only do these records 'provide a window into the legal system's regulation of everyday family, community and work life', they also accentuate the rapid changes as 'the penal contract labor system was dismantled' (Merry, 2000: 8). Just as Finnane and Moore found that Melanesian workers were more likely to attract the attention of the law when they began to move more freely into colonial culture, Merry finds that as the law intervened into 'everyday life' it redefined some activities as 'criminal' and the courts 'disproportionately prosecuted low-status outsiders' (Merry, 2000: 189).

Merry describes her work as an ethnographic account of the 'colonizing project' in Hawai'i (Merry, 2000: 26). This is perhaps most apparent in her treatment of sexuality, marriage and the body where these intersected with 'crime' and made their way into Hawaiian courts. But her investigations into criminality and its construction in this context, despite offering court records as her major source, seem limited because she reads them as 'mediated by the language of the law' (Merry, 2000: 9) and, unlike Kelly, she denies them their 'smells, sights, feelings and noise'. The transcripts of several cases included in Merry's appendices show that deeper readings of the 'evidence' are possible. Kelly's work offers a more complex, layered and nuanced 'ethnography' than Merry's work. He makes multiple readings of the legal archive materials within his micro-study.

Concluding remarks

One purpose of this chapter was to identify this Australia, New Zealand and Pacific region as a potential 'new' site of historical investigation about crime and colonialism, meaning that it should be revisited as a space for regional and comparative studies. It should also take account of the important and rich scholarship that already exists: work by Clive Moore, Mark Finnane, Jacqueline Leckie and Doug Munro and others. A brief survey of this field reveals that work about labour in the South Pacific and patterns of resistance and accommodation has sometimes sought to take crime as a central theme of investigation, including the work by Finnane and Moore in Queensland. New work by Tracey Banivanua-Mar, already mentioned, also focused on Queensland, examines the violence of colonialism with regard to these problems and relates the control over indentured labourers to the control of Aboriginal people. As work on this region continues to appear, it should take account of the possibilities in the archive, especially the legal archive. As Knafla suggested in 2002, studies about 'crime and justice are rarely written from single sources or from a single focus'; themes like 'class, gender and sexuality … are usually depicted within the institutions of the police, the military, the courts, and local and central governments' (Knafla, 2002: xiv) and are affected by 'an interplay' of social forces. By referring to the work by John D. Kelly, I have suggested not only 'ways of seeing' but also 'ways of doing' legal-historical scholarship that explore this new site of historical work in a post-colonial vein. These might offer some new challenges to historians interested in these problems and specifically in the operations of the criminal law in colonial contexts.

Acknowledgments

Special thanks to Graeme Dunstall and Barry Godfrey for organising the two-day conference held at the University of Canterbury, Christchurch, New Zealand, in October 2003, and for providing the opportunity to present an earlier version of this chapter. Participants at that conference were extremely helpful and suggested further questions. Participants at an earlier symposium at the University of Waikato, New Zealand in 2002, and at the 2003 Australian and New Zealand Law and History Society conference in Brisbane, Australia, also provided valuable responses to the ideas expressed here.

Notes

1. See, for instance, the recent collection of articles, 'Making law visible: past and present histories and postcolonial theory', edited by Nan Seuffert and Catharine Coleborne in *Law Text Culture*, vol. 7, 2003. Earlier volumes of *Social and Legal Studies* (1996) and *Law and Critique* (1995), both co-edited by Eve Darian-Smith and Peter Fitzpatrick, have focused on law and post-colonialism. Darian-Smith and Fitzpatrick also co-edited *Laws of the Postcolonial* (University of Michigan Press, 1999). *Law and History Review* (Fall, 2003) also comments on the possibilities of post-colonial scholarship for law and history.

2. There is a range of archival and documentary sources available to historians of colonial crime and legal worlds, including statistical records generated by government reports, court records, policing records, judges' notebooks, institutional sources and private journals or diaries. This chapter only explores suggestive examples of these sources.

3. Peter Gibbons and I taught a second-year history course called 'Oceania' at the University of Waikato for the first time in 2002. Some of the ideas expressed in this chapter were articulated by him in our conversations about that course, and I owe him thanks for helping me to realise some of the ideas here, while the flaws are my own.

4. 'Comparative crime history' is explored in different ways by Hempenstall (2000) and Morrison (2003).

5. Historians including McClintock, Stoler and Manderson have examined the intersections between gender, class and 'race' in Africa and South-East Asia. In one piece of work Stoler (1997) specifically deals with laws regulating 'mixed marriages' in what was known as French Indochina in 1898, and the effects of these on articulations of gender and 'race'. Other historians have already begun to examine the specific histories of indigenous peoples in settler colonies and the complex range of gendered relations between indigenous peoples and Europeans, acknowledging law as central to these histories.

6. The justification for including Hawai'i in this survey study is provided in more detail by Flynn, Giráldez and Sobredo (2002: 4–5).

7. For instance, one contemporary account written after a year in the New Hebrides in 1872 by a European named F. A. Campbell who was un-sympathetic to the labour trade estimated that 20 per cent of indigenous peoples who left to enter this trade went out of a sense of curiosity and to obtain European goods. He also estimated that many others were forced,

taken through deceit, purchased or driven off their lands. See F. A. Campbell, *A Year in the New Hebrides, Loyalty Islands, and New Caledonia.* Geelong: G. Mercer, 1873.

8. We might also consider the implications of scholarship around legal pluralism here. See Merry (2000: 18).

References

Ballantyne, T. 'Reading the archive and opening up the nation-state: colonial knowledge in South Asia (and beyond)', in Burton, A. (ed.), *After the Imperial Turn: Thinking with and through the Nation.* Duke University Press, 2003, pp. 102–21.

Banivanua-Mar, T. 'Stabilising violence in colonial rule: settlement and the indentured labour trade in Queensland in the 1870s', in Banivanua-Mar, T. and Evans, J. (eds), *Writing Colonial Histories: Comparative Perspectives.* University of Melbourne, 2002, pp. 145–63.

Benton, L. *Law and Colonial Cultures: Legal Regimes in World History, 1400–1900.* Cambridge University Press, 2002.

Bjork, K. 'Race and the right kind of island: immigration policy in Hawaii and Cuba under US auspices, 1899–1912', in Flynn, D.O., Giráldez, A. and Sorbredo, J. (eds), *Studies in Pacific History: Economies, Politics, and Migration.* Ashgate, 2002, pp. 140–54.

Byrnes, G. *Boundary Markers: Land Surveying and the Colonisation of New Zealand.* Bridget Williams Books, 2001.

Creed, B. and Hoorn, J. *Body Trade: Captivity, Cannibalism and Colonialism in the Pacific.* University of Otago Press, 2001.

Curthoys, A. 'Does Australian history have a future?', *Australian Historical Studies* Special Issue: 'Challenging Histories: Reflections on Australian History', 118, 2002, pp. 140–52.

Dalley, B. 'Creeping in sideways: reading sexuality in the archives', *Archifacts*, October 2001, pp. 35–41.

Denoon, D. and Mein-Smith, P. *A History of Australia, New Zealand and the Pacific.* Blackwell, 2000.

Emsley, C. and Knafla, L. (eds) *Crime History and Histories of Crime: Studies in the Historiography of Crime and Criminal Justice in Modern History.* Greenwood Press, 1996.

Finnane, M. and Moore, C. 'Kanaka slaves or willing workers? Melanesian workers and the Queensland criminal justice system in the 1890s', *Criminal Justice History*, 1992, pp. 141–60.

Flynn, D., Dennis, O., Giráldez, A. and Sobredo, J. (eds), *Studies in Pacific History: Economies, Politics, and Migration*, Aldershot, UK and Vermont, USA: Ashgate, 2002.

Garton, S. 'The convict taint: Australia and New Zealand', in Emsley, C. and Knafla, L. (eds), *Crime History and Histories of Crime: Studies in the Historiography of Crime and Criminal Justice in Modern History.* Greenwood Press, 1996, pp. 271–90.

Gallagher, N. 'Postcolonialism', in Boyd, K. (ed.), *Encyclopedia of Historians and Historical Writing.* Fitzroy Dearborn Publishers, 1999, pp. 951–2.

Gibbons, P. J. 'The climate of opinion' in Rice, G. (ed.), *The Oxford History of New Zealand,* 2nd edn. Oxford University Press, 1992.

Gibbons, P. 'The far side of the search for identity: reconsidering New Zealand history', *New Zealand Journal of History,* 37, 1, 2003, pp. 38–49.

Guha, R. *Dominance without Hegemony: History and Power in Colonial India.* Harvard University Press, 1997.

Hempenstall, P. ' "My place": finding a voice within Pacific colonial studies', in Lal, B. V. (ed.), *Pacific Islands History: Journeys and Transformations, Journal of Pacific History,* Special Edition, 1992, pp. 60–78.

Hempenstall, P. 'Releasing the voices: historicizing colonial encounters in the Pacific', in Borofsky, R. (ed.), *Remembrance of Pacific Pasts: An Invitation to Remake History.* University of Hawai'i Press, 2000, pp. 43–61.

Howe, K. R. *Nature, Culture, and History: The 'Knowing' of Oceania.* Honolulu: University of Hawai'i Press, 2000.

Kelly, J. 'Gaze and grasp: plantations, desires, indentured Indians, and colonial law in Fiji', in Manderson, L. and Jolly, M. (eds), *Sites of Desire, Economies of Pleasure: Sexualities in Asia and the Pacific.* University of Chicago Press, 1997, pp. 72–98.

Kercher, B. *An Unruly Child: A History of Law in Australia.* Allen & Unwin, 1995.

King, P. 'Locating histories of crime: a bibliographical study', *British Journal of Criminology,* 39, 1, 1999, pp. 161–74.

Knafla, L. (ed.) *Crime, Gender and Sexuality in Criminal Prosecutions.* Greenwood Press, *Criminal Justice History,* Special Edition, 17, 2002.

Knapman, C. *White Women in Fiji 1835–1930: The Ruin of Empire?* Allen & Unwin, 1986.

Lal, B., Munro, D. and Beechert, E. D. (eds), *Plantation Workers: Resistance and Accommodation.* University of Hawai'i Press, 1993.

Mein-Smith, P. 'New Zealand Federation Commissioners in Australia: one past, two historiographies', *Australian Historical Studies,* 34, 122, 2003, pp. 305–25.

Merry, S. *Colonizing Hawai'i: The Cultural Power of Law.* Princeton University Press, 2000.

Mills, J. *Madness, Cannabis and Colonialism: The Native-Only Lunatic Asylums of British India, 1857–1900.* Macmillan and St Martin's Press, 2000.

Moore, C. 'A precious few: Melanesian and Asian women in Northern Australia', in Saunders, K. and Evans, R. (eds), *Gender Relations in Australia: Domination and Negotiation.* Harcourt Brace, 1996, pp. 59–81.

Moore, C., Leckie, J. and Munro, D. (eds), *Labour in the South Pacific.* James Cook University of Northern Queensland, 1990.

Morrison, B. 'Practical and philosophical dilemmas in cross-cultural research: the future of comparative crime history?', in Godfrey, B., Emsley, C. and Dunstall, G. (eds), *Comparative Histories of Crime.* Willan Publishing, 2003, pp. 195–212.

Moss, M. 'Archives, the historian and the future', in Ben Hey, M. (ed.), *Companion to Historiography*. Routledge, 1997, pp. 960–73.

Ralston, C. *Grass Huts and Warehouses: Pacific Beach Communities of the Nineteenth Century*. Australian National University, 1977.

Spiller, P., Finn, J. and Boast, R. *A New Zealand Legal History*. Brookers, 2001.

Stoler, A. 'Sexual affronts and racial frontiers: European identities and the cultural politics of exclusion in colonial Southeast Asia', in Cooper, F. and Stoler, A. (eds), *Tensions of Empire: Colonial Cultures in a Bourgeois World*. University of California Press, 1997, pp. 198–237.

Stoler, A. 'Colonial archives and the arts of governance: on the content and the form', in Hamilton, C. *et al.* (eds), *Refiguring the Archive*. Kluwer Academic, 2002, pp. 83–100.

Taylor, N. M. (ed.), *Early Travellers in New Zealand*. Clarendon Press, 1959.

Chapter 8

Traces and transmissions: techno-scientific symbolism in early twentieth-century policing

Dean Wilson

David Garland has suggested that punishment is not just an instrument of control but is also an expressive institution, a cultural performance. Through its portrayals of social authority and social relations, punishment contributes meaning to the social world (Garland, 1990, 1991). Drawing upon Garland's observations, there has recently been greater interest in the ways in which policing also communicates social meanings and actively constitutes culture (Walker, 1996; Loader, 1997; Loader and Mulcahy, 2003). Nevertheless, while scholars have begun to address the importance of what Nigel Walker (1996) terms 'the symbolic dimension' of policing, there has been less attention paid to how this symbolic dimension shapes and is shaped by historical change. In this chapter I wish to explore the historical transformation of the symbolic dimension of policing through an Australian case study – that of Melbourne. While the Melbourne case study bears local inflections, it is nevertheless indicative of similar trans-formations of police symbolism across jurisdictions that accompanied the altered time-space relations of modernity (Harvey, 1990; Giddens, 1990).

This chapter will first focus on the symbolic meanings inherent in beat policing. Beat policing was introduced to Melbourne in 1854, and the police constable on patrol was mobilised as a pivotal emblem of central authority. My observations draw upon Wilbur Miller's innovative work on the presentation of the London constable (1977). I then wish to consider why the beat constable, initially the focal point through which the symbolic dimension of policing was deployed, shed this wider cultural purpose. By the early twentieth century the beat constable was surpassed as the central symbol of policing by new techno-scientific symbols: fingerprinting and radio communications. In Melbourne fingerprinting, introduced in 1903, and the commencement of a motorised wireless patrol in 1922 are crucial elements in a paradigm situating the birth of modern scientific policing in the early decades of the twentieth century. In standard institutional police histories – inevitably written from an insider perspective (for Victoria see O'Brien, 1960; Victoria Police Management Services Bureau, 1980) – the wireless patrol and fingerprinting have become emblems of the break with nineteenth-century policing character-ised by beat patrols, Irishness and amateurism. The wireless patrol (see Figure 8.1) and fingerprinting are pivotal in triumphal and teleological narratives that inevitably culminate in adulatory references to contemporary technologies such as DNA and computer data matching. The development of this symbolism is of considerable interest, as it continues to fashion perceptions of policing both among police themselves and throughout wider culture.

In the early twentieth century Australian police authorities, like their counterparts in the United States, Canada and New Zealand (Walker,

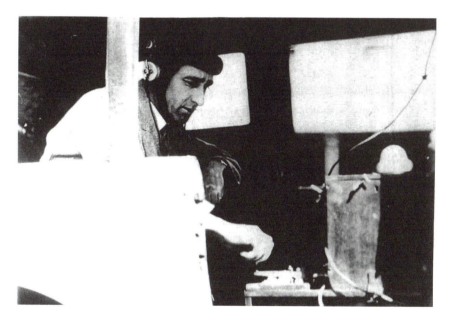

Figure 8.1   Wireless operator.

1977: 72–3; Marquis, 1993: 72–4; Hill, 1995: 165–74), were keen to promote technical innovations that portrayed their police forces as innovative, modern and progressive. They were aided by an eager press, already given to relating scientific advances to readers, which was more than ready to disseminate stories discursively fusing law enforcement with technological and scientific development. By focusing attention on the glamorous world of criminal detection, these technological developments made police forces – which were often underfinanced, undermanned, and suffering poor morale within the ranks – appear modern and efficient to a wider public. But I would suggest they indicate an even more important transformation in the symbolic dimension of policing. Images of science and modernity detached the symbolic dimension of policing from routine practice. Symbols were constituted in which policing was 'disembedded', to use Anthony Giddens' term, from the constraints of time and space (1990: 21–9). Moreover new technological symbols continued the development of panoptic principles that were also intrinsic to theories of the police beat. To understand the significance of this transformation, I first wish to consider the importance of symbolism in mid-nineteenth-century policing.

Beat constable as symbol

Wilbur Miller has noted the importance of police symbolism in the nineteenth-century London Metropolitan Police centred upon the creation of the 'automatic policeman'. Through discipline, drill, uniforms and the regular patrol of the beat, the London constable assumed a powerful symbolic function as the neutral and objective representative of impersonal central authority, idealised as the embodiment of the collective will of the people (Miller, 1977: 39–40). In London, the constable as symbol of impartially and rationally applied authority was primarily engaged to hasten acceptance of full-time professional police (De Lint, 1999: 37). In Melbourne, however, where police forces with varying levels of adherence to metropolitan standards had existed for over a decade, the theories of London policing were redeployed to confront uniquely colonial problems of authority and government (Wilson, 2003: 198).

Indeed the symbolism of the automatic policeman assumed added significance in the tumultuous social climate of gold-rush Melbourne. In the midst of upheaval and chaos, anxious government administrators placed great faith in public symbols to articulate aspirations of permanent and stable government authority. Many of the city's key cultural institutions – the University of Melbourne, the public library, mechanics institutes, botanic gardens and the museum – were founded to promote order and a respect for English cultural values among the populace. There was somehow a faith that the transplantation of these institutions from Britain would create order almost of themselves (Goodman, 1994: 88; Goodman, 1990; Fox, 1988). Police constables, too, were enrolled as symbolic representatives of the aspirations and ideals of colonial authorities seeking to fashion a more stable and cohesive society. Of all symbols of state power, the police were arguably the most significant. As Alan Silver has remarked, the policeman represented 'the penetration and continual presence of central political authority throughout daily life' (1967: 12–13).

Despite the local inflections of a gold-rush society informing the deployment of beat policing in Melbourne, the corporeal regulation and discipline of the police constable mirrored similar developments in other jurisdictions (De Lint, 1999, 2000; Emsley, 1996: 214–15; Miller, 1977). The shaping of the police constable into the symbolic representative of a benign and rationally applied central authority was to be achieved through the strict regulation of appearance and conduct (see Figure 8.2). The public purpose of the policeman was unmistakably indicated by his distinctive uniform, which signified his separation from the general

Figure 8.2 Melbourne police constables.

population and his mission as an impersonal agent of state power. As the bearer of institutional authority, any signs of individuality were to be erased. The governing of the individual constable even went to the level of facial hair, with moustaches to be short and trimmed, and policemen were not to 'indulge in fancy styles or fashion, nor wear long hair, nor allow the beard to grow of unseemly dimensions' (Police Department, Colony of Victoria, 1877: 3). Police rulebooks even strove to shape and mobilise the subjectivity of the police constable in the service of the state. The police personality was to be one of taciturn aloofness, and the constable was to be 'guarded as to his demeanor' (Police Department, Colony of Victoria, 1877: 17).

Of particular concern to authorities was the deportment of the constable. Drill was specifically incorporated into training as it would prevent policemen 'slouching down the street in an unseemly way' (Select Committee on the Police Force, 1863: 27–8). In 1888 a Police Guide informed constables of the importance of correct posture noting that 'nothing…seems worse in the eyes of the public than to see a constable lounging about in a lazy slovenly manner, as if it were a burden to him to carry his own weight' (Barry, 1888: 4–5). However, the symbolic dimension of policing was not only expressed through the person of the constable but also through the organisation of police work. The uniform and rational conduct of the constable was extended throughout space by the division of police work into discrete spatial units: police beats. Police beats were introduced to Melbourne in 1854, and, devised by a former officer of the London Metropolitan Police, divided the city into discrete units to provide round-the-clock surveillance (Wilson, 2003: 203). The regularity of spatial division was to complement the regulated body of the constable. By 1888 the walking pace of two miles an hour was judged to be the correct pace to observe 'people and places' (Barry, 1888: 7). The beat system was envisaged as a giant outdoor incarnation of Bentham's panopticon – a massive vision machine in motion constructed from a multitude of human moving parts.

Importantly the beat system comprising well-regulated constables extended symbolic metaphors of the police institution as rational and consistent. The rationality and benevolence of the state was to be consistently performed through interactions with the constable on the street, whose predictable movement made him both accessible and ever present. The aims were indeed broader than crime control. The constable was deployed as a model of idealised citizenship. In theory, police not only observed, noted and prevented infringements and deviations. They were also to provide a model of virtuous conduct to those policed, which, it was hoped, might be emulated.

Nevertheless the centrality of the constable as the key symbol of policing was increasingly eroded in the later nineteenth and early twentieth century. Partially this might be attributed to the difficulty of crafting individual policemen into appropriate symbols. The aspirations of beat policing were indeed expansive and, for those charged with putting them into effect, exacting. It is hardly surprising therefore that the men who daily buttoned up their blue tunics and walked their beats seldom lived up to such rigorous expectations. Despite the promise of round-the-clock policing members of the public complained throughout the nineteenth century that beat police could never be found when needed (Wilson, 2001: 92). Officers despaired as the mechanical functioning of the beat system faltered through human failing, as constables under their command fell asleep in doorways, wandered the streets in various states of drunkenness or simply disappeared from the streets to fraternise with the community they were supposed to be policing, and inevitably it seemed they fraternised with the least respectable sections of that community (Wilson, 2001: 50–4).

However, there were more significant reasons why the wisdom of uniformed beat patrol as the dominant symbol of policing was increasingly strained in the second quarter of the nineteenth century. Critiques emerged that highlighted the weakness of beat policing as a system that was spatially and temporally constrained. Uniformed beat patrols were increasingly criticised for their sheer predictability. Studious criminals, it was argued, could easily learn the monotonous path the policeman walked night after night. Such knowledge permitted criminals to commit offences safe in the knowledge that the constable was far away on another part of his beat. Similar criticisms were also directed at the visibility of the constable's uniform. The uniform had been heralded as one of the strengths of preventive policing. As one senior officer commented in 1882, the purpose of the police uniform was to make constables highly visible 'so that they can be seen at a long distance, like lighthouses, so that when people want a policeman they may be able to distinguish him at a long distance' (Royal Commission on Police, 1883: 192). However, as both members of the public and ordinary policemen increasingly pointed out, law-breakers could also see the policeman at a great distance, a fact which made their chances of evading capture that much greater.

Serious doubt also emerged as to whether uniformed beat policing even achieved the core function of protecting property through deterring the commission of offences. Although, in theory, the beat constable instilled in the criminal and potentially criminal awareness that they were being watched, attentive law-breakers were also able to calculate when the constable's gaze would be turned the other way. Those investigating the police in 1882 were troubled by the knowledge that 'the measured tread of a constable going along the street in the still hour of night can be heard at a great distance'. Burglars, it was feared, would quickly make their escape as the noisy boot of the constable echoed in the distance. Felt slippers or India-rubber soles were suggested to silence police at night, but many police had already taken the initiative, removing the nails from their boots – the cause of the offending noise (Royal Commission on Police, 1883: 27). In 1906 a story was circulating in Melbourne that one well-known criminal had boasted to a senior police officer that he knew exactly where and when all the constables in one section of the City could be found at any given time (Royal Commission on the Victorian Police Force (RCVPF), 1906: 34). In the same year, Inspector Henry Cawsey also claimed numerous burglaries in Melbourne's central area took place at five o'clock in the morning – precisely the hour when the night and day duty beats changed over. Such criticism was also heard from a wider public (RCVPF, 1906: 111–12). In 1904 the *Argus* newspaper was suggesting police on fixed beats protected neither person nor property, and advocated they be replaced with a more flexible method of patrol (5 July 1904: 9).

Such criticisms serve to underline the increasing fragility of the constable on the beat as the central symbol of policing by the later nineteenth century. While the fragility of the police beat symbol can partially be attributed to its own deficiencies, it was also due in some degree to its failure to function as an enabling device for emerging conceptions of police work. By the early twentieth century some senior police officials were advocating an increased detective function for ordinary police, and a corresponding increase in the number of men patrolling in plain clothes. Inspector Henry Cawsey was a strong advocate of increased plain-clothes policing, commenting that 'the thief cannot know where the plain clothes man is … a plain clothes man may pop up at any moment' (RCVPF, 1906: 113). In 1906, the desirability of increasing the numbers of plain-clothes police and having them work city beats 'irregularly and contrawise to the uniformed men', was one of the key recommendations of a Royal Commission established to investigate the organisation of the Police Force (RCVPF, 196: 113).

Increases in plain-clothes patrols were one manifestation of a more general erosion of the preventive policing principles so dominant in the mid-nineteenth century. Another was the elevation of detection rather than prevention as a police priority. Increasingly in the early twentieth century, police administrators talked of criminal detection as the core police function (RCVPF, 1906: 119). The work of policing was conceived more exclusively in terms of detecting and catching criminals, rather than maintaining a loosely defined 'order', or indeed of preventing crime from occurring. At the theoretical level at least then, there was an increasing individualisation of the objects of policing (cf. Garland, 1985: 115–16). The constable on the beat was the symbolic mobilisation of preventive policing principles. Highly visible beat policing conflated moral education, law enforcement and performance of the state. The new language of detection, however, shed the expansive project of social education in favour of isolating, locating and containing the aberrant individual.

Traces

If the patrol constable on the beat was faltering as the symbolic embodiment of policing, two new technologies – fingerprinting and the wireless patrol – offered redolent potential and were enthusiastically mobilised to signal transformed and modernised law enforcement. If the police beat represented regularity, visibility, predictability and confinement within space and time, both fingerprinting and the wireless patrol represented fluidity, invisibility and the transcendence of spatial and temporal strictures. They postulated an imagined world of seamless policing in which individuals could be rapidly tracked and located both temporally and spatially without the need for the continual physical presence that constrained and limited the beat constable.

By the first years of the twentieth century fingerprinting had become the official means of identification in Argentina, the United States, England and Australia (Joseph and Winter, 1996: 196; Cole, 2001: 152). A meeting of the State Commissioners of Police held in Melbourne in 1903 agreed on the establishment of a uniform system of fingerprint identification, and on the importance of the exchange of fingerprint data (Finnane, 1994: 80). Victorian police were followers rather than leaders in their adaptation of fingerprinting, but it was significant that the police force was seen to embrace new methods – new methods seen to place them on a par with major metropolitan police forces in Britain and the United States.

Fingerprinting was warmly embraced by the Melbourne press who deployed arguments already familiar in England to hail fingerprinting as a modern and scientific advance in criminal detection. Fingerprinting was promoted as offering a potentially omnipotent police archive, facilitating the rapid detection of offenders. Police administrators and journalists became positively giddy with the potential of fingerprint technology. In 1912 a feature article in the *Argus* newspaper informed readers:

The system is in fact a very much more delicate and accurate application of the clumsy Bertillon plan, which relied upon certain physical measurements in relation to others … The fingerprint expert relies upon certain coincident formations in relation to the central ridges. These formations never alter. The ridges formed upon the fingers before birth persist until the individual dies. (14 March 1912: 6).

Considering the potential applications of fingerprint technology for the future the writer became even more excited:

It is not difficult, indeed, to foresee the day when some state or nation, desiring a ready means of identification of any citizen at a moment's notice, may take a census of finger-tip impressions. In such an event no citizen could die unknown, the kidnapping and substitution of millionaires' babies would become a lost industry, and crime would become a very dangerous profession indeed, even for the beginner. Not the least extraordinary thing about such a fancy is its absolute ease of realization. (14 March 1912: 6)

Fingerprinting imbued policing with the infallibility and precision of science, reinventing the detective as an expert in the field of criminal investigation. One commentator remarked of fingerprinting that 'to talk of it as a "fad" is as absurd as a similar definition of wireless telegraphy or aeroplanes … it is a serious and scientific department of criminal investigation' (*Argus*, 16 June 1913: 12). Examples of criminals brought to justice by way of their fingerprints proliferated in the press, usefully projecting an image of policing as an exact and scientific enterprise. The following hypothetical case – that of housebreaker William Sykes – is one of many such stories published in Melbourne's daily press illustrating the utility of the new technology and the skill of its practitioners.

William Sykes breaks into a house at Malvern. His prints have been taken when he was in gaol in New South Wales for assault and robbery. He is not progressive, and does not wear gloves. Upon the lid of a steel cash box which he prises open he leaves a varied assortment of faint finger prints. Some of these are smudged as he moved his fingers when they were made. But some are not. Detective Potter comes to the house, and brushes a fine powder over the prints. He picks out those he wants, photographs them, and enlarges them at the detective office. He looks through his records, and does not find the print. But the copy sent to New South Wales receives its answer. Inspector Childs has such a print and sends the duplicate down. Then comes minute examination. The inner line of the 'loop' nucleus is broken in a certain place. Just level with this the next line out 'forks'. The third line, at a point opposite these aberrations, breaks, continues as a dot, breaks again, and then runs on unbroken. The fourth line is perfect, and the fifth forks at a certain point. These minutiae are faithfully reproduced on one of the prints upon the cash box. Detective Potter goes further, until he has about 20 points of resemblance and Sykes is traced and arrested. (*Argus*, 16 January 1913: 12)

The narrative of William Sykes's identification through the fingerprint is a story of the conquest of knowledge and science over anonymity. Moreover, the narrative suggests a virtually unlimited police potential to trace the individual. Detective Potter was able to map Sykes's movements, discover his past and uncover his present all from the small ridged lines on his finger. Most importantly Sykes only appears at the end of the narrative, by which time the knowledge necessary to convict him has already been accumulated. The science of fingerprinting had enabled detectives to assemble and catalogue a biography from a trace peripheral to the physical crime, and one which Sykes was unconscious of having left. This was record-keeping *par excellence.* Such publicity solidified both popular and police conceptions that the proper work of policing was criminal investigation and the tracing of offenders.

Intertwined with this celebration of fingerprinting was a new conception of police work as a highly professionalised occupation involving the mastery of complex technology. Policing was envisaged as more than its uniformed representatives, the sum of its fallible human parts – but as an expert system. This modernised conception of police work privileged scientific know-how and a quick intellect over the muscle and common sense of the nineteenth-century cop. Detective Potter, hunched over enlarged images of whorls, arches and loops in the police darkroom, is reminiscent of a pathologist gazing into the microscope to trace the origins of some as yet unknown disease.

The symbolic power of such an image was its suggestion that policing might claim an ultimate victory over crime through the routinised application of innovative scientific techniques. It also held out the promise of an infinite archive capable of conquering the spatial complexity and anonymity of the modern city. As the *Argus* phrased it, 'the identification of any print would be as easy to the expert as the finding of a word in a well-ordered dictionary' (14 March 1912: 6). The fingerprint archive also transcended time, as identities could be stored and retrieved whenever necessary (cf. Ericson and Shearing, 1986: 141). Importantly for police administrators, technologies of criminal investigation such as finger-printing projected an image of police modernisation propelled by scientific advances with the (imagined) capacity to eradicate criminal activity entirely.

Transmissions

Various scholars have noted the potential of technological innovations in police work to enhance the surveillance of police over citizens while simultaneously escalating the level of bureaucratic control over the policeman on the street (Ericson and Shearing, 1986; De Lint, 2000; Dandeker, 1990: 127–8; Walker, 1977: 136–7). As De Lint notes, 'with each new technology, a fuller and more penetrating gaze has been envisioned, both of the police into the polity and of police supervision on police officer mobilisation' (2000: 70). This has been especially relevant in the case of radio communications, an innovation adapted in both North America and Australia in the 1920s and 1930s. Radio communications with patrol cars compressed space and time while facilitating an intensification of supervision over the police constable (De Lint, 2000: 69). Nevertheless, while scholars have grasped the organisational and societal significance of the introduction of radio communications to police work, the symbolic ramifications of these developments are less well charted.

The symbolic currency of radio communications is evident in Melbourne with the introduction of motorised wireless patrols, an experiment seen as placing the Australian city's police at the forefront of technological innovation. In November 1922, a 15-mile test broadcast was made to a waiting police patrol car. The roving patrol could now receive information of incidents in real time, responding rapidly and randomly (Haldane, 1986: 191–4). The wireless patrol became the darling of the Melbourne press with its development widely publicised. A plethora of news stories reinforced the perception that policing aided by technology could be anywhere at anytime – and quickly (see examples in Amalgamated Wireless Company, 1923). Wireless radio seemed to offer up the possibility of omnipotent policing. It was flexible, concealed, rapid and very modern. As the Chief Commissioner commented 'many thieves and house-breakers will be afraid to operate when there is the possibility of the sudden arrival of a car load of police, bound to no particular beat, but likely to appear at any time in any street' (Amalgamated Wireless Company, 1923: 23).

For contemporaries the promise of this technologically driven rapid policing was the certainty of detection. This was well articulated by the Amalgamated Wireless Company, which, in its promotional booklet *Police Radio: Scientific Aid in the Detection and Suppression of Crime*, noted the 'importance of time':

> Time is the all-important factor when the police are on the track of the 'wanted' criminal. The quicker that the description can be circulated, the less chance of evading capture; indeed, it is doubtful whether, in any other sphere of activity, the value of time is of such paramount importance. It cannot be gainsaid that a brief description, widely circulated within a short period of time is worth volumes circulated a few hours later. (1923: 2)

Rapid communications were thus viewed as a panacea for the altered space-time relations of modernity confronting policing in the early twentieth century. Whether such technologies actually captured anyone was perhaps less important than the powerful image of police modernisation they advanced. The radio offered a symbol of policing as thoroughly modern and in step with, even ahead of, new configurations of law-breaking. As the *Age* newspaper commented in 1923, 'The police force has been the starveling among State Departments. Undermanned, and generally ill-provided for, it has acquired no reputation for modern methods in either administration or activities.' The wireless patrol thereby combated previously dominant symbols of policing, such as the uniform beat constable, that were rigid, predictable, visible and historically bound to the police institution's mid-nineteenth-century birth. Obversely the wireless patrol offered a potent symbol of modern policing as fluid, innovative, discreet and utterly contemporary. As the report went on to say of the motor police, 'wireless sets, modern cars and good equipment, have made this branch undoubtedly the most up-to-date in the Department' (*Age*, 16 January 1923, cited in Amalgamated Wireless Company, 1923: 18). The *Argus* announced: 'The old-style policeman with his bull's eye lantern, truncheon and rattle has faded into the past, and the Melbourne police are well on the way to being ranked with the most efficient and best equipped forces in the world' (cited in O'Brien, 1960: 142).

In common with fingerprinting, the wireless patrol also hinted at the potentials of a mode of policing which was invisible yet omnipotent. Both technologies offered on a symbolic level the possibility of Jeremy Bentham's 'invisible inspector' at the centre of the panopticon – seeing but never seen. Beat policing had attempted to envisage this project through physical observation. However, Bentham himself conceded the practical impossibility of such an undertaking. Rather, Bentham suggested, 'the next thing to be wished for is, that, at every instant, seeing as reason to believe as much, and not being able to satisfy himself to the contrary, he should conceive himself to be so' (Bentham, 1995: 34). The wireless patrol embodied this notion of concealed observation.

Unlike the plodding cop on the beat, who might be easily outwitted by the observant burglar who could time his absence, wireless and fingerprinting projected a vision of policing as invisible and everywhere.

While these images of modern policing were promoted, the ordinary constable in uniform trudging the beat became increasingly denigrated as the symbol of a bygone era of flawed and ineffectual policing – an anachronism in the modern city of speed, technology and anonymity (cf. Manning, 1977: 347–53). By 1922, even Melbourne's senior police official, Chief Commissioner Alexander Nicholson, exhibited scant respect for the ordinary policeman trudging the beat. Praising motor patrols, Nicholson remarked that 'the system by which a burglar can see a constable in uniform standing on one corner and go around the next street and break into a house is out of date'. For Nicholson, the future of police work lay with the motorcar, which allowed random patrols and swift unpredictable movements over space. The motorised police constable would outsmart law-breakers, as 'criminals will not know where a police-man is at any given time' (*Argus*, 14 June 1922: 11).

Conclusion

A series of new images consequently circulated through society linking policing firmly with contemporary urban life – detectives racing to the scene of the crime in motor cars, or the policeman in the photographic darkroom piecing together clues with the aid of science, solving crime as a white-coated scientist might discover the cure to a mysterious disease. Techno-scientific symbolism severed the symbolism of policing from the immediacy of social relations, reconfiguring it within wider culture as an expert system. I would be careful here to say that the 'symbolism' of policing was disembedded, as police still trudged their beats, arrested and patrolled. Nevertheless, by the early twentieth century the constable on patrol had largely been stripped of symbolic resonance. Part of this rested in the limitation of the constable as a physical presence constrained by time and place. Moreover the symbolic role of the constable was also fused with a generalised conception of police as a comprehensive instrument of social regulation and education.

Techno-scientific symbols gathered momentum through the evocation of modes of policing with the capacity to saturate time and space. In so doing they evoked a fantasy of total panopticism that retains cultural salience in the present. Swift movement and archives could identify from a distance, symbolically releasing policing from the shackles of co-presence and physical observation. Policing could also abandon the broad social purpose of the constable in the community, focusing on the identification and capture of the individual offender. In the nineteenth century the symbolic dimension of policing was corporeally inscribed on the police constable and interwoven with the routine work of policing. However, by the early twentieth century the symbols of policing were cast adrift from the quotidian drudgery of police work. These techno-scientific symbols of policing emerging from the early twentieth century have proven remarkably resilient. They continue to inform our cultural understandings of policing and authority, while simultaneously growing evermore distant from routine police practice.

References

Amalgamated Wireless (Australasia) Ltd. *Police Radio: Scientific Aid in the Detection and Supression of Crime*. Amalgamated Wireless, 1923.

Barry, J. *Victorian Police Guide containing practical and legal instructions for police constables*. J. W. Burrows, 1888.

Bentham, J. *The Panopticon Writings*, ed. M. Bozovic. Verso, 1995.

Cole, S. *Suspect Identities: A History of Fingerprinting and Criminal Identification*. Harvard University Press, 2001.

Dandeker, C. *Surveillance, Power and Modernity: Bureaucracy and Discipline from 1700 to the Present Day*. Polity, 1990.

De Lint, W. 'Nineteenth century disciplinary reform and the prohibition against talking policemen', *Policing and Society*, 9, 1, 1999, pp. 33–58.

De Lint, W. 'Autonomy, regulation and the police beat', *Social and Legal Studies*, 9, 1, 2000, pp. 55–83.

Emsley, C. *The English Police: A Political and Social History*, 2nd edn. Longman, 1996.

Ericson, R. and Shearing, C. 'The scientification of police work', in Bohme, G. and Stehr, N. (eds), *The Knowledge Society: The Growing Impact of Scientific Relations on Social Relations*. D. Reidel, 1986.

Finnane, M. *Police and Government: Histories of Policing in Australia*. Oxford University Press, 1994.

Fox, P. 'The State Library of Victoria: science and civilisation', *Transition*, Spring 1988, pp. 14–26.

Garland, D. 'The criminal and his science', *British Journal of Criminology*, 25, 1, 1985, pp. 109–37.

Garland, D. *Punishment and Modern Society: A Study in Social Theory*, University of Chicago Press, 1990.

Garland, D. 'Punishment and culture: the symbolic dimension of criminal justice', *Studies in Law, Politics and Society*, 11, 1991, pp. 191–222.

Giddens, A. *The Consequences of Modernity*. Stanford University Press, 1990.

Goodman, D. 'Fear of circuses: founding the National Museum of Victoria', *Continuum*, 3, 1, 1990, pp. 18–34.

Goodman, D. *Goldseeking: Victoria and California in the 1850s*. Allen & Unwin, 1994.

Haldane, R. *The People's Force: A History of the Victoria Police*. Melbourne University Press, 1986.

Harvey, D. *The Condition of Postmodernity*. Blackwell, 1990.

Hill, R. *The Iron Hand in the Velvet Glove: The Modernisation of Policing in New Zealand, 1886-1917*. Dunmore Press, 1995.

Joseph, A. and Winter, A. 'Making the match: human traces, forensic experts and the public imagination', in Spufford, F. and Uglow, J. (eds), *Cultural Babbage: Technology, Time and Invention*. Faber & Faber, 1996.

Loader, I. 'Policing and the social: questions of symbolic power', *British Journal of Sociology*, 48, 1, 1997, pp. 1–18.

Loader, I. and Mulcahy, A. *Policing and the Condition of England: Memory, Politics, and Culture*. Oxford University Press, 2003.

Manning, P. *Police Work: The Social Organisation of Policing*. MIT Press, 1977.

Marquis, G. *Policing Canada's Century: A History of the Canadian Association of Chiefs of Police*. University of Toronto Press, 1993.

Miller, W. R. *Cops and Bobbies: Police Authority in New York and London, 1830–1870*. University of Chicago Press, 1977.

O'Brien, G. *The Australian Police Forces*. Oxford University Press, 1960.

Police Department Colony of Victoria *Regulations for the Guidance of the Constabulary of Victoria*. John Ferres Government Printer, 1877.

Report from the Select Committee on the Police Force, 1863, *Votes and Proceedings of the Legislative Assembly of Victoria*, 1862–3.

Royal Commission on Police. 'The Proceedings of the Commission, minutes of evidence, appendices, etc.' *Victorian Parliamentary Papers*, 1883.

Royal Commission on the Victoria Police, 1906, *Victorian Parliamentary Papers*. 1906.

Silver, A. 'The demand for order in civil society: a review of some themes in the history of urban crime, police and riot', in Bordua, D. (ed.), *The Police: Six Sociological Essays*. John Wiley, 1967.

Victoria Police Management Services Bureau. *Police in Victoria 1836–1908*. Melbourne: Victoria Police Department, 1980.

Walker, N. 'Defining core police tasks: the neglect of the symbolic dimension', *Policing and Society*, 6, 1, 1996, pp. 53–71.

Walker, S. *A Critical History of Police Reform: The Emergence of Professionalism*. D. C. Heath, 1977.

Wilson, D. 'On the beat: police work in Melbourne, 1853–1923', unpublished PhD thesis, Monash University, 2001.

Wilson, D. 'The Melbourne constable as automatic policeman', *Victorian Historical Journal*, 74, 2, 2003, pp. 197–224.

Chapter 9

The English model? Policing in late nineteenth-century Tasmania

Stefan Petrow

In the late nineteenth century Tasmania was the only Australian colony to retain a decentralised system of policing based on the English model and here I want to examine why that system was adopted, how it worked in practice and why centralisation was introduced in 1899. The connecting theme of the paper is therefore the tension between centralised and decentralised forms of policing. Who should control the police? Should it be the local community alert to local needs and allowing for variety in the enforcement of laws or the central government free from the pressure of local interests, sentiments or prejudices and able to enforce uniform standards for all citizens? This debate has been revived recently by the think-tank Policy Exchange, which, with the number of English police forces reduced to 43 by 2003, has called for a return of police forces to local councils and less central government interference (Loveday and Reid, 2004). In both Tasmania and England the debate – to about 1900 at least – was 'essentially concerned with accountability, control and form' and not function (Emsley, 1999: 42).

England

In England policing had long been a local function at parish level but between 1829 and 1856 there occurred much active police reform in response, broadly speaking, to fear of crime and disorder. Emsley has described police reform as 'a slow process involving experiment, debate, and compromise; debates over, and experiments with, a variety of different models were to continue throughout the 1840s and early 1850s' (Emsley, 1996: 42). Philips and Storch (1999: 7) stress that debates about police reform 'did not simply pit against each other those who favoured the new police and those who did not. There were many camps and a great cacophony of voices.' In what became 'a wider struggle over the distribution of power within various elements of the English state', the gentry battled hard to preserve 'their status and authority'. I cannot consider all the proposals for reform here, but can identify the four main policing models to emerge.

Perhaps the best known was the model of the Metropolitan Police. Formed under the Metropolitan Police Act 1829, this force of initially 3,000 uniformed men was organised in a centralised, hierarchical and rigid body to patrol London streets (Miller, 1999). This model of 'state civilian force' relied on management by two Commissioners, who were controlled by the Home Office and were answerable to Parliament (Emsley, 1999: 36). The second model, or 'civilian municipal police', arose from the Municipal Corporations Act 1835. It created watch committees to establish and supervise police forces in incorporated boroughs. The 1835 Act ensured that all boroughs organised police forces along the same lines but was not compulsory. By 1850 perhaps as many as 23 of 178 boroughs had no police force (Emsley, 1996: 43). Some forces were very large, many were small. The watch committees appointed head constables and police forces, did the hiring, firing and disciplining, and sought to influence day-to-day management. The head constables were very much the social inferiors of the watch committees and, as these committees met weekly, the head constables had little autonomy.

Crime fighting was not the major function of borough forces. Police carried out many petty administrative and welfare duties such as acting as mace-bearers on civic occasions, collecting market tolls, acting as inspectors of weights and measures, lodging houses, cattle and nuisances, collecting licences, and serving as Poor Law relieving officers and assistant surveyors of highways. As town councils and watch committees regarded the police as 'their servants who could be used at their discretion, and not simply for the prevention of crime', duties piled up as the century continued (Emsley, 1996: 44, 84). As economy was the catch-cry of borough elections, police wages and numbers depended upon the rates local electors were prepared to pay. The main problem with this model was that the police forces were too small to deal with serious riots and, argues Taylor (1997: 33), most forces failed to adopt new policing practices.

For our third model we turn to the Rural Constabulary Acts 1839 and 1840, which gave control of the police to the magistrates who ran local government at the county level and empowered county benches to create a constabulary by authorising them to set a rate (Emsley, 1996: 40–5). As this Act was also not compulsory, it seems that by the mid-1850s only 35 of the 54 counties had established police forces and some were very small indeed. The Police Committees appointed Head Constables, who were the social equals of the magistrates (military officers or landed gentry). Their appointment had to be approved by the Home Secretary. The county benches only met quarterly and thus left much discretion in the hands of head constables. Ratepayers sent petitions to the quarter sessions if they felt too much money was spent on the police or if the police were inefficient. In addition to expense and inefficiency ratepayers claimed that police tried too hard to prosecute offences (Emsley, 1996: 49).

Dissatisfaction with this system led to new proposals for reform of the more traditional system of local policing. In this final model the Parish Constables Act 1842 required magistrates to compile lists of fit ratepayers of good character between 25 and 55 who would be sworn in as parish constables (Emsley, 1996: 48–9). They would be supervised by new superintending constables appointed by the quarter sessions and paid from the county rate. Proponents argued that this system would not only be more efficient and less expensive, but that, as ratepayers, the police would have a greater incentive to protect property. The Superintending Constables Act 1850 empowered quarter sessions to appoint these officers for each petty sessional division of their county. While superintending constables were professional policemen, they found it difficult to raise the policing standards of part-time parish constables. Superintendents also became overburdened with duties. Despite acknowledged deficiencies, many English counties implemented the legislation, but the system was giving 'diminishing satisfaction by the mid-1850s' (Philips and Storch, 1999: 213–19, 231).

Despite problems with particular models, ruling elites became accustomed to 'the idea of professional policing' and approved of the impact of the new police, especially in imposing order (Emsley, 1996: 49). Storch (1976) sees them as domestic missionaries bringing civilisation and decorum to working-class communities armed with a battery of legislation. Policemen made themselves useful by discharging welfare and administrative tasks, but to what extent these impeded their efficiency in maintaining order or crime fighting is hard to say. Often these duties were not onerous and may have provided part of the basis for police legitimacy, although some, such as tax collecting, were unpopular.

While Storch (1975) has stressed the initial level of lower-class resistance to intervention by the new police, we see a change in attitudes. By the mid-1850s 'all social groups', but especially national and provincial ruling elites, had, argue Philips and Storch (1999: 3, 8–9, 221), decided that the traditional system of parochial police could not be improved and, impressed with the county forces as 'powerful order-imposing machines', wanted a more uniform system of policing to deal with various problems and fears. These included the ending of transportation to eastern Australia and the need to cope with criminals at home; the return of soldiers from the Crimean War; a rise in vagrancy, petty crime and disorder; and the increased mobility of criminals due to the spread of the railways (Emsley, 1996: 49–54). After a period of debate revealed support for reform from all sides of politics, the final piece in the legislative jigsaw puzzle, the County and Borough Police Act 1856, was passed easily because, Philips and Storch (1999: 233) stress, it was the culmination of 'a long and complex process of both ideological change and practical experiment in the countryside'.

The 1856 Act made it obligatory to set up uniformed, bureaucratic, hierarchical police forces at county and borough level (Emsley, 1996: 54). It established a national inspectorate of three to assess annually the efficiency of police forces and impose basic standards and uniform procedures. To counteract criticism of the expense, central government agreed to contribute one quarter of the cost of pay and clothing for forces certified as efficient by the Inspectors. Chief Constables had to supply the Inspectors with annual reports of the crime occurring in their districts. Thus local control was retained and central government contributed to the cost of the new police. But the Act did indicate that the needs of an increasingly urbanised and industrialised society made the parish system inappropriate as the unit of policing. The other major change occurred at the county level in 1888. The Local Government Act established joint standing committees comprised half of magistrates and half of elected councillors as the county police authority, but local control remained strong (Emsley, 1996: 85). Centralisation at the national level was still not popular because of fears for civil liberties and the tyranny of the continental model of policing. So we find the triumph, as Carolyn Steedman (1984: 3–6) sees it, of the 'provincial vision of the rural police as a kind of soldiery', a paramilitary force, 'the defensive arm of local property owners' as well as 'the administrative agency of local magistrates and watch committees'.

Despite opposition to police centralisation, we can identify a gradual trend in this direction with the Inspectors using efficiency certificates 'to enforce a degree of uniformity, specifying what did and what did not constitute proper policing tasks, and urging forces to adopt what they considered to be good and sensible practice from elsewhere' (Emsley, 1996: 91–2). The Inspectors determined efficiency by the men's performance at drill, but mainly by the number of constables in relation to population (one policeman to 900 people was standard) and the number of senior officers to supervise constables. As policing became more professional and specialised, central government tried to avoid the police authorities and dealt directly with chief and head constables, giving them executive power independently of local authorities (Emsley, 1996: 85, 88, 92–5). To secure greater supervision and control of provincial police, the Treasury grant was increased from one quarter to one half in 1874. A drop in the number of police forces occurred after the Local Government Act 1888 abolished police forces in towns with a population less than 10,000. This reduced the number of police forces from 231 in 1888 to 183 in 1889, but the number rose again to 197 in 1900 when additional boroughs were incorporated (Critchley, 1978: 133). If centralisation did become stronger after 1900, it continued to be not 'as consistent ruling-class policy, but more as piecemeal responses to evolving policy' (Miller, 1993: 194).

Tasmania

While in England decentralised models of policing predominated in the nineteenth century, in Australia the colonies were evenly divided between decentralised and centralised models of policing by 1856. Tasmania, South Australia and Victoria followed centralised models, and in succession Western Australia, New South Wales and Queensland had followed suit by 1863 (Finnane, 1994). The existence of a large convict and ex-convict population, a recalcitrant indigenous population, the upheavals caused by the discovery of gold and serious outbreaks of bushranging propelled the formation of powerful centralised forces akin to the Irish Constabulary. Yet at a time when other colonies were centralising their police, Tasmania, which had experienced the most heavily centralised police force for 30 years, decided to adopt the English decentralised municipal model in 1858 (Moore, 1991: 112).[1]

How do we explain this reversal of policy and how did it work in practice? Tasmanians had been scarred by the way the French-like centralised police, mostly ex-convicts, had abused their powers, spied on free citizens, provided little protection of person and property and infringed liberties under the supervision of paid magistrates answerable to the Lieutenant-Governor (Petrow, 2000a, 2001). Many colonists remained very suspicious of government and wanted to control their own police. This view was particularly strong in rural areas dominated by the landed elites (an ersatz aristocracy as the British politician Charles Dilke later described them), who wanted to use their regional power bases to resist efforts by government to impose central control or taxes or to interfere with their property (Reynolds, 1969a). During the convict era, colonists had paid heavily for the large police forces established by the lieutenant-governors and many property owners wanted to control the costs of policing themselves.

During the tenure of Lieutenant-Governor William Denison (1847–55) the future of policing under self-government was hotly debated in the local press. The proposals had echoes of English models. The *Launceston Examiner* (30 April, 8 December 1853) thought only the most 'trustworthy and efficient' police should be retained and the rest should be replaced by citizens sworn in as special constables. This form of parish policing would reduce police expenses to a tenth of the current cost and provide 'ten times more security'. Others suggested placing the police under the control of existing local councils in Hobart Town and Launceston before extending the system to other areas (*Hobart Town Courier*, 15 September 1853). Yet others argued that the police should be controlled by a legislature elected by the people, who would then no longer be 'a community of slaves' with their 'liberty taken away' or their money 'filched' by convict police (*Cornwall Chronicle*, 16 May 1849). Later, the *Colonial Times* (20 September, 17 November 1856) advocated the Metropolitan Police system under parliamentary control. This model proposed one force for the island controlled by a Chief Commissioner, with Superintendents for the northern and southern districts. Until his retirement in 1857, Chief Police Magistrate Francis Burgess, who managed the centralised police, strongly argued against change in the police, which was an organisation of 'a military character, and where centralisation is so essential to its vigorous growth and action' (Jackman, 1966: 82–3).

Unlike other Australian colonies, from 1856 Tasmania experienced no serious threats to social order to justify a centralised police: white settlement had destroyed the Aboriginal population, no goldfields had yet developed, bushrangers had long stopped terrifying colonists in any organised way and the ex-convict population did not threaten – indeed many ex-convicts seemed to flee the island as soon as they could (Reynolds, 1969b: 21–2). Tasmania was not a very urbanised colony, industry was underdeveloped and the population was widely dispersed so a decentralised force seemed to suit social, economic and geographical circumstances (Hartwell, 1954).

Significantly, the new colonial government was obsessed with cutting expenditure and divesting itself of expensive, unpopular and contentious functions such as policing. It thus encouraged local communities to control their own police forces. Much impetus for responsible government came from large rural landowners, who sought to preserve political power by creating a weak central government subservient to a parliament they dominated (Reynolds, 1969a: 67–8). The government justified its decision to devolve policing by following the recommendation of a Royal Commission on the State of the Public Service, which reported in September 1857. The commissioners described the centralised Irish Constabulary force as 'the best organised and most efficient body of men working for the preservation of order', but they were expensive and Tasmania had no order problems necessitating such a force (Petrow, 1995: 168). The commissioners favoured the 'widely different' English system, where police were managed by 'local bodies, who determine the amount of force that the police necessities of the district demand, and provide the revenue which is necessary to defray the expenditure'. The commissioners recommended that Tasmania be divided into districts defined by area, population or geographical position; that municipal councils be established to appoint, control and manage the police of their districts as well as other municipal functions; and that each municipal council be empowered to levy rates to fund their policing and other duties.

But, like the pre-1856 English system, the government did not require local areas to form their own councils: under the Rural Municipalities Act 1858 50 ratepayers could request the Governor to declare a municipal council in towns, or electoral, or road or police districts. By 1866 19 rural municipalities, most in old settled areas with well-established landed elites, were formed to add to the Hobart and Launceston councils which were already formed under their own Acts in 1858 (Petrow, 1998). Each council had its own police force. To save money, the government retained stipendiary magistrates only in the two largest towns, and required wardens of rural councils to sit on local benches as the senior lay magistrates. The rural municipalities varied in physical size. In 1867 the smallest was Glenorchy with six police to protect its population of 1,265 people inhabiting 24,000 acres (Petrow, 1998: 245–6). The largest was Hamilton where six policemen had charge of 1,497 people over 2,959,000 acres. Only two rural municipalities exceeded 5,000 people. Only one municipality had ten or more police, not including the two urban forces, which were the largest. In rural municipalities the ratio of policemen to population ranged from 1 to 93 in Spring Bay to 1 to 693 in Westbury. The size of police forces fluctuated over later decades depending on economy drives by local councillors, but by 1898 only Hobart and Launceston had more policemen than in 1867.

Although the 21 police forces were autonomous, some central interference was possible. The Inspector of Police, who controlled the police in
the initial eight non-municipal or police districts, was the agent of the
Colonial Secretary. The Inspector was empowered to report on the
efficiency of municipal police forces, to write general rules for their
guidance (O'Sullivan, 1980: 198), and to apply for a writ of mandamus in
the Supreme Court if councillors cut numbers to below adequate levels
(Petrow, 1998: 246). Helping to subsidise police costs gave central government an opening to interfere with municipal police when necessary. But
interference rarely occurred, despite claims over the next two decades that
the system was plagued with abuses, abuses partly inherent in any
decentralised system of policing and partly arising from retaining a form
of magisterial control of the police.

Abuses of the decentralised system

As there were so many police forces and so few have been studied in
detail, we have to rely on government inquiries and newspaper accounts
for information on how the system worked. A major area of disquiet
concerned a lack of impartiality in the administration and enforcement of
justice (Petrow, 1998: 247). Municipal policemen were 'restrained from an
honest and fearless discharge of their duty' by avoiding offending 'some
one dressed in a little brief authority' or their friends and relatives.
Subservience to 'a local and ever changing management' injured effective
policing because someone prosecuted one year might be a councillor in the
next and have the power of dismissal, against which there was no power of
appeal. One policeman complained that he had been 'hampered,
humbugged, or misruled' by councillors who were 'wholly illiterate' and
lacked competency to manage a police force. That was not necessarily a
feature of all forces. In Bothwell the warden and councillors did not appear
to interfere with their police force or to have used the police to further their
own interests (Petrow, 2000b: 113).

Councillors usually exercised their power in subtle ways and constables
soon learnt 'when to open their eyes and when to keep them shut' (Petrow,
1998: 247–8). If this meant passive policing and overlooking the faults of
councillors' friends, then the *Cornwall Chronicle* (11 July 1878), though
critical, thought that little 'mischief' was done. But if, as had happened, it
meant finding 'a fault in one who may happen to be at variance' with the
views of a councillor, then it produced 'the greatest and most intolerable
injustice'. In Brighton police supposedly allowed influential ratepayers to
break laws, which acted as a precedent for others. More illegalities

occurred, even innocuous legislation like the Californian Thistles Act was not enforced, and the law was treated contemptuously by the local community (Petrow, 1998: 247).

Sometimes wardens took into account how many votes at municipal elections suitors possessed and for political reasons would dismiss cases brought by policemen (Petrow, 1998: 247). Wardens also tried to bolster municipal funds by imposing heavy fines. Wardens were 'utterly unacquainted' with the law and citizens had little confidence in their decisions. Few cases of injustice were discovered because court pro-ceedings in rural areas were not reported. In 1873 respected Launceston lawyer and Town Clerk, C. W. Rocher, held that incompetent municipal magistrates were 'spoken of with derision' and charged 'openly with favouritism and corruption' (Petrow, 1998: 247-8). Rocher predicted that, if a poll was held, three-quarters of rural voters would support police centralisation and the abolition of 'judicial powers in municipalities'.

Another serious defect arose from a desire to save money by combining the positions of Superintendent and Council Clerk (Petrow, 1998: 248). It was inconsistent with established practice for the Superintendent to be the prosecutor as well as the clerk who recorded the depositions. It placed the Superintendent in 'the anomalous position' of taking down a prisoner's statement, then his depositions, and later prosecuting him in court. This jeopardised the 'impartial and unsuspected administration of justice' and injured 'the proper conducting of office and police business'. For a miserly saving, councillors paralysed the administration of the laws and com-promised 'the securities with which life and property are protected'.

The third abuse was the diverse way in which laws were administered in different municipalities (Petrow, 1998: 248). Some were 'fair and tolerant' and enforced 'the spirit and not the penal letter of the law'. But some councillors were 'culpably remiss' and failed to check their Superintendent's 'ever varying and oppressive caprices, whether they be of a meanly vindictive nature or of a fawning species of favouritism'. Influenced more by local sentiment than legal standards, some wardens refused to allow their police to cooperate with the government and supply the names of carriage owners who defaulted in their payment of a carriage tax (Petrow, 1997a). In the major towns of Hobart and Launceston the police often overlooked the way publicans infringed the licensing laws because the drink interest was well represented on their respective councils (Petrow, 1995, 1997c).

Sometimes police exercised discretion in enforcing laws out of respect for community values. While serving at Jerusalem in the Richmond municipality in the 1880s, Sub-Inspector C. S. Lynch followed established police custom and 'never interfered' if residents, especially old pensioners, collected dead wood 'as long as they did not sell it' (Petrow, 2003: 22). If they sold the wood, he required them to pay for a licence. Lynch advised Sub-Inspector Curley not to let any man 'monopolize the wood trade' in Spring Hill Bottom unless they would provide reliable information on sheep stealers.

Some critics thought the 'abuse of patronage' was 'the greatest danger' in establishing the rural police (Petrow, 1998: 248). At times, councillors appointed a local resident as Superintendent because he needed a job or for other reasons needed help from fellow residents. At Deloraine the son of a settler and the brother of one of the councillors was appointed Superintendent despite his young age and lack of police experience. At Bothwell, James Gill McDowall, the son of a councillor, was appointed Superintendent in 1871, but the next year resigned after complaints about his inefficiency (Petrow, 2000b: 114). At Richmond a serving councillor Edwin Kearney was appointed Superintendent in 1890 (Petrow, 2003: 13). As the century progressed, superintendents tended to be appointed because of their experience gained in other districts, but mostly local knowledge and connections were regarded more highly than police experience.

Councillors expected favours for their patronage. According to the *Tasmanian Tribune* (3 January 1873), most rural policemen were 'little better than messengers' to councillors. Councillors who owned stores routinely 'compelled' policemen to buy their goods from them 'even at exorbitant prices'. The *Cornwall Chronicle* (9 February 1872) held that a policeman should not be 'the obsequious attendant upon some local magnate', but an 'independent' public functionary 'swayed neither by affection nor favour'. But the restrictive rural franchise meant that only a small number of ratepayers were eligible to stand as councillors or even to vote (Reynolds, 1969a). No wonder, then, that policemen kowtowed to councillors and treated smaller ratepayers with barely disguised contempt.

The pay and conditions of rural policemen also attracted criticism. Policemen were expected, thought Hobart's *Mercury* (29 April 1869), to be 'not only shrewd and intelligent, but men of principle, maintaining a good character', who were 'trustworthy and trusted'. The best encouragement to good character was 'a fair pay', enabling policemen to maintain their position with 'credit and respectability'. Inadequate pay forced a policeman 'to eke out his subsistence as he best may' by taking tips. In 1869 the Oatlands Municipal Council reduced police pay to four shillings a day, which was insufficient to sustain a wife and family. This opened the door to bribery. As lowering municipal costs was popular with ratepayers, policemen always lived with the 'uncertainty' that their wages would be reduced to unacceptable levels. In some instances police were not reimbursed for incurring legitimate expenses in tracking sheep stealers and thus 'independent and intelligent' action was discouraged. No rural force had a superannuation scheme.

The last major criticism was the inability to cope with disorder. When riots broke out in Launceston in 1874 over the requirement to pay a railway rate and in Hobart Town in 1879 when Irishmen took exception to the anti-Catholic comments of Pastor Charles Chiniquy and stopped him from lecturing, the small municipal forces displayed their incapacity and the central government had to restore order (Petrow, 1997b).

The end of decentralisation

Despite abuses and defects, the decentralised system lasted 40 years until centralisation was reintroduced in 1899. Why did it last so long? One possible reason is that the municipal police system received the kudos for the low level of crime in Tasmania. According to Reynolds (1969b: 22), by the 1880s Tasmania 'probably had a lower incidence of crime than any of the other Australian colonies', although this was largely due to the old convict class dying out as much as police efficiency. There is no evidence that crime statistics were manipulated to give the appearance that Tasmania was a safe haven from crime. If we take Bothwell and Richmond as case studies, we find that crime was not regarded as a problem and police managed to contain the minor crime and disorder that did occur (Petrow, 2000b, 2003). When sheep stealing became prevalent in the 1860s Bothwell cooperated with adjoining municipalities and the Inspector of Police in the deployment of men (Petrow, 2000b: 116–17). The municipal police were asked to perform a number of functions such as distributing charitable relief, acting as inspectors for rabbit, codlin moth[2] and truancy laws and as inspectors of weights and measures, collecting agricultural statistics and unpaid dog licences, performing work for the Court of Requests and sanitary inspection (Breen, 2001: 120). Breen calls these social order functions, which enabled the police 'to maintain close contact with their local towns', enhanced their 'primary tasks of surveillance and peace-keeping' and justified the costs of maintaining forces. These powers with others like those over vagrancy gave the police supreme control over local populations and kept crime low, Breen suggests. An alternative explanation might stress that police were so tied up with administrative functions or pleasing councillors that they did not have the time (or the ability) to chase criminals and therefore ratepayers did not bother to report crime.

The major reason why decentralised policing lasted so long was the power of the rural elites, who, through a restrictive franchise, dominated the Tasmanian Parliament until the mid-1880s: their experience of the convict era made them reluctant to strengthen central powers (Petrow, 1998: 261). By the mid-1880s these men were dying off, the proportion of the population with experience of the convict era was much smaller, and the franchise had become more democratic. The arguments of the central government, which had tried to claw back police control from the 1870s, benefited from the changed nature of society which no longer tolerated rural oligarchies.

The central government had typically argued that training, discipline, pay and conditions would be more uniform under one head than 21, that a unified force would improve promotion prospects, that moving policemen from one district to another would break up compromising local ties, and that criminals, who were not confined to one municipality, would be more hotly pursued wherever they went (Petrow, 1998: 256–60). The central government could also point to the more efficient and economic working of the Territorial Police since placed under the command of a Commissioner of Police in 1890 (Jackman, 1966: 78–81). By the 1890s most municipalities felt less inclined to cling to their police forces and saw no threats to individual liberties from a police force controlled by a more democratically elected government. The clinching point was the Braddon government's capitulation to Legislative Council pressure to levy a four pence police rate in 1899 and 1900 and thereafter to fund the total cost of the police. Few municipalities could resist a proposal which would reduce their police rate and achieve more efficient policing.

Underlying all these points was the changing attitude to the relative responsibilities of central and local government. During most of the decentralised period policing for most councils was their most important function and justified their existence, so they were reluctant to hand their 'kingly power' back to the government (Breen, 2001: 147). Increasingly from the 1880s the larger councils in particular felt that too much time was taken up with policing matters and diverted aldermanic attention and ratepayer money from modernising and taking on new responsibilities to improve the comfort and convenience of their constituents. The Tasmanian government looked less to England and more to the governments of the other Australian colonies, which managed their own increasingly large and bureaucratic police forces and could thus ensure that the laws passed by Parliament were uniformly enforced. As Launceston's *Daily Telegraph* argued in 1898, 'the administration of the law of the country is essentially a State prerogative' (Breen, 2001: 146). It laid down the 'broad principle' that the laws passed by parliament should be enforced by officers responsible to Parliament. Thus was introduced a third type of police organisation and control under a Police Commissioner reporting to a

Minister, the Attorney-General, who was in turn responsible to a democratically elected Parliament (Finnane, 1994). Although not free of imperfections or of attempts at reform from about 1880, this model worked well in the other Australian colonies, aimed to strike a balance between police independence and public accountability, and represented the police as the servants of the public and not the slaves of sectional or local interests.

Notes

1. It might be noted here that by the 1830s Lands Commissioners divided the island into counties, hundreds and parishes, but these divisions did not have the same local government significance as in England: they acted more as 'aids in the description of land titles' and were renamed land districts in 1962 (Wettenhall, 1968: 81–2).
2. A codlin moth was a moth whose larvae caused worm-eaten apples to fall prematurely. The police enforced legislation requiring the use of arsenical spraying and fungicides to control the pest.

References

Breen, S. *Contested Places: Tasmania's Northern Districts from Ancient Times to 1900*, Centre for Tasmanian Historical Studies, 2001.

Critchley, T.A. *A History of Police in England and Wales*. London: Constable, 1978.

Emsley, C. 'A typology of nineteenth-century police', *Crime, histoire et sociétés/Crime, History and Societies*, 3, 1, 1999, pp. 29–44.

Emsley, C. *The English Police: A Political and Social History*, 2nd edn. Longman, 1996.

Finnane, M. *Police and Government: Histories of Policing in Australia*. Oxford University Press, 1994.

Hartwell, R. M. *The Economic Development of Van Diemen's Land 1820–1850*. Melbourne University Press, 1954.

Jackman, A. K. 'Development of Police Administration in Tasmania 1804–1960', unpublished Diploma of Public Administration thesis, University of Tasmania, 1966.

Launceston Examiner, references as cited in the text.

Loveday, B. and Reid, A. *Going Local: Who Should Run Britain's Police*. Available at: www.policyexchange.org.au, 2004.

Mercury, references as cited in the text.

Miller, W. R. 'Review of C. Emsley, The English Police: A Political and Social History, New York: St. Martin's Press, 1991', *Law and History Review*, 11, 1993, pp. 190–4.

Miller, W. R. *Cops and Bobbies: Police Authority in New York and London, 1830–1870*, 2nd edn. Ohio State University Press, 1999.

Moore, D., 'Origins of the police mandate: the Australian case reconsidered', *Police Studies*, 4, 1991, pp. 107–20.

O'Sullivan, J. *Mounted Police of Victoria and Tasmania*. Rigby, 1980.

Petrow, S. 'The Hobart Town Municipal Police 1858–1878', *Tasmanian Historical Research Association Papers and Proceedings*, 42, 1995, pp. 165–84.

Petrow, S. 'Carriages and scab: elite contention against the law in nineteenth-century Tasmania', *Newcastle Law Review*, 2, 2, 1997a, pp. 70–91.

Petrow, S. 'Turbulent Tasmanians: anti-railway rate and sectarian riots and police reform in the 1870s', *Australian Journal of Legal History*, 3, 1997b, pp. 1–24.

Petrow, S. 'Tolerant town, model force: the Launceston municipal police 1858 to 1898', *University of Tasmania Law Review*, 16, 1997c, pp. 235–65.

Petrow, S. 'Economy, efficiency, and impartiality: police centralisation in nineteenth century Tasmania', *Australian and New Zealand Journal of Criminology*, 31, 3, 1998, pp. 242–66.

Petrow, S. 'Policing in a penal colony: Governor George Arthur's system of police in Van Diemen's Land, 1826–1836', *Law and History Review*, 18, 2000a, pp. 351–95.

Petrow, S. 'Policing in Rural Tasmania: Bothwell 1863–1898', *Tasmanian Historical Research Association Papers and Proceedings,* 47, 2000b, pp. 112–25.

Petrow, S. 'After Arthur: Policing in Van Diemen's Land 1837–1846', in Enders, M. and Dupont, B. (eds), *Policing the Lucky Country*. Hawkins Press, 2001, pp. 176–98.

Petrow, S. 'Policing in a Rural Mausoleum? Richmond 1861–1898', *Coal Valley History*, 2, 2003, pp. 8–27.

Philips, D. and Storch, R. D. *Policing Provincial England, 1829–1856: The Politics of Reform*. Leicester University Press, 1999.

Reynolds, H. '"Men of honour and deservedly good repute": the Tasmanian gentry 1856–1875', *Australian Journal of Politics and History,* 15, 1969a, pp. 61–72.

Reynolds, H. '"That hated stain": the aftermath of transportation in Tasmania', *Historical Studies Australia and New Zealand*, 14, 1969b, pp. 19–31.

Steedman, C. *Policing the Victorian Community: the Formation of the English Provincial Police Forces 1856–80*. Routledge, 1984.

Storch, R. D. '"The plague of blue locusts"; police reform and popular resistance in Northern England, 1840–1857', *International Review of Social History*, 20, 1975, pp. 61–90.

Storch, R. D. 'The policeman as domestic missionary: urban discipline and popular culture in Northern England, 1850–1880', *Journal of Social History*, 9, 1976, pp. 481–509.

Taylor, D. *The New Police in Nineteenth-Century England: Crime, Conflict, and Control*. Manchester University Press, 1997.

Wettenhall, R. *A Guide to Tasmanian Government Administration*. Platypus Publications, 1968.

Chapter 10

The growth of crime and crime control in developing towns: Timaru and Crewe, 1850–1920[1]

Barry S. Godfrey and Graeme Dunstall

This chapter discusses some questions that we have been attempting to answer through a joint research project on rapidly developing small towns in the nineteenth century. This project is just in its infancy, but we hope to comment here on two areas of criminological interest – on the growth of crime and control in 'boom' towns; and on how a study of this kind might contribute to debates on the 'atomised' nature of 'home' and colonial communities.

In his collection of studies of Victorian cities Asa Briggs (1963), an admirer of Australian cities, talked of a few English Victorian towns being 'as new as cities of the British Empire'.[2] Indeed he called the booming iron town of Middlesbrough the 'British Ballarat'. Similarly, in his study of crime and policing in that town, David Taylor (2002) implicitly compares the 'Infant Hercules' of industrial production with the Victorian gold rush town. Middlesbrough grew rapidly from a group of cottages at the start of the nineteenth century to a town containing almost 40,000 people in 1871.[3] Like Ballarat, it quickly acquired a reputation for violence, disorder and general lawlessness[4] and Taylor has written a detailed empirical study of how police services coped in this apparent cockpit of vice. He shows that Middlesbrough's crime levels roughly followed general crime trends in Victorian England. Judicial statistics appear to show that serious crime per capita generally rose higher in Middlesbrough than the national average when the town was developing, and started to fall after the 1860s when, mirroring the situation in the rest of the country, social and economic conditions were more stable. Changes in the level of minor offences are harder to chart because the court records are lost or were never kept (the preservation of public records was not always a high priority for hard-pressed administrators in small towns that were fast growing into major ones). However, there is sufficient court- and media-generated data for Taylor to state that:

> Middlesbrough was not a typical Victorian town. Its peculiar economic and demographic characteristics set it apart but, despite its singularities, the town experienced, albeit in more acute form than most, more common problems of establishing the rule of law and of imposing order and decorum at a time of rapid urbanization. [Nonetheless the] brash and often brutal 'British Ballarat' gradually succumbed to the forces of order. The anxieties and fears … were gradually, though partially, dispelled. The town never entirely threw off its reputation for violence but, even though it had spilled over its original borders, it gradually lost its frontier characteristics. (Taylor, 2002: 182, our italics)

Although keen to raise the idea that Middlesbrough could be considered a frontier town like some of those in Australia or America,[5] he does not present a depth of empirical evidence on this point. If Middlesbrough was like Ballarat, what was Ballarat like? How do the towns of the so-called English and Welsh (and possibly Scottish) 'urban frontier' compare with the colonial 'frontier towns' of New Zealand and Australia?

The towns selected for this study were both shaped by one dominant industry, enjoyed rapid growth over a comparatively short period of time, and acted as 'social nets' which dragged in labour from near and far, forcing people to develop social relationships and form communities very quickly. They could both be considered 'frontier towns', and indeed have been depicted as such. In academic historiography, four markers of 'frontiership' can be identified in both the Old and New Worlds.

First, commonly, the term 'frontier' is synonymous with a zone of recent colonisation where a set of social conditions differs from that prevailing in longer established settlements. Typically, they were 'new towns' in locations where pre-existing social structures and institutions were rudimentary and struggled to cope with rapid population growth, such as that experienced by the towns selected for this study.[6] For example, the population of Crewe increased by 126 per cent between 1861 and 1871, reaching 19,904 in 1871 and 42,000 in 1901; Timaru had a population of 1,418 in 1871, reaching 35,589 by 1911.

Secondly, the outcome of rapid growth by long-distance migration to new towns was an imbalance of the sexes, with a predominance of young, unmarried, generally kinless and transient adult males. For Timaru, in the 'frontier phase' of its development, the proportion of the male population (and of the total population) aged between 20 and 40 was significantly over-represented. However, in Crewe, family migration, encouraged by the railway company, engendered a relatively balanced, albeit youthful, population at an early stage.

The third 'marker' was the links between existing regional populations and the new communities, and the type of in-migration which could be varied. For example, particularly in its first decade, Ballarat saw an on-going turnover of long-distance migrants of diverse backgrounds. In 1881, 64 per cent of the males and 58 per cent of the females in Timaru were born overseas, constituting virtually all of the adult population. By contrast, 58 per cent of Crewe residents in 1881 had been born locally. The recruitment of labour from the locale (say, within a 30-mile radius of Crewe) from the outset helped to preserve kinship networks in the region, and to embed the new community within the group of north-western industrial towns.

The fourth marker was the high level of crime and disorder in frontier towns. Public order offences and violent crime were markedly higher than in more settled communities. As the new communities took on a more settled profile, the gender imbalances lessened, police services became more extensive and crime rates receded. Even so, a reputation for lawlessness may pertain for many years after they no longer match the reality. The pilot study of two of our towns suggests that the situation is much more complex than the existing literature describes. Individual trends for categories of crime (good order, violence, property, regulatory) suggest that there are more sophisticated processes of naturalisation, civilising processes, policing and demographic changes taking place.

Crime and demographic change

There are marked differences in levels of prosecutions in Crewe and Timaru in the categories of good order, violence and property crime (we use the proxy measures of number of proceedings against drunkenness, assault and minor larcenies here – see Figures 10.1–10.3). The Timaru figures clearly suggest the ongoing presence of 'frontier characteristics' in the New World town by contrast with Crewe during the late nineteenth century.[7]

What then of the trends for violence, drunkenness and offences against property? In Timaru, after relatively high rates of assault, from 1878 there

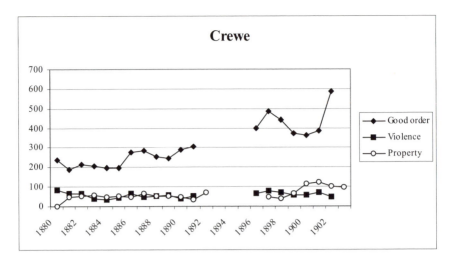

Figure 10.1   Prosecutions in Crewe 1880–1902.

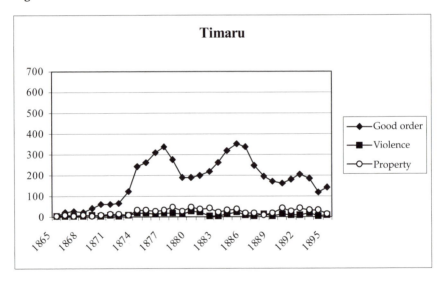

Figure 10.2   Prosecutions in Timaru 1865–1895.

was an uneven long-term decline in prosecutions to a low point in the early 1930s. Similar trends for violence are found in Crewe where per capita rates of assault practically halved between 1881 and 1901.

As with the early prosecutions for assault, the small numbers charged (and convicted) of drunkenness between 1859 and 1862 (rising from 7 to 22

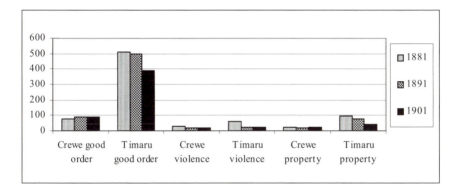

Figure 10.3 Crewe and Timaru: offences per 10,000 population 1881–1901.

males) represented a high rate for Timaru's small population. Thereafter, until 1869, the numbers arrested did not increase significantly and the rate declined. Coinciding exactly with the trend of convictions for violence, there was a pronounced upswing in drunkenness convictions in 1874 (from 93 to 218), reaching a peak in 1876, then declining sharply between 1878 and 1880. The common pattern of a sharp upswing and decline indicates a strong association between alcohol and much disorder during the 1870s. Between the mid-1880s and the First World War the overall fall in the rate of drunkenness convictions was much more sluggish than that for assaults. For a proportion of males at least, propensities for unruly behaviour in public spaces died hard. Nevertheless, the per capita drift was down and falling throughout the 1890s and 1900s. Again Timaru's raw and per capita figures put Crewe's in the shadows (they were about a quarter of Timaru's per capita totals). The trend, however, ran contrary to Timaru. Drunkenness in Crewe rose in the 1880s and continued to rise in the 1890s and early 1900s, before falling again in 1911 to 27.55 per 10,000 population. Thereafter, between the wars, motoring replaced drunkenness as the largest crime category (and police priority); for example, in 1927 assault cases, drunkenness and larcenies totalled 83, while motoring (not including horse-drawn traffic or bicycles) totalled 237.

At Timaru, the overall rate of convictions for offences against property (mainly various forms of larceny, including horse and sheep stealing) shows no clear trend in the late nineteenth century. The numbers of convictions increased from 4 in 1873 to 29 in 1874 and did not decline significantly thereafter. While there is a coincidence during the mid and late 1870s in the upswing and decline in the rates per capita of convictions for assault, drunkenness and theft, this coincidence does not persist from the early 1880s. If anything, there tends to be an inverse relationship between drunkenness and theft rates in their fluctuations during the 1880s and 1890s – suggesting the influence of changes in the local economic climate and the labour market – but the tendency is not strong. A consistent link between changes in the economic climate and in drunkenness and theft rates is not apparent from such statistical measures (the trend in wage rates and savings bank deposits) that have been employed to test it. In the trend that could be taken to be indicative of a shift to a more stable urban society, the ratio of convictions for theft to those of assault rose as the assault rate declined between the 1880s and the 1930s. Crewe's property offences were equally diverse, and included thefts of sweets, cigarettes and food from shops, bicycles from the streets, money from gas meters and the odd housebreaking. Where Timaru's figures halved between 1881 and 1901, Crewe's stayed stable. (Timaru had four times the per capita rate of Crewe in 1881 and twice the rate by 1901.)

The figures as a whole seem to confirm that by 1901 Timaru had not 'matured' into a town with 'normal' levels of disorderliness like the Old World town of Crewe. This could be due to the different socio-economic structures (for example, the informal control exercised by the railway employers in Crewe), demography and cultures of masculinity, or the efficiency of public policing. However, those framing explanations will have to account not just for the high figures in Timaru, but also why crime trends in the two towns were moving in opposite directions at various times, and detail how demographic changes and economic conditions structured crime figures.

Social control and economic structures as protective factors

Through its workshop rules and punishments, its role as the dominant landlord and in civic governance more generally, the railway company could have been more determined and effective in applying social discipline to Crewe's wage-earning population at an early stage in the development of the town than were Timaru's petty proprietors to its mobile workforce in this period. Moreover, the predominantly irregular pre-industrial modes of employment in Timaru contrasted with that of the dominant group of skilled artisans in Crewe's railway workshops, with their culture of respectability and improvement (symbolised by use made of the Mechanics Institute). Differences in occupational and drinking cultures (of stereotypical artisanal moderation by contrast with the excesses engendered by irregular work patterns – the colonial 'spree' and the convention of 'shouting', for example) might also account for different levels of disorder. To give weight to this comparison, however, the extent to which there were differences in the occupational structure of offending in each town has yet to be examined. If demographic changes (including changing occupational profiles) can account for general trends in crime, can they explain differential trends across types of offences? The decline of violence is posited by crime historians for the late Victorian period – is this declining trend also apparent in frontier towns, and is it more shallow or more steep? English, Australian and New Zealand national crime rates show an increase in prosecutions for drunkenness at the time when our towns are maturing into more settled demographics. Were patterns of drinking in new communities resistant to the pressures on habitual drunkenness in the 1880s and 1890s? A number of subsidiary questions about comparative crime rates have yet to be investigated.

Masculinity and crime

As stated, in all of the towns under consideration the 'frontier' demography provided considerable potential for disorder or 'turbulence', especially when fuelled by alcohol.[8] Fundamental to the conception of frontier turbulence is its linkage to a preponderance of young and single men whose work and leisure was largely spent solely in the company of their peers. But how far was frontier town violence the product of an unbridled masculine culture of impulsive aggression, with fighting for recreation, to redress insults or grievances, or to settle disputes? Such a conception has been implicit or explicit in interpretations of frontier masculinity in America, Australia and New Zealand.[9] However, in the New Zealand context at least, the existence of a 'macho' male culture and its influence on the level of frontier violence has been discounted by an interpretation which emphasises, instead, the consequences of social atomisation. In short, according to Miles Fairburn, tidal waves of long-distance migration to colonial New Zealand and the rapid expansion of the frontier between the 1850s and the 1870s had an atomising effect.[10] For a period, a majority of colonists were transient and strangers to one another, with little time or few institutions for mixing and meeting. To Fairburn, weak social bonds meant misunderstandings of others' motives and intentions, and also weak pressures to curb excessive drinking or violence. The masculine cultural explanations for the decline of frontier violence emphasise the consequences of a demographic rebalancing (with an evening-up of the sex ratios and a growing proportion of married males) along with a changing 'moral climate' associated with a late nineteenth-century 'drive for compulsory respectability'.[11] Fairburn, by contrast, emphasises the effects of growing social bonding – by linking the demographic rebalancing to a declining rate of immigration and the growth of a settled population in 'intensely cohesive' communities, which provided informal and increasingly effective mechanisms of social control from the 1880s.[12]

Fairburn's model of the colonial social pattern has been controversial. Critics have questioned the extent of social bondlessness it posits, and the extent to which it accounts for the rates of colonial drunkenness and violence, but it has proved to be remarkably robust. Certainly it has dominated discussions of the nature of society in colonial Australia and New Zealand. We wish to investigate, first, its applicability to industrial 'frontier towns' in early and mid-nineteenth century Britain. The debates over the extent of atomisation, weak social ties and transitional shifting populations in developing colonial societies, to some extent, overlap the recent debates in Europe and the UK over the scale of recidivism. The data we have started to collect in Crewe and Timaru offers the possibility of examining one aspect of the atomisation debate – that most crimes were committed by transient males moving through the region, and not by established residents who 'put down roots' and developed stronger community ties. Thus far the conclusions drawn from a preliminary analysis of data gathered at Crewe and Timaru are suggestive rather than conclusive regarding the issue of persistence and social atomisation. The numbers and rates of persistence over time, and the occupational background of the persisters, have yet to be firmly established. If significant differences appear regarding persistence and persisters in Crewe and Timaru, then important distinctions will be indicated about crime and policing in new towns in the New and Old Worlds.

The control of crime and the regulation of society

We will document levels of formal policing in conjunction with crime levels generally, and with particular offences (not least because, in Timaru, prosecutions appear to have risen proportionately to police levels). Additionally, we will examine the diversity of policing structures and practices in the differing economic, climactic and geographic conditions. Where our study differs from many historical studies of crime in specific regions or towns is its emphasis on regulatory offences – such as market bye-laws, lighting offences, chimney keeping and so on. This category of offending constituted 27.3 per cent of all criminal cases dealt with at Crewe petty sessions (1880–1905) and an average 37 per cent of all convictions in Timaru (1881–91). The use of quasi-policing agencies (health inspectors, education and truancy officers, nuisance inspectors and a range of other regulatory services) is relatively unresearched and, in fact, rarely acknowledged.[13] We will be able to chart relative changes in the proportion of regulatory offences prosecuted over time. Why were quasi-police agencies so active, and are they an attempt to impose legitimate authority on rapidly changing communities? Are they used to facilitate commerce and capitalistic development, maintain good order, civilise a 'rough' population, or for other purposes? Just how marginal were the police to the 'policed society'? This is an impressive list of questions, but in about two years' time we hope to bring forth some answers, or at least a more refined set of questions.

Notes

1. This chapter presents data collected by Barry Godfrey (Keele University) and Graeme Dunstall (Canterbury University, NZ) and funded by The British Academy. The 'Crime in Developing Townships Project' focuses on three small but rapidly developing towns in the UK (Crewe), NZ (Timaru) and Australia (Ballarat).
2. Briggs (1968: 29).
3. Taylor (2002: 19).
4. Because low-quality housing was thrown up so quickly in Middlesbrough, covering all available space, including that which might have been reserved for places of worship to be built, it became known as the 'Godless Town'.
5. As does Briggs (1968: 250).
6. Briggs (1968: 242); Taylor (2002: 7); Bate (1978: chapter 1).
7. Yet it has been argued that Timaru's demographic structure began to resemble that of a mature town in the Old World from the 1880s. This is not apparent from drunkenness and property offence rates.
8. Briggs (1968: 245–6); Taylor (2002: 53, 66–9); Bate (1978: 22–4) – Bate pays little attention to 'turbulence'.
9. See Courtwright (1996: 3 and chapters 2, 5).
10. See Fairburn (1986: 89–126); Fairburn (1989: 191–3 and chapter 7).
11. Courtwright (1996: chapter 7); Phillips (1987: chapter 2).
12. Fairburn (1989: chapter 8).
13. Brown-May's (1998) study of Melbourne is a valuable exception to this rule.

References

Bate, W. *Lucky City. The First Generation at Ballarat 1851–1901*. Melbourne University Press, 1978.
Briggs, A. *Victorian Cities*. London, 1963.

Brown-May, A. *Melbourne Street Life*. Australia Scholarly/Arcadia, 1998.

Chaloner, W. *The Social and Economic Development of Crewe, 1780–1923*. Manchester University Press, 1950.

Courtwright, D. *Violent Land. Single Men and Social Disorder from the Frontier to the Inner City*. Harvard University Press, 1996.

Drummond, D. *Crewe: Railway Town, Company and People, 1840–1914*. Scolar Press, 1995.

Fairburn, M. 'Violent crime in old and new societies – a case study based on New Zealand 1853–1940', *Journal of Social History*, Fall 1986, pp. 89–126.

Fairburn, M. *The Ideal Society and its Enemies: the Foundations of Modern New Zealand Society, 1850–1900*. Auckland University Press, 1989, pp. 191–3, and chapter 7.

Jones D. J. V. *Crime, Protest, Community and Police in Nineteenth-Century Britain*. Routledge and Kegan Paul, 1982.

Jones, D. J. V. *Crime in Nineteenth Century Wales*. Cardiff, 1992.

Reed, B. *Crewe Locomotive Works and Its Men*. David & Charles, 1982.

Taylor, D. *Policing the Victorian Town. The Development of the Police in Middlesbrough c.1840–1914*. Palgrave, 2002.

Chapter 11

(Re)presenting scandal: Charles Reade's advocacy of professionalism within the English prison system

Sarah Anderson

More than a decade after Charles Dickens famously presented audiences with literary images illustrating the excesses of prison life, another English novelist, Charles Reade (1814–84), sought to expose the potential for malpractice within prisons. Setting out, in 1852, to write a successful fictional documentary, Reade explored the prison with meticulous care, hoping to provide an exposé of mid-Victorian prison experience. Four years later, he published *It Is Never Too Late to Mend* (1856), the most thoroughly documented prison novel of the nineteenth century. Drawing on the details of the scandal of prisoner abuse and suicide at Birmingham gaol which emerged in 1854, Reade's novel has rarely been considered anything more than self-serving sensationalism. This chapter suggests, however, that not only did Reade capitalise on the publicity the Birmingham case received, but his novel *It Is Never Too Late to Mend* (*NTLM*) also offers both a timely, and significant, critique of local justice administration and amateurism within English penal arrangements. It is argued that Reade's critical appraisal of local justice ineptitude in his novel effectively promotes, reinforces and reaffirms the need for central state bureaucratic control and professional inspection within English prisons, even if, ironically, the bureaucratic machinery then created provided new forms of crushing rigidity within the prisons. It is the purpose of this essay to examine the penological context in which Reade's ideas and campaign developed, and to explore his novel's prison sketch in more detail than previous accounts have done, in order to assess the role of this literary work in the development of prison policy in the second half of the nineteenth century.

Reade wrote, set and published his novel in an era when English prisons were the responsibility of both central and local governmental authorities. By the mid-nineteenth century, England's two-tiered prison system of national and local prisons was subjected to increased government intervention and scrutiny. Successive legislative moves to reconfigure England's prison system around a centralised regulatory body were initiated by the government with the implementation of the 1835 Prisons Act. The legislation allowed for the establishment of a prison inspectorate which marked the beginning of the central government's attempts to regulate and maintain acceptable levels of punishment within English prisons. While the Act effectively gave central government control of convict prisons and the power to inspect and regulate local gaols, it did little, however, to remove the control of local gaols from their respective authorities. It enabled prison inspectors to publicise abuses but not to close prisons or demand significant changes. Further legislation was passed in 1839 granting increased powers to the Home Secretary and providing local authorities with directives for the implementation of the separate system. In the following decade, central government continued its attempts to influence the course of local prison policy: Pentonville was presented as a national model for the separate system, which was subsequently adopted in several localities,[1] and the Home Office focused on achieving uniformity in prison conditions through attempts to standardise dietary scales and tread-wheel labour.

Reade began researching and writing his prison novel at a time when local prison governance was increasingly under threat. By the mid-nineteenth century, the convict service, administered mainly by army officers, emphasised strict discipline and public works programmes, while the local system fostered a tradition of civic involvement and philanthropic enterprise in prison management. The latter's supervisory arrangements became the increasing focus of official inquiry and scrutiny; a Select Committee recommended that greater powers should be vested in a central authority which would be given the responsibility of 'enforcing uniform adherence to rules laid down from time to time by Parliament' (*Report of the Select Committee on Prison Discipline*, 1850: iii). Investigations into disciplinary practices disclosed a wide variety of methods employed within local prisons; inspectors discovered that some prisons were using fetters and extended periods of solitary confinement – neither of which were authorised punishments – to discipline refractory prisoners (*Report of the Inspectors of Prisons (Home District)*, 1845). A growing belief that all

English prisons should be brought under centralised governmental control was further strengthened when a scandal of prisoner abuse and suicide emerged at Birmingham gaol in 1853.

Under Lieutenant William Austin's governorship, disturbing rumours circulated about oppressive and brutal treatments to which Birmingham's prisoners were subjected. Eventually, after suffering from repeated punishments and a restricted diet, one young prisoner, Edward Andrews,[2] hung himself in his cell in May 1853. The prisoner's death prompted a Royal Commission of Inquiry, which found that Austin had practised deliberate cruelties on his prisoners. It discovered that Andrews was made to perform hard labour upon a crank that weighed four times more than was recommended, and was routinely punished for failing to meet his task. Other prisoners were discovered to have been forced to work under the rigours of hard labour until they eventually collapsed; some were denied critical medical treatment, and several had been subjected to repeated beatings, water drenches and other torments (*Report of the Royal Commission into the Condition and Treatment of the Prisoners Confined to Birmingham Borough Prison*, 1854: xi–xviii).

In order to avoid similar malpractice, demands for a central regulatory body to ensure the standard of performance of individual members, were sanctioned by the *Select Committee of the House of Lords on Prison Discipline* (1863: 10) which recommended that 'without delay a system [should be implemented] approaching as nearly as may be practicable to a uniformity of labour, diet and treatment'. Increasingly such matters were seen as responsibilities for the state to determine and manage rather than as matters for local justices, reform-minded individuals or private organisations. Under mounting pressure, the future of local prison governance was tenuous, and in 1865 the Prisons Act was passed, essentially depriving local bodies of their previous autonomy. Essentially, the Act established a uniform code of hard labour and segregated cellular confinement in both convict as well as the locally financed and administered prisons; rules determined precise diet, hours of education, exercise, warden/prisoner relations and punishment. Diet was spare, educational and religious instruction minimal. While the Act did not legislate for centralisation, it symbolised a move away from local prison management, and provided a basis for a modern bureaucratic institution with professional regulatory mechanisms to develop. Opposed to any form of local control and non-professional intervention, Edmund Du Cane, as Director of Convict Prisons, pressed unremittingly from 1869 to centralise all prison administration in England and Wales under one department in the interest of efficiency, economy and uniformity, and by the late 1870s he was successful.

In 1877, the Prison Act was introduced, effectively removing the local prisons from the jurisdiction of local authorities and making them the responsibility of a powerful new arm of government, the Prison Commission. The Act was nothing less than the nationalisation of the local prisons. All public prisons in boroughs and counties, previously owned by local communities and administered by locally elected or appointed justices, were transferred to central government. Prison real estate became national property, and prison employees civil servants. Prisons were now to be administered by the Home Office and funded by the Treasury from taxation. This shift in penal policy put the local prisons on the same administrative and financial basis as the convict system. In addition, it minimised the rights and duties of Justices of the Peace and thus removed the prison from the influence of the voluntary sector. Hereafter, English prisons were the responsibility of a centralised state bureaucracy.

Central authorities were not the only group to apply pressure and scrutiny to local prison governance in the mid-nineteenth century. Indeed, the publication of Charles Reade's *It Is Never Too Late to Mend* in 1856 posed a further, and more public, critique of local justice autonomy. Reade's fictional documentary of prison life presented the literary public with a vivid display of the gratuitous and illegal brutality allowed to occur in a prison that remained the responsibility of local justice authorities. Moreover, Reade's novel was a powerful reminder of the excesses that could occur within a prison system devoid of a bureaucratic structure or without professional regulatory mechanisms.

Reade is largely unknown nowadays, for his works were so contemporary that they rapidly became irrelevant and redundant; as George Orwell observed of him, 'it is unusual to meet anyone who has voluntarily read him' (Orwell, 1943: 34). Reade had neither Charles Dickens's personal insight nor his inventive genius; rather his approach to writing was more formulaic, more often than not as a series of melodramas in which virtue always triumphs.

Reade's early literary accomplishments as both a dramatist and novelist were modest.[3] His first two novels – *Peg Woffington* (1851) and *Christie Johnstone* (1852) – were largely unnoticed in the age of Dickens and serialised works. Prior to the publication of *It Is Never Too Late to Mend*, Reade had yet to compose a successful work of fiction, despite his aspiration to do so; 'I want to show people that, I can *invent* too, if I choose to take the trouble. And it is a trouble to me I confess' (Reade's italics, cited in Reade and Reade, 1887, vol. 1: 326). In the interim, he published *Gold*, a contemporary drama based on the 1851 Australian gold rush, which he believed had the potential to be an enduring and significant social documentary. Despite Reade's ill-fated prediction – the play's success was short-lived – his research for material on the play's convicted thief led him to visit Durham gaol and to study the lives of its various prisoners (Reade and Reade, 1887, vol. 1: 323; Burns, 1961: 156). This initial association with the English prison provided Reade with both the stimulus and subject matter from which he began preparations to create a fictional documentary with important political and social themes. This early interest in the prison as a potential literary focus was further encouraged by the recent success of Harriet Beecher Stowe's portrayal of slave exploitation in her (1852) novel, *A Key to Uncle Tom's Cabin*. Inspired to produce a work of comparable depth and popularity, Reade began his fictional representation of a locally administered English prison. [4]

In the (1856) novel's infancy, Reade realised that in order to successfully duplicate Stowe's achievement, he required sensational material which meant: 'visit[ing] all the London prisons, [to] get warm facts for the Robinson business' (Reade and Reade, 1887, vol. 1: 333). Only weeks later, however, the Birmingham scandal emerged in the pages of *The Times* (6–16 September 1853), providing Reade with the ultimate answer to his concerns. An article appeared in *The Times* on 8 September 1853 that detailed the sufferings endured by four prisoners of Birmingham gaol which 'touched [Reade's] heart, and flamed [his] imagination' (Reade, 1883: 323). Four days later, details of the sufferings and suicide of Edward Andrews emerged, and Reade discovered the case that would serve as the centrepiece of his prison sketch. The scandal at Birmingham gaol provided Reade with the opportunity to write (like Stowe) a novel of social importance and impact.

The central story of *It Is Never Too Late to Mend* focuses on the fortunes and misfortunes of its main character, Thomas Robinson. Robinson is committed to helping his friend George Fielding rescue his farm from financial ruin so that Fielding can marry his love, Susan Merton, and urges his friend to emigrate to the Australian gold fields. Fielding takes Robinson's advice. However, rival suitors desire Merton, one of whom has Robinson arrested, convicted and imprisoned for theft. In prison, Robinson endures great suffering and witnesses the brutal treatment of Josephs, a fellow convict. However, with the efforts of a zealous chaplain, Robinson is penitent, and eventually transported to Australia where he meets up with his old friend Fielding and the pair strike gold. After a number of narrow escapes from the unscrupulous schemes of rivals, they return to England where Fielding and Merton are happily reunited.

Of particular interest here is Thomas Robinson's stay in prison as the sketch reflects firstly the way in which Reade capitalises on the publicity of the Birmingham scandal, and secondly his advocacy of professionalism within the English prison system. Indeed, Reade draws heavily on information that emerged from the inquiry, as the 34 chapters which centre on Robinson's imprisonment are largely based on the evidence presented to the Commission. At times, it seems as if Reade over-relies on this evidence, perhaps compensating for his somewhat limited creative ability. Furthermore, Reade made little attempt to conceal his use of the more conspicuous aspects of the subsequent inquiry; rather than invent a fictitious name for his prison, he simply blanks the prison's name with a line (—— gaol). Even certain characters replicate actual individuals; for example, Birmingham's Governor, William Austin, became the fictional Mr Hawes, and the 15-year-old convict Edward Andrews, who committed suicide while in Austin's charge, became Josephs. From this basis, there seems to be little question that he sought to bring Birmingham's Governor, William Austin, and his officers to a kind of moral justice through the publicity his novel could bring to the facts of the case. Most importantly, though, in exposing these individuals Reade effectively condemns the ineptitude of officials who allowed such abuses of power to occur and by extension, condemns the unreformed system of prison administration.

While imprisoned, Robinson, the novel's protagonist, is subjected to repeated harassment and brutal treatment from the malicious Governor, Mr Hawes. He suffers a range of punishments supervised by Hawes, which include restricted diets, serious beatings and repeated water drenchings. After a series of such punishments, Robinson nearly dies when left in the punishment jacket, turning 'black in the face, his lips livid, insensible, throttled and dying', and his flesh turns 'red and blood' (Reade, 1856: 100) under the scrubbing he receives from the warders trying to revive him. Portraying such brutality and excess highlights Reade's desire to draw attention to the arbitrary and corrupt practices in a system with amateur regulation.

However, the focal point of Reade's presentation of the Birmingham scandal is the portrayal of the abuse inflicted by the brutal prison governor, Hawes, on the ill-fated Josephs. Through their interaction, Reade shows what arbitrary and illegal abuse can occur when the inspection process is amateur and unprofessional. As had been the case with the real-life Edward Andrews and his fellow inmates, Robinson is able to hear the anguished cries of Josephs nearby as he suffers in the punishment jacket. Robinson's first sight of Josephs strapped in the device reveals the physical pain the boy suffered at the hands of abusive officials: he was 'white, his lips livid, his eyes ... nearly glazed, and his teeth chatter[ing] with cold and pain' (Reade, 1856: 96). This description resembles the medical testimony included in the Inspector's Report on Birmingham gaol, which describes 'ecchymosis'[5] and other physical effects of severe constriction in such a device (Allday, 1853: 13).

Over the course of Robinson's stay, Reade intensifies the conflict between the brutal governor and the helpless prisoner. Hawes subjects Josephs to dietary restrictions, he deprives him of bedding and lighting, and constantly places him in the punishment jacket, complete with a water drenching to prevent Josephs's feigning unconsciousness. The prisoner's body is scarred and maimed by the physical effects of Hawes's brutality. Josephs's physical state is weakened as a result of his treatment, 'his flesh withered on his bones; his eyes were dim, and seemed to lie at the bottom of two caverns; he crawled stiffly and slowly instead of walking' (Reade, 1856: 203).

Reade repeatedly presents similar descriptions of Josephs's case as with the real-life sufferings of Andrews. The duration of Josephs's punishment in the jacket is supported by evidence from the inquiry. Although the falsified and incomplete records kept by Austin's administration make it difficult to judge whether Andrews was punished as frequently and severely as Josephs was, the Inspector's report indicated that under Austin's regime 'it is the custom to accumulate all these punishments at once upon a single offender' (Allday, 1853: 13).

Josephs's suffering culminates in the final hours that he spends alive in his separate cell devoid of bedding and light, according to Hawes's orders. Worn out from a poor diet, hard labour and maltreatment, he decides to put an end to his torture (Reade, 1856: 211). Finally, Josephs prays for God's and his mother's forgiveness, and hangs himself while he still can, before his 'hands [become] crippled with cold' (Reade, 1856: 212).

Despite repetitive complaints from critics that Reade distorted and exaggerated the facts of the Birmingham case, the novel's portrayal of abuse and scandal is both recognisable and essentially faithful to the evidence found by the inquiry. In fact, a number of individual stories have been taken directly from the Royal Commission's report with little embellishment.

Even the darkest and most disturbing incidents that Reade includes within his portrayal of prison life actually originate from the evidence revealed in the Birmingham scandal. The true extent of Hawes's brutality is exposed in a disturbing portrayal of the physical abuse of a half-mad prisoner named Carter. The prisoner suffers the torments of Hawes, his deputy, Fry, and the surgeon, as they stuff handfuls of salt into his mouth each time he yells in pain and fear from the punishment jacket. The end of the punishment ritual occurs when Carter is left for a considerable period in the pillory where his 'prolonged pain brings on cruel thirst' (Reade, 1856: 200). This scene is not simply the result of Reade's desire to further blacken the prison officials; rather, Carter's sufferings are based upon Austin's treatment of an idiotic prisoner named Samuel Hunt. Such facts were duly revealed in the governmental inquiry: 'Salt was brought, and the surgeon in the governor's presence, whenever the prisoner opened his mouth to shout or bite, thrust into it a quantity of salt, repeating this proceeding until the prisoner was subdued, and became quiet' (*Report of the Royal Commission into the Condition and Treatment of the Prisoners Confined to Birmingham Borough Prison*, 1854: xxvi).

Most importantly, Reade draws on evidence from the Royal Commission to highlight and document what he sees as the failings of a disciplinary system devoid of professional regulatory mechanisms. By closely paralleling the series of events that led to the demise of Alexander Maconochie's tenure as prison governor at Birmingham gaol, Reade seeks to question the largely unmonitored role and decision-making capabilities of the Visiting Magistrates. As the inquiry discovered, Maconochie was relieved of his duties at Birmingham by the Visiting Magistrates for an ostensible mismanagement of prison funds. In reality, dissatisfied with his lenient and humane approach to prison discipline, and having listened to the timely protests of the deputy governor, Lieutenant William Austin, the Magistrates removed Maconochie in favour of a sterner disciplinarian. Similarly, in Reade's (1856) novel, Governor Hawes replaces an official named O'Connor as the head of Birmingham Gaol, who (like Maconochie) 'had been one of the first dissatisfied with the old system, and had written very intelligent books of crime and punishment, which are supposed to have done their share in opening the nation's eyes to the necessity of regenerating its prisons' (Reade, 1856: 85). Moreover, though Birmingham's magistrates did not state the matter so bluntly, Reade tells us that the broad-minded O'Connor was dismissed in favour of a new regime of 'severe punishment of body and mind' (Reade, 1856: 85) and forced to end his career because of allegations that he had mismanaged funds.

A disciplinary system without centralised and professional regulations is open to, in Reade's mind, manipulation by non-accountable and amateur prison officials. Therefore, it is not surprising that when Hawes's prison records are eventually presented to the Home Office, Reade's reform-minded character, Mr Eden, indicts them as being 'a tissue of frauds, equivocations, exaggerations, diminutions, and direct falsehoods' (Reade, 1856: 177). Similarly, Eden denounces the legitimacy of Hawes's official reports to the Home Office condemning them as 'a tissue of the same frauds, suppressions, inventions, and direct falsehoods' (Reade, 1856: 177).

Reade continues to build his case against locally administered prisons with his portrayal of the Visiting Magistrates' reluctance to acknowledge and reproach existing malpractices. In an obstinate manner, Reade's Visiting Magistrates continue to resist the chaplain's assertions of illegalities and abuse on the part of the governor, looking more and more like wilfully blind and brutal prison overseers themselves. According to the version of events recorded by the Commission, it seems that Reade's picture of these zealously loyal magistrates was accurate. The Commission found that the real-life chaplain, Mr Sherwin, had 'frequently recorded in his journal the complaints and sufferings of prisoners: but this journal, though it was formally laid before the visiting justices at their board meetings, was never read by them' (*Report of the Royal Commission into the Condition and Treatment of the Prisoners Confined to Birmingham Borough Prison*, 1854: xxxvi). Only when called to account for themselves, and facing the prospect of looking foolish and cruel before the English public, did the Visiting Magistrates finally renounce the very disciplinary approach that they had hired Austin to pursue.

The ineptitude displayed by the Visiting Magistrates, who were supposed to regulate injustices at the local level, bore the brunt of Reade's disapproving pen. Indeed, the author scorns the fact that county magistrates are given unregulated discretionary power and derides the notion that this group can order and authorise a warden to flog a prisoner. The group's failure to do anything more than request assurances from the governor that all operations in the prison were in working order led Reade to argue for the professionalisation of their role. Indeed, Reade felt that the only way to rid the prison system of the illegal and brutal practices, like those depicted in his prison sketch, was through the professionalisation of the roles of prison officials. He typifies the more general rise to middle-class professionalism of the period in his following statement:

> No body of men ever gave nothing for anything worth anything, nor ever will. Now knowledge of law is worth something; zeal, independent judgement, honesty, humanity, diligence are worth something … yet the state, greedy goose, hopes to get them out of a body of men for nothing. (Reade, 1856: 259)

In Reade's mind, the discipline and regulation of England's prison population was an area of Victorian life that required professional and regulated, as opposed to amateur, standards.

Although Reade places a heavy emphasis on the abuse and corruption of certain prison officials, nonetheless he does not entirely denounce the separate system of discipline; rather he confines his criticism to specific operational matters. Moreover, his representation suggests that while the separate system is fundamentally sound in its reformative capacity, it is also vulnerable to potential corruption and manipulation. Indeed, Reade's research into the separate system led him to believe in the reformative objectives and capabilities of the disciplinary regime. He described his novel as a story of reform, 'in which a bad man is ... not despaired of by a wise and good man but encouraged, softened, converted'; this he called the 'immortal part of the work', a sentiment that is reinforced by the optimistic message in the novel's title *It Is Never Too Late to Mend* (Reade in an undated letter to his American publisher James T. Fields, cited in Burns, 1961: 155).

From the moment Thomas Robinson is imprisoned in an English separate system prison, after being apprehended for theft, both its physical and theoretical descriptions are taken from Reade's research into the separate system. The novel takes its readers with Robinson on his entry into prison, and through the narrator we are told about the changes to the prison that have occurred since Robinson's last prison stay; not yet 'four years ... since his last visit, [and] great changes had begun to take place' (Reade, 1856: 85).

Placing Robinson within a separate system prison provides Reade with the opportunity to elaborate his view of the disciplinary regime. What ultimately results is a detailed description of life inside a locally administered, Victorian penal institution. Reade provides a clear picture of the interior of Robinson's cell emphasising its modern and comfortable features, almost as if he were a separate system advocate. Indeed, he describes the furnishings of Robinson's 'homely ... [and] exquisitely clean' cell, focusing upon the 'mattress (made of cocoa bark) ... [and the] water-spout so ingeniously contrived, that, turned to the right, it sends a small stream into a copper basin, and to the left, into a bottomless close stool at some distance' (Reade, 1856: 84). In order to reinforce the image of a clean and sanitised prison cell, the narrator notes the 'leathern knee-guards used in polishing the room', and he goes so far, in fact, to suggest that as the 'furniture is so clean you might eat off it' (Reade, 1856: 84). By providing such a positive representation of the cell conditions within an English separate system prison clearly suggests that Reade believed in the potential, and operation, of the separate system when practised properly.

Furthermore, Reade is careful to portray the prison as a disciplinary system, particularly as a tool for transforming the prisoners it confines. He methodically reports on Robinson's advancement into despair and self-reflection with an hour-by-hour rundown of his progress, ultimately towards his reformation. In his first hour, Robinson occupies himself by slowly ingesting his bread and water and trying to sleep away his solitude. By the third hour, Robinson is trying to avoid thought altogether rather than to suffer the torments of his 'past ... coming with all its weight upon him' (Reade, 1856: 141). Finally, he relents and contemplates his past, reflecting on his transgressions and discovering his guilt about them. By uncovering his guilt, Reade then plunges Robinson into despair and a new self-understanding, effectively recreating the 'ideal' outcome for the operation of the separate system. Ultimately, Reade's (1856) novel is a story of reform; Thomas Robinson is eventually transformed from thief to hero through self-reflection.

Reade, therefore, reaffirms his faith in the ability of the separate system to achieve its reformatory objectives, reinforcing his optimistic message in the novel's title. His story of reform ends up validating separate discipline, with demonstrable proof of its efficacy in the form of Thomas Robinson, who is transformed from thief to repentant by the power of the prison. In comparison with other mid-nineteenth-century literary representations, Reade's account presented a more hopeful and positive view of the reformative English prison. By 1856, Charles Dickens had abandoned any such confident expectations of the reformative English prison, and since visiting the US in 1842 he had opposed the idea of separate confinement in particular, and in 1850 he both wrote of his grave objections to separate confinement, and lampooned the religious insincerity of 'model prisoners' in his novel *David Copperfield*.

Defenders of the prison failed to see this positive reinforcement of the separate system, arguing instead that Reade's novel was simply a piece of propaganda designed to discredit Birmingham Gaol and its officials.[6] While to some extent Reade's novel does unashamedly capitalise upon the atrocities that occurred at Birmingham, it does more than this. Through its satirical representation of the ineptitude of officials to prevent abuses of power, Reade's novel promotes the need for central state bureaucratic control and professional inspection. Using evidence from the Birmingham scandal, Reade is determined for his portrayal to be a timely reminder of the excesses that can occur when prison officials, who are not accountable to any credible or efficient regulatory mechanisms, are left to exploit their discretion.

In other words, his representation suggests that while the separate system is fundamentally sound in its reformative capacity, it is also vulnerable to potential manipulation. Robinson's comfortable cell conditions and his eventual reformation illustrate Reade's confidence in the reformative potential of the separate system, whereas Hawes's repeated brutality highlights Reade's desire to draw attention to possible corruptive elements with the system. Whether intentional or not, what Reade is doing by representing the separate system in such a way is helping to establish the parameters for modern prison development. Not only does his representation positively reinforce the reformative capacity of the separate system, it also strongly suggests that brutality and corrupt practices should have no place in the workings of a modern system of penal discipline. Furthermore, the way to rid the penal system of them is to have a centralised, professional bureaucracy – to set standards and enforce them throughout.

Essentially, Reade's prison sketch in *It Is Never Too Late to Mend* is an argument for middle-class professionalism and bureaucracy as opposed to the 'noblesse oblige' of the old social structure. In turn, this line of reasoning is exactly what was prescribed in the Prisons Acts of 1865 and 1877, which put prisons on a modern footing and turned them into bureaucratic institutions that prevented arbitrariness, but certainly did not stop abuses. What Reade had not anticipated – perhaps because of his faith in bureaucracy and professionalisation as opposed to the old amateurism and inefficiency in prison governance – was the way in which this then generated new scandals and barbarities. Several decades of prisoner biographies testified to this; for example, Austin Bidwell (1895: 459–60) equated the experience of imprisonment within an English prison to the workings of a remorseless machine:

An English prison is a vast machine in which a man counts for just nothing at all … The vast machine of which he is an item keeps undisturbed on its course. Move with it and all is well. Resist, and you will be crushed as inevitably as the man who plants himself on the railroad track when the express is coming. Without passion, without prejudice, but also without pity and without remorse, the machine crushes and passes on.

Although new bureaucratic structures and professional standards were in place across the English prison system by the late nineteenth century, not all scandals or injustices were eliminated as the *Report from the Departmental Committee on Prisons [Gladstone Committee]* (1895) was ultimately prepared to recognise:

While much attention has been given to organisation, finance, order, health of the prisoners and prison statistics, the prisoners have been treated too much as a hopeless or worthless element of the community, and the mood as well as the legal responsibility of the prison authorities has been held to cease when they pass outside of the prison gates. (1895: 7)

Notes

1. By 1850, ten new prisons had been built based on the Pentonville model, and ten more converted to the separate system. Separate confinement was also popular throughout Europe at this time (Evans, 1982: 384), and certain features of the Pentonville model had been replicated in Australia (Finnane, 1997: 23–4).
2. Fifteen year-old Edward Andrews was imprisoned for theft of a piece of beef and was described by Birmingham's chaplain Sherwin Ambrose as a 'mild, quiet, docile boy' (*Royal Commission into the Condition and Treatment of the Prisoners Confined to Birmingham Borough Prison*, 1854: vi).
3. Reade's early dramatic accomplishments included a number of unperformed plays adapted from the French stage or from older English novels, such as Tobias Smollett's (1751) *Peregrine Pickle*, and a handful of moderately successful collaborations with Tom Taylor (see Smith, 1976: 15–28).
4. Apart from his exploration of the prison, Reade also condemned English madhouses and lunatic laws in *Hard Cash* (1863) coffin-ships in *Foul Play* (1868), and trade union conflicts in *Put Yourself in His Place* (1870), all of which novels were designed to illustrate abuses and injustices.
5. Ecchymosis is the bruising resulting from bleeding under the skin.
6. Matthew Davenport Hill argued that Reade had 'cruelly distorted and exaggerated the facts' (Davenport Hill and Davenport Hill, 1878: 332). Walter Clay, in writing up his father's memoirs as the chaplain at Preston Gaol, blamed Reade for resurrecting public interest in a 'tragedy [that] was almost forgotten', and for creating a 'grotesquely absurd caricature of the actual facts' (Clay, 1855: 262).

References:

Allday, J. (ed.) *'Truth is Stranger than Fiction': A True Account of the Proceedings Leading to, and a Full and Authentic Report of, The Searching Inquiry, by Her Majesty's Commissioners, into the Horrible System of Discipline Practised at the Borough Gaol of Birmingham*. John Tonks, 1853.

Bidwell, A. *From Wall Street to Newgate*. Bidwell Publishing Co., 1895.

Burns, W. *Charles Reade: A Study in Victorian Authorship*. Bookman Associates, 1961.

Clay, W. *The Prison Chaplain: A Memoir of the Reverend John Clay*. Patterson Smith, 1855.

Davenport Hill, R. and Davenport Hill, F. *The Recorder of Birmingham: A Memoir of Matthew Davenport Hill, with Selections from His Correspondence*. Macmillian & Co., 1878.

Evans, R. *The Fabrication of Virtue: English Prison Architecture, 1750–1840*. Cambridge University Press, 1982.

Finnane, M. *Punishment in Australian Society*. Oxford University Press, 1997.

Orwell, G. 'Charles Reade', in Orwell, S. and Angus, I. (eds), *The Collected Essays, Journalism, and Letters of George Orwell: My Country Right or Left*. Harcourt, Brace & World, 1943.

Reade, C. *It Is Never Too Late to Mend*. London, 1856.

Reade, C. *Readiana, Comments on Current Events*. Chatto & Windus, 1883.

Reade, C. L. and Reade, Rev. C. *Charles Reade; Dramatist, Novelist, Journalist: A Memoir Compiled Chiefly from His Literary Remains*. Chapman & Hall, 1887.

Report from the Departmental Committee on Prisons [Gladstone Committee]. Parliamentary Papers (PP), LVI, London, 1895.

Report from the Select Committee of the House of Lords on the Present State of Discipline in Gaols and Houses of Corrections. PP, IX, London, 1863.

Report of the Inspectors of Prisons (Home District). PP, XXIII, London, 1845.

Report of the Select Committee on Prison Discipline. PP, XVII, London, 1850.

Report of the Royal Commission into the Condition and Treatment of the Prisoners Confined to Birmingham Borough Prison. PP, XXXI, London, 1854.

Smith, E. *Charles Reade*, Twayne, 1976.

Chapter 12

'Saving our unfortunate sisters'[1]? Establishing the first separate prison for women in New Zealand

Anna McKenzie

The appointment of Dr (later Sir) John Findlay as New Zealand's Minister of Justice in 1909, and the subsequent retirement of Arthur Hume as the Inspector of Prisons, indicated that the penal system in New Zealand was ready for change. Hume had been the head of the Prisons Department for nearly 30 years, and many politicians, including Findlay, believed that the system of penal institutions in New Zealand had stagnated over this time: 'I do not say that in the past our prisons system has not been conducted fairly and intelligently; but it is idle to deny that the present system in New Zealand, and that which has been in existence here for many years, is antiquated, and is no more than the system which was in existence in England in 1860 and 1870.'[2]

The basis for this criticism was the fact that from the late nineteenth-century, there had been considerable international growth in the use and popularity of 'scientific' penology. This had become particularly well established in America and had then gone on to influence other countries, including New Zealand.[3] The idea that crime was a scientifically 'measurable' disease, rather than a moral deviance, had been established by some of the early researchers, but by the early twentieth century the 'cult of science' unquestionably focused on the medical interpretation of crime as a disease.

One result of this new way of 'scientifically' inquiring into the causes of crime was that it focused, somewhat disproportionately, on crime committed by women. A large number of so-called 'cacogenic' family studies were published between 1874 and 1926 (see Hahn, 1980; Rafter 1997). These studies played a major part in the development of the idea that the innate defect of criminality was passed from one generation to the next by biology and genetics. Such a belief then meant that the nature of women, as the 'life-givers' in the population, was even more important; 'bad' women would conceive 'bad' children.[4] The 'cacogenic' studies also served to reframe the sexual and moral dangers of certain women into more modern biological terms, which then led to their elevation to the status of a more serious social menace. This meant that specialist institutions, known as reformatories, needed to be established to house these women and to cater for their specialist needs.

All of this new rhetoric about the use of 'scientific' methods and tests, the resulting changes in American penal policy, and the establishment of reformatories was quite attractive to other countries struggling with their own social problems with little apparent success. In New Zealand, Findlay was very attracted to the new 'eugenic' policies, and he began a more concerted effort to raise the profile of prison reform and to point thinking in this 'modern' direction. In an effort to make the Members of Parliament realise that reform of the prison system was vital, he cited the progress made internationally in dealing with inmates:

> Other countries have made progress along lines which have ceased to be experimental, and which have proved to be effective in their purpose, and I think the time has come when we should bring ourselves abreast of countries like … America … and not allow our prison system to be pointed at – in this most progressive country – as one of the most backward systems in existence … I want to remind honourable members of what everyone knows – that a new spirit, and a new purpose, and a new measure of criminal punishment has arrived.[5]

In order to achieve this new system, Findlay argued that the very foundation of New Zealand's penal thought needed to change, and that prisons needed to have a more reformative function at every level, stating that '… vengeance in the old barbaric, brutal way has given way to considerations of intention'.[6] Inmates deemed to be a threat would simply be held until they were 'reformed'.[7] Such an attitude indicates that Findlay believed that numbers of offenders could be redeemed, in spite of the international research which noted the biological and therefore essentially determined nature of criminal behaviour. This statement is one of the first incidences of the contradictions in Findlay's beliefs regarding offenders, which became more frequent over his tenure as Minister of Justice, particularly when he was discussing female inmates.

While it is clear that Findlay wanted to address the apparent stagnation of New Zealand's prison system under Hume by employing modern penological theory, it is not as clear whether he was actually proposing reforms to deal with the perceived issues women inmates caused within the system. The significantly larger numbers of female inmates in America meant that they caused a considerably larger problem and so needed to be addressed specifically. In New Zealand, however, the numbers of women sentenced to prison terms were much smaller and it is debatable whether they caused any significant issues for the Department's administration of prisons. Findlay may have been more interested in utilising modern theories about incarceration and reformation for *male* prisoners in New Zealand; the fact that internationally *female* inmates were the focus of a large number of these theories was a useful consequence, and would serve to placate the high levels of feminist agitation in New Zealand (see Coney, 1993; Dalton, 1993; Dalziel 1993; Nicholls, 1996; Page, 1996; Tennant, 1976 for further detail on feminist campaigning in New Zealand). Compared with America the numbers of women in prison in New Zealand over the early years of the twentieth century were actually quite small. Between 1900 and 1910, the daily average number of women held in the various prisons throughout New Zealand was approximately 68, which was still close to 10 per cent of the total prison population.[8]

Supporting the idea that Findlay considered women inmates as an addendum to his main reformative aims is the fact that, although he had a definite eugenic aim in his legislation, there were a number of contradictions in his beliefs, especially those relating to women. A clear example of this is from 1910 when he noted that, 'it is unfortunately true that where you have a woman an habitual criminal, in ninety cases out of a hundred her case is hopeless'.[9] Yet, when Findlay proposed his reformation of the New Zealand prison system later that same year, he allowed for the classification of women criminals as either incorrigible or reformable to be relatively fluid so that they could move from one type of institution to the other.[10]

Despite his lack of definitive ideas about women inmates, Findlay was obviously persuaded by international and local concerns about, especially young, women, who did not conform to the 'ideal woman' stereotype, and passed the landmark Reformatory Institutions Act 1909. This mirrored legislation that had been passed in America in the late 1880s, and marked the first moves in New Zealand towards the 'problematisation' of young women offenders at an official level. Essentially this legislation created a new type of criminal female – a 'reformable subject' (Hannah-Moffat,

2001: 53) – one who was wayward, potentially chaste, more 'sinned against than sinner' (Rafter, 1990: 49) but, more importantly, redeemable. This type of offender was not thought to be inherently criminal, but simply in need of some kind of educational assistance and guidance to help them back to their 'true' role as a woman, wife and mother (see Brenzel, 1983; Cox, 2003; Freedman, 1981; Hannah-Moffat, 2001; Rafter, 1990). In contrast, the more wicked, hardened and recidivist women offenders would never be redeemed and therefore any consideration of them was pointless (Hannah-Moffat, 2001; Rafter, 1990).

As further consolidation of his eugenist beliefs, and indicating the depth of impact on him of international changes, Findlay went on to propose a complete reordering of the prison system. His *Scheme for the Reorganization of the Prison System of New Zealand*,[11] a corollary to the Crimes Amendment Act 1910, contained a large number of new types of institutions. Each of these would treat the inmates according to eugenist principles – the all-important goal of reformation would be achieved through efficient and scientific classification. For men, seven different types of criminals were identified: professional criminals, 'sexual perverts', those of 'unsound mind', drunkards, 'incipient and pseudo' criminals, 'corrigible criminals' and the remainder of the criminal class.[12] For women, it was believed that there were four criminal types: those classified as 'incorrigible', 'corrigible', 'incipient and pseudo' criminals and those of 'unsound mind'.[13] Although Findlay did not give any indications about what he actually meant by these descriptions, it is clear that he believed that although there were a number of different types of women offenders, facilities for them could essentially be broken down into two main categories, a reformatory or a penitentiary.[14] The 'problematisation' of young women offenders, which had its genesis in the Reformatory Institutions Act 1909, had now reached a new level and was further enshrined in penal policy.

To cater for a different type of criminal there would be a number of different types of institution. For male offenders there would be penitentiaries for professional criminals, criminal asylums for sexual and mentally unstable offenders, an inebriate institution for habitual drunkards, a reformatory for the corrigibles or redeemables, camps for offenders showing good conduct, and 'private institutions' for the incipient and pseudo criminals.[15] For women inmates, however, Findlay advocated just one institution to hold all types of offenders. This decision was because of the relatively small numbers of women sentenced to prison.[16] In 1909, 5,769 prisoners were received into the various gaols throughout New Zealand, 562, or around 9 per cent, of whom were women.[17]

This single female institution would be divided into two sections, the inmates of each division having no direct contact with those in the other. This separation of reformable and more hardened offenders was very important, as it was a commonly held belief that younger, more vulnerable offenders would be contaminated by any contact with older, habitual offenders, and saving them from a life of crime would be much more difficult.[18]

The first division would be the reformatory. Women sent to this facility would be the so-called 'petty offenders', whose ability to reform was considered more hopeful.[19] This included offenders whose crimes were for minor drunkenness, those arrested for 'prostitution' and others who had first become 'problematised' by the Reformatory Institutions Act 1909. In line with the belief that the inmates in the reformatory needed appropriate education and guidance to help them return to society, in Findlay's proposed institution they were to be instructed in all areas of domestic service and housekeeping, with special, advanced classes being offered for those who showed aptitude in any of the lessons. There would also be supplementary lessons in health, nursing, first aid, child and infant care, flower cultivation and school training for those with 'deficient education'.[20] This system of training women in the 'domestic arts' ('For improved domesticity', 1909) was to be a parallel to the existing system of farm training for deviant young men,[21] and would make up for their deficient childhoods.

Findlay's reformulation and expansion of the 'fallen woman' concept first introduced in the 1909 legislation indicates how important it was, at this time, for girls and young women to conform to a more traditional stereotype of appropriate female behaviour. The international and local disquiet about 'modern girls' (see Alexander, 1995; Faith, 1993; Hannah-Moffat, 2001; Nathanson, 1991; Odem, 1995; Oliver, 1994, 1998; Strange, 1985, 1991; Strange and Loo, 1997) caused Findlay to publicly note 'the noticeable [trend] among our young women [towards] a reduced domesticity' ('For improved domesticity', 1909).

Findlay also saw this apparent trend had led to more selfish behaviour so that 'the young woman, of "wider activities", [is] doing more good for herself ... than the old woman, of the more thoroughly domestic days'. This anxiety about the lack of popularity of 'domesticity, the homely arts and crafts' ('For improved domesticity', 1909) probably contributed to the emphasis on domestic training in the proposed reformatory, and is again indicative of the direction of thought about criminal women at this time. However, the changes in legislation may also indicate that Findlay was simply following international trends and populist public concern by legislating against such a population, as there is no significant evidence that 'modern girls' were causing any particular problem in New Zealand at this time. For example, from 1900 to 1908, only 62 girls and young women had passed through the Education Department operated Te Oranga Reformatory near Christchurch, and it only received an average of 15 inmates per year over its 18 years of operation (Dalley, 1992).

The second division of Findlay's proposed women's prison would be the penitentiary for the habitual and incorrigible criminals. In keeping with beliefs about the causes of their offending, the regime for these offenders would be quite different from that envisaged for the women in the reformatory, and would operate more along traditional prison lines. In this part of the institution, women would be kept employed at more punitive, industrial tasks such as making prison clothing and doing laundry for both the prison and the local hospital. Release from the penitentiary was also dependent on the behaviour of the inmate, a suitable job being found and proper supervision for a probationary period of not less than 12 months.[22] This type of institution would, therefore, function along punishment and deterrent lines – remarkably similar to those used in New Zealand since Hume's arrival.[23]

Although the reformatory and penitentiary sections were to be physically separate, Findlay envisaged that inmates would be able to move from one section to the other, depending on conduct within the institution and an inmate's perceived desire to reform. A woman from the penitentiary could be removed to the reformatory if she could give 'conclusive proof' that she intended to amend her life, and alternatively, if a reformatory inmate was seen to be 'successfully resisting' the reformatory discipline, she could also be transferred to the harsher environment of the penitentiary.[24] This aspect of Findlay's scheme indicates, again, the contradictory, or possibly negotiable, nature of some of his beliefs about women. In this case, while he felt there were two separate categories of women criminals, Findlay was also willing to accept that these were not definitive, and that some women would inevitably move between the categories.

In spite of the fact that Findlay proposed to establish a reformatory to hold women convicted of minor crimes, in his discussion of the scheme in the House, he noted that, on current statistics, the number of women that would be eligible for this institution was 'not very large'.[25] Findlay recognised that a massive majority of female inmates, somewhere around 90 per cent of female convicts, would be classified as 'habitual criminals' and incorrigible.[26] The establishment of a reformatory for such a small population (numbering around 50 total inmates per year) raises significant questions about Findlay's real level of commitment to eugenic goals for women inmates. He obviously believed it was possible to simply transplant American systems into New Zealand and achieve the same results, without considering the appropriateness of the system on a much smaller, and therefore different, population.

Further questions about his dedication to eugenic concerns relating to women arise when we note that Findlay intended the new women's institution to be located in Wellington, ostensibly to make use of existing facilities.[27] Findlay himself described Wellington (Terrace) prison as 'somewhat puzzling … It is an old-new gaol – partly both',[28] and it had a number of buildings of various ages, the most recent of which was a rather hasty addition to the women's wing built in 1903.[29] The thinking of the time argued that large cities were the cause of many social problems and international opinion about women's institutions, and reformatories in particular, was that they worked best when located in a rural area – a rural life meant a moral life (Brenzel, 1983: 43–4; Freedman, 1981: 117). Most, if not all, international reformers believed that when offenders were moved away from contaminating influences, including cities that actually induced criminal behaviour, and placed in rural settings, given plenty of healthy, fresh air and forced to exercise, they might be cured of their disease – crime (Rafter, 1990: 35).

New Zealand politicians, including Findlay, also supported this way of thinking. Henry Ell (MP for Christchurch South from 1905 to 1919 and an influential advocate of social reform) recommended 'more open-air [and] country work for prisoners in the gaols. The gaols ought to be in the country, not in the cities; for the work that could be provided in the country for the prisoners would be better for them physically and morally.'[30] Findlay directly linked increasing urbanisation to the 'decay' of New Zealand's society (Fleming, 1981: 78; *White Ribbon* (WR), 1911, 17/ 194: 9). For this reason, Findlay's decision to base the women's institution in Wellington is yet another action that seems to contradict his eugenic beliefs, and also departs, rather dramatically, from the American system on which it was based. The Wellington location offered no potential for the agricultural activities which characterised the similar reformatories in America (see Brenzel, 1983; Freedman, 1981; Rafter, 1990), and while the penitentiary would allow inmates to raise vegetables and keep poultry, the reformatory women would not come anywhere near to the rural ideal, which meant it was going to be a significantly different institution. However, when considering the educational and industrial programmes Findlay proposed for the reformatory – cookery, dressmaking, millinery, health and first aid, infant care, plant and flower cultivation[31] – it is obvious that the location of any such facility was almost irrelevant, as most of the training and work available to inmates could be carried out indoors.

Along with the apparent contradictions and complexities involved in Findlay's beliefs about women criminals, the practicalities of the New Zealand situation, particularly the amount of money available for the construction of new institutions, must have also tempered many of Findlay's grand plans to reform the prison system. The sheer size of the perceived problems in New Zealand's penal system meant that realistically not everything could be done immediately and it appears that Findlay concentrated more on the reform of male institutions, with women inmates being a secondary consideration. For women, cost constraints meant that an institution that was a combined penitentiary and reformatory located in an urban area represented the extent to which the government was able to reform aspects of the penal system relating to women.

National response to Findlay's proposals, particularly from the women lobbyists, was generally good. Unfortunately though, the local Wellington newspaper makes no specific mention of the proposal to establish a women's only institution, which is somewhat telling in itself. However, all of the general commentary about the new legislation was very complimentary about Findlay and what he was aiming to do (see 'Crimes act', 1910; 'Crimes amendment', 1910; 'Criminals and crimes', 1910; 'The gospel of humanity', 1910; 'Prison methods', 1910; 'Prison reform', 1910a, 1910b; 'Reforming the criminal', 1910).

Despite the fact that Findlay's initial idea to use Wellington's Terrace Gaol as a base for women inmates was well received by members of the public, it was far less acceptable to those involved in prison administration. One of the most important concerns was premised on the fact that the Terrace Gaol in Wellington was, at the time, the second largest prison in New Zealand, after Auckland Gaol. The ramifications of it becoming a women's institution would have been considerable, as it would mean that Wellington, New Zealand's capital, would have no facility for men with long prison sentences. This again reflected the gap between the rhetoric about changing imprisonment for women and the lack of willingness to put these theories into action, especially if imprisonment for men would be affected.

The main alternative to Findlay's plan for using the Terrace Gaol was to convert the Samaritan Home in Addington, Christchurch (which had originally been a gaol) back into a prison for women.[32] This building had originally been opened as a prison in the 1870s,[33] but in 1896 it had been converted into a Samaritan Home for young pregnant women and elderly, destitute men and women (Tennant, 1992: 74). This alternative solution was, however, not without problems of its own; since its initial construction in the 1870s, many aspects of the institution had been considered 'defective'.[34] When it had been eventually closed to prisoners in 1890, the unsuitability of the building was further noted and that 'the cells in present use [at Lyttelton where the women from Addington had been moved to] are more healthy and better suited for a female prison than those at Addington'.[35] However, despite the numerous problems, Addington reopened in 1896 as a Samaritan Home, and functioned as such for more than a decade.

Publication of the plan to use Addington as a prison again led to a petition from the local residents asking that use of the Samaritan Home as accommodation for criminals, 'degenerates … and other "undesirables" be ceased'.[36] However, this petition was quickly dismissed by the Under-Secretary of Justice and by 1912, the decision was made to move all the women prisoners in New Zealand to the Addington site.[37]

By this time, two years since Findlay announced his plan to reorganise the prison system, there had been large changes in the imprisonment of men in New Zealand, including the closure of a number of older prisons. The imprisonment of women, however, had not gone beyond the stage of allocating a specific, and at this stage woefully inadequate, institution. The slow pace with which the Department moved regarding female imprisonment indicates the lack of any real commitment to reformation from Findlay, his successors and the Department. The women lobbyists and reformers so active in the late nineteenth and early twentieth centuries seemed to have been happily placated by the 1910 reform suggestions. As there had been major changes in terms of men's imprisonment, it seems that the issue of reforming female prisons did not have the same sense of urgency.

To further complicate matters, there were a number of significant political changes occurring. The major change came in July 1912 when the Liberal party, which had prospered in nearly 20 years of government, finally lost its grip on the country and was voted out of office (see Hamer, 1988). As a result of the change in government, Findlay lost his seat and was no longer the Minister of Justice. Fortunately, although the Department had lost the minister who had designed the massive reorganisation of the prison system, the moves towards adopting a more modern and scientific method of dealing with inmates progressed under the new ministers (AJHR, 1912, H20).

When the women's facility at Addington finally opened to receive inmates on 17 April 1913, it bore little resemblance to the initial plans of Findlay.[38] The first major problem was the building in which the women were housed. Although a high fence had been built around the grounds and a number of the older buildings had been pulled down, the main building of the prison was still in need of considerable work (AJHR, 1913, H20: 6). The main problem lay in the way the prison was configured, as it left little room for the complete separation of the penitentiary and reformatory inmates that Findlay had envisaged, and inmates mixed easily with each other. The best that could realistically be achieved was to try and keep each class of offender to separate floors of the building.[39]

The problem with the structural design of the Addington facility clearly embodies the almost indifference shown to women inmates by the Department. International penological theory argued that women prison inmates needed specialist care because of their gender (see Colvin, 1997; Freedman, 1981; Hannah-Moffat, 1997, 2001; Oliver, 1994; Rafter, 1990; Strange, 1985). However, as previously noted, this theory was premised on a significantly larger number of women in the penal system, which made specialist care far more cost-effective. In New Zealand, the very small numbers of women prison inmates (in 1912 the daily average of women in prison in New Zealand was just 64) meant they were not a significant part of the total prison population. They were further problematised because they were not like the rest of the (male) population and could not be treated in the same way. As Hume had pointed out in 1898, the numbers of women in prison were so small as to be inconvenient;[40] specialist care for such a small population was therefore not justifiable. Although Findlay, in his plan to reorganise the entire prison system, was able to satisfactorily address some of the concerns about women's imprisonment, he had not made any commitment to real change.

The second major problem with Addington, and where it differed even more significantly from the institution Findlay had proposed, was the regime for the prisoners. As it was not possible to completely separate different classes of inmates, there was no real difference in the work given. Those held in the reformatory section of the prison did not receive '[instruction] in all branches of domestic service and housekeeping, advanced classes in cookery, dressmaking, and millinery',[41] as the 1910 proposal had outlined, but instead followed the more punitive lines of the penitentiary regime. The lack of classification meant that all the women held at Addington were employed in cleaning, sewing, knitting, washing and repairing the clothing for the Lyttelton prison (now only holding males), and keeping the grounds in order.[42]

Labour at Addington became even more focused on indoor industry when, at the end of 1913, the inmates began to manufacture knitted wool socks and cardigans for distribution to inmates at Invercargill prison.[43] It was further expanded to include the making of heavy calico clothing bags, shirts for Lyttelton and all items for Addington.[44] This was significantly different from the variety of outdoor work available for male prisoners, who were employed in a wide range of occupations including quarrying, metal-crushing, road making, earthworks, manufacture of bricks, tiles and drainpipes, boot making and tree planting.[45] At Addington, the employment problem was further compounded by the fact that there was very little room outside the confines of the prison wing for any occupation (see Lingard, 1936 for a thorough overview of prison labour in New Zealand up to 1935).

A further problem that became apparent at Addington in its early years was the lack of inmates, a fact that may have confirmed to the Department the lack of any material need for a central women's facility. Although Addington had been opened with the expectation that it would hold every woman sentenced in New Zealand to six months or more in prison, in reality this did not happen. In 1913, the year Addington reopened for women, it received 78 inmates. However, the Wellington Gaol received 245 women, Auckland Gaol 129, and several other minor prisons a total of 81 inmates.[46] This carried on throughout the next decade, with Wellington and Auckland continuing to receive numbers of sentenced women far exceeding those at Addington. In 1920, Addington received just 49 inmates compared with 114 at Wellington and 83 in Auckland.[47]

These figures also illustrate two trends: firstly, the decline in numbers of women being sent to prison over the early part of the twentieth century as already discussed, and secondly, the absence of any real commitment from northern prisons to send women inmates south to Addington. The most probable reason for the northern prisons failing to send women to Addington is quite simple – money. While Findlay's initial 1910 proposal for women's imprisonment had planned for a central autonomous prison to be used to hold all women sentenced in New Zealand, the expense and delay of sending women to the South Island (an issue which Findlay did not identify) meant that in actual fact Addington operated more along the lines of a women's division in a mixed institution, rather than a female prison in its own right.[48] The gaoler from Lyttelton continued to make weekly inspections, and there were a number of male guards who held positions of responsibility within Addington, making the institution less than autonomous and the Matron and her assistants almost subordinate in their own institution.[49]

So, while Findlay's 1910 proposal and the resulting establishment of the women-only prison at Addington were indicative of a desire to save 'our unfortunate sisters',[50] they lacked any real commitment both at a political and financial level from the government, and because of this were only partially, but more importantly defectively, implemented. Findlay's actions, and those of the Department following his replacement, indicate that the idea of reforming prison for women was simply not within the scope of the government at this time but was incidental to the reform of the prison system as a whole.

Such a lack of commitment naturally leads to a questioning of Findlay's true motive in suggesting the reform of imprisonment for women. The actions towards reforming women's imprisonment over the early 1910s were half-hearted attempts to replicate the far more progressive system from America and to appease the public calls for moves in that direction. Although the theory of replacing the Victorian punitiveness by a more modern and reformative practice for dealing with offenders was admirable, the small numbers of women and apparent reluctance of the Department to commit to a realistic programme of reorganising imprisonment for women meant that the resulting situation was almost worse for incarcerated women. In spite of Findlay's rhetoric about there being a new spirit of criminal punishment in play, for women, the more traditional treatment of being neglected and overlooked remained, and the system of women's imprisonment returned to a level of stagnation until well into the twentieth century.

Notes

1. New Zealand Parliamentary Debates (NZPD), 1910, vol. 150, p. 346.
2. NZPD, 1909, 147, p. 458.
3. See Appendices to the Journals of the House of Representatives (AJHR), 1892, H13, p. 2 where Hume briefly mentions America.
4. This was argued as being evident in the fact that the birth rate of the 'criminal' classes was increasing at a faster rate than that of the middle classes (Bacchi, 1980; Haller, 1963; Rafter, 1997; Zedner, 1991).
5. NZPD, 1909, 147, p. 458.
6. NZPD, 1909, 147, p. 459.
7. NZPD, 1909, 147, p. 461.
8. See Statistics of New Zealand (SNZ), 1900–1910.
9. NZPD, 1910, 150, p. 357.
10. AJHR, 1910, H20B, p. 7.
11. AJHR, 1910, H20B, pp. 1–8.
12. AJHR, 1910, H20B, p. 2.
13. AJHR, 1910, H20B, p. 2.
14. AJHR, 1910, H20B, p. 6.
15. AJHR, 1910, H20B, p. 2.
16. NZPD, 1910, 150, p. 357.
17. SNZ, 1883–1909.
18. NZPD, 1904, 129, p. 469; 1905, 132, p. 554; 1906, 137, p. 173.
19. AJHR, 1910, H20B, p. 7.
20. AJHR, 1910, H20B, pp. 6–7.
21. NZPD, 1910, 150, p. 357.
22. AJHR, 1910, H20, p. 7.
23. AJHR, 1910, H20, p. 7.

24. AJHR, 1910, H20, p. 7.
25. NZPD, 1910, 150, p. 357.
26. NZPD, 1910, 150, p. 357.
27. NZPD, 1910, 150, p. 357.
28. NZPD, 1910, 150, p. 353.
29. AJHR, 1904, H20, p. 9.
30. NZPD, 1907, 140, p. 194.
31. AJHR, 1910, H20B, p. 7.
32. AJHR, 1910, H20, p. 2.
33. Information contained in registration proposal form for historic places regarding Addington Prison, submitted by G. Wright in 1998. Held by New Zealand Historic Places Trust, Christchurch.
34. AJHR, 1886, H4, p. 4.
35. AJHR, 1890, H4, p. 3.
36. National Archives (NA), Justice Series 40 (J40), Prisons Department (PD) Box 152, 1911/20/35, Forwarding petition that old gaol building (Samaritan Home) at Addington be not further used for accommodation of criminals.
37. AJHR, 1911, H20, p. 1.
38. AJHR, 1914, H20, p. 10.
39. NA, J40, PD Box 231, 1921/20/63: Matthews to Minister, 19/10/17.
40. AJHR, 1898, H20, p. 3.
41. AJHR, 1910, H20B, p. 7.
42. AJHR, 1914, H20, p. 10.
43. NA, J40, PD Box 169, 1914/8: Hawkins to Jordan, 18/12/13.
44. NA, J40, PD Box 185, 1915/275: Maher to Jordan, 9/8/15.
45. AJHR, 1914–1950, H20.
46. AJHR, 1914, H20, p. 16.
47. AJHR, 1921–22, H20, p. 13.
48. NA, J40, PD Box 231, 1921/20/63: Handwritten note on Matthews to Minister, 19/10/17.
49. AJHR, 1919, H20, p. 12; NA, J40, PD Box 193, 1916/196: Jordan to Public Works Department, 5/12/13.
50. NZPD, 1910, 150, p. 346.

References

Alexander, R. *The 'Girl Problem': Female Sexual Delinquency in New York, 1900–1930*. Cornell University Press, 1995.

Bacchi, C. 'Evolution, eugenics and women: the impact of scientific theories on attitudes towards women, 1870–1920', in Windschuttle, E. (ed.), *Women, Class and History: Feminist Perspectives on Australia 1788–1978*. Fontana, 1980.

Brenzel, B. *Daughters of the State: A Social Portrait of the First Reform School for Girls in North America, 1856–1905*. MIT Press, 1983.

Colvin, M. *Penitentiaries, Reformatories, and Chain Gangs: Social Theory and the History of Punishment in Nineteenth-Century America*. Macmillan Press, 1997.

Coney, S. *Standing in the Sunshine: A History of New Zealand Women since They Won the Vote*. Penguin, 1993.

Cox, P. *Gender, Justice and Welfare: Bad Girls in Britain, 1900–1950*. Palgrave Macmillan, 2003.

'Crimes act', *Evening Post*, 9 August 1910, pp. 7–8.

'Crimes amendment', *Evening Post*, 14 September 1910, p. 6.

'Criminals and crimes', *Evening Post*, 18 August 1910, p. 3.

Dalley, B. 'From demi-mondes to slaveys: aspects of the management of the Te Oranga Reformatory for delinquent young women, 1900–1918', in Brookes, B., Macdonald, C. and Tennant, M. (eds), *Women in History 2*. Bridget Williams Books, 1992.

Dalley, B. 'Women's imprisonment in New Zealand, 1880–1920', unpublished PhD thesis, Otago University, 1991.

Dalley, B. 'Prisons without Men: the development of a separate women's prison in New Zeland', *New Zealand Journal of History*, 27, 1, 1993a, pp. 37–60.

Dalley, B. 'Making Bricks Without Straw: Feminism and Prison Reform in New Zealand, 1896–1925', *Women's Studies Journal*, 9, 2, 1993b, pp. 30–50.

Dalton, S. 'The Pure in Heart: The NZWCTU and Social Purity 1885–1930', unpublished MA thesis, Victoria University, Wellington, 1993.

Dalziel, R. 'New Zealand Women's Christian Temperance Union 1885–', in Else, A. (ed.), *Women Together: A History of Women's Organisations in New Zealand*. Historical Branch, Deptment of Internal Affairs/Daphne Brasell Associates Press, 1993.

Faith, K. *Unruly Women: The Politics of Confinement and Resistance*. Press Gang, 1993.

Fleming, P. 'Eugenics in New Zealand 1900–1940', unpublished MA thesis, Massey University, Palmerston North, 1981.

'For improved domesticity', *Evening Post*, 17 August 1909, p. 6.

Freedman, E. *Their Sisters' Keepers: Women's Prison Reform in America, 1830–1930*. University of Michigan Press, 1981.

'The gospel of humanity', *Evening Post*, 10 August 1910, p. 6.

Hahn, N. 'Too dumb to know better: cacogenic family studies and the criminology of women', *Criminology*, 18, 1, 1980, pp. 3–25.

Haller, M. *Eugenics: Hereditarian Attitudes in American Thought*. Rutgers University Press, 1963.

Hamer, D. *The New Zealand Liberals: The Years of Power, 1891–1912*. Auckland University Press, 1988.

Hannah-Moffat, K. 'From Christian Maternalism to Risk Technologies: Penal Powers and Women's Knowledges in the Governance of Female Prisons', unpublished PhD thesis, University of Toronto, 1997.

Hannah-Moffat, K. *Punishment in Disguise: Penal Governance and Federal Imprisonment of Women in Canada*. University of Toronto Press, 2001.

Lingard, F. *Prison Labour in New Zealand: A Historical, Statistical and Analytical Survey*. Government Printer, 1936.

Nathanson, C. *Dangerous Passage: The Social Control of Sexuality in Women's Adolescence*. Temple University Press, 1991.

Nicholls, R. *The Women's Parliament: The National Council of the Women of New Zealand, 1896–1920*. Victoria University Press, 1996.

Odem, M. *Delinquent Daughters: Protecting and Policing Adolescent Female Sexuality in the United States, 1885–1920*. University of North Carolina Press, 1995.

Oliver, P. '"To govern by kindness": the first two decades of the Mercer reformatory for women', in Phillips, J., Loo, T. and Lewthwaite, S. (eds), *Essays in the History of Canadian Law: Crime and Criminal Justice*, vol. 5. Osgoode Society for Canadian Legal History, 1994.

Oliver, P. *'Terror to Evil-Doers': Prisons and Punishments in Nineteenth-century Ontario*. University of Toronto Press, 1998.

Page, D. *The National Council of Women: A Centennial History*. Auckland University Press/Bridget Williams Books/National Council of Women, 1996.

Page, D. *The National Council of Women*. Pratt, J. Punishment in a Perfect Society. Victoria University Press, 1992.

Pratt, J. *Punishment in a perfect society: the New Zealand penal system, 1840–1939*. Victoria University Press, 1992.

'Prison methods', *Evening Post*, 19 August 1910, p. 4.

'Prison reform', *Evening Post*, 11 August 1910a, p. 6.

'Prison reform', *Evening Post*, 20 August 1910b, p. 9.

Rafter, N. *Partial Justice: Women, Prisons and Social Control*, 2nd ed. Transaction, 1990.

Rafter, N. *Creating Born Criminals*. University of Illinois Press, 1997.

'Reforming the criminal', *Evening Post*, 10 August 1910, p. 3.

Strange, C. '"The criminal and fallen of their sex": the establishment of Canada's first women's prison, 1874–1901', *Canadian Journal of Women and the Law*, 1, 1985, pp. 79–92.

Strange, C. 'The Perils and Pleasures of the City: Single, Wage-Earning Women in Toronto, 1880–1930', unpublished PhD thesis, Rutgers University, 1991.

Strange, C. and Loo, T. *Making Good: Law and Moral Regulation in Canada, 1867–1939*. University of Toronto Press, 1997.

Tennant, M. 'Matrons with a Mission: Women's Organisations in New Zealand, 1893–1915', unpublished MA thesis, Massey University, 1976.

Tennant, M. '"Magdalens and moral imbeciles": women's homes in nineteenth-century New Zealand', in Brookes, B., Macdonald, C. and Tennant, M. (eds), *Women in History 2*. Bridget Williams Books, 1992.

White Ribbon (Women's Christian Temperance Union of New Zealand), 1991, 17–194.

Zedner, L. 'Women, crime, and penal responses: a historical account', in Tonry, M. (ed.), *Crime and Justice: A Review of Research*, vol. 14. University of Chicago Press, 1991.

Chapter 13

Maori police personnel and the *rangatiratanga* discourse

Richard S. Hill

Examining matters of imperial intent and method, and of indigenous aspirations and responses to the colonisers, goes to the heart of the colonising project – a project whose results continued to underpin life in New Zealand in post-colonial times. This chapter introduces one key aspect of the relationship between the Crown and Maori. 'The Crown' is used synonymously with 'the state', representing as it does the lego-constitutional ruling authority in New Zealand since annexation by Britain in 1840. The configuration of personnel and lines of responsibility within the state, of course, changes through time – from governors (until the 1850s) to ministers and their officials. The state's constitutional profiles are those of Crown Colony until 1853, Colony (with internal self-government from 1856) until 1907, Dominion until 1947 and independent realm thereafter. The discussion draws upon my work on both policing history in New Zealand (Hill, 1986, 1989, 1995) and the history and contemporary practice of relations between Maori and the Crown (Hill, 2000, 2003, 2004).

In relatively recent times, a great deal of research and debate has occurred within the parameters of what might be called the *rangatiratanga* discourse. Accordingly, much modern historiography in the field of the Treaty of Waitangi (signed between the Crown and Maori in 1840) and 'race relations' studies has constituted, in effect, an investigation of the Maori quest for *rangatiratanga*, a term broadly interpretable as autonomy (Belich, 1986; Orange, 1987; Walker, 1990; Cox, 1993; O'Malley, 1998). This emphasis has been so marked that the concept has entered the works of recent additions to the literature produced by the 'North American academic visitor' (Alves, 1999; Kersey, 2002). It is now generally believed that the promise of *rangatiratanga*, embedded in Article Two of the Maori language version of the Treaty of Waitangi, was the inducement for chiefs to sign the document, and that attempting to get this promise implemented has been, for Maori collectively organised, the most significant aspect of their relations with the state ever since (Waitangi Tribunal, 1996; Durie, 1998; Byrnes, 2004).

The Crown, on the contrary, saw Article One as conferring indivisible sovereignty upon itself, and has been exceedingly loath to share power or even (until recently) to accommodate indigenous culture or lifestyle. None the less, since 1840 Maori have tried to force or persuade state authorities to implement power-sharing, partnership, devolution or other arrangements that would respect *rangatiratanga* (Hill and O'Malley, 2000; Hill, 2004). As a result, tension has been endemic, and where there is tension there is policing.

Policing has always, therefore, been a key site of test and contest in the endemically troubled interface between Crown governance and Maori *rangatiratanga*/autonomy. 'Maori' is used in this chapter as a shorthand way of covering many and varied collective organisations (usually tribally focused) which have had a relationship with the Crown. Such an expansive definition of organisational expression of Maori aspirations recognises the complexities of the race relations history of New Zealand. It also answers criticism of the *rangatiratanga* discourse – for example, that of Lyndsay Head, who argues that this discourse demonises or ignores nineteenth-century Maori who were supportive of the Crown. Depicting the Maori search for autonomy as taking many and varied tactics and strategies, including actions accommodative of the Crown (such as allying with it against tribal enemies), addresses such conceptual problems. It also takes into account other arguments, such as that a notion of a European-derived 'law-based citizenship' developed amongst Maori, shaping their actions (Head, 2001: 97–9, 116).

To sum up this chapter's perspective on the *rangatiratanga* discourse: Maori have always collectively organised in a self-determinationist way, seeking in effect a partnership with the Crown within a nation that might, were such a relationship to be forged, more accurately be called 'New Zealand/Aotearoa' (Hill, 2004; Boenisch-Brednich and Hill, 2004). But Maori ways and means – and indeed their ends – have varied as circumstances and opportunity require or provide. Policing has been a constant theme in this long and evolving story, integrally involved in both the numerous Maori quests for *rangatiratanga* and the Crown's responses.

State responses to autonomist aspirations are governed by the fact that policing, in the final analysis, provides the capacity for legitimated coercion over citizens. Policing action will result, for example, when the search for autonomy is perceived by the Crown to violate 'indivisible sovereignty' or offend its concepts of public (or private) order. At the most extreme level of coercion, when Maori were perceived to be rebelling against the Crown, they were militarily suppressed, often by or in conjunction with militarised police forces tasked with later occupying the conquered areas.

Coercive policing is the central paradigm for interpreting the state relationship with Maori in the first decades of the colony, when mobile armed units constituted the major policing formations. In 1886 Maori were deemed to have been sufficiently subjugated (and the non-Maori, or Pakeha, population sufficiently 'settled') for the police to be disarmed for purposes of normal daily work. Retaining the capacity for maximum coercive response, however, they were geared for use against 'Maori disobedience' – in preference to deployment of the military, for such reasons as readiness, expense and minimising provocation. The suppression by the New Zealand Police Force of the prophet Rua Kenana's attempt to assert *rangatiratanga* at his stronghold at Maungapohatu in 1916, for example, led to 'in effect the last shooting in the Anglo-Maori wars' (Ward, 1967: 167; Binney *et al.*, 1979; Webster, 1979).

Yet policing is a more complex task than that of overt coercion. From the earliest days of British interest in Aotearoa, the imperial priority was to tame the new frontier. This implied, at least ultimately, supplanting *rangatiratanga* and (in the words of a constable) 'reconciling the Maori to pakeha rule' (Hill, 1995: 62). Maori being both numerous and warlike made such a task difficult. Moreover, the colonial mission in New Zealand, since it was one of very many in the British empire, needed to be carried out cheaply (and therefore, preferably, non-militarily). Police were to have a central role in the taming of the Maori as well as of the Pakeha frontier; and their methods were to range, strategically and tactically, along a continuum of control measures from overtly coercive to benignly hegemonic. This chapter proposes ways of patterning the intricacies of state policing which included use of Maori personnel in mechanisms of both direct and indirect control.

At the time of an imminent historiographical revolution on race relations in New Zealand (Veracini, 2001), I drew some preliminary conclusions about policing Maori and Maori police in the nineteenth century (Hill, 1985). This chapter re-examines these conclusions in the light of historiographical developments in the last two decades, and also applies them to the twentieth century. The previous scoping effort came at a time of changing perceptions among New Zealand historians which partly reflected a recent politico-cultural 'Maori Renaissance' – itself a manifestation of what Ranginui Walker has called the Maori 'struggle without end' for autonomy (Walker, 1990). In this way, the practice and dissemination of history became interconnected with the quest for *rangatiratanga*, and tensions in the Crown–Maori interface drew attention to the nature and purposes of policing. While policing operates at shifting points along a control continuum, several broad paradigms of control can be discerned.

The first of these, from the outset of colonisation in the 1840s, involves the state utilising Maori *expert* or *specialist* knowledge and skills. However coercive the policing methods used in different circumstances in the early colonial years, specialist Maori knowledge and techniques were often considered essential. Knowledge needed to be gained from Maori about their own or other tribes, about the physical, political and cultural environments of Maoridom. Through such knowledge and its application, already developed and theorised imperial ways and means of controlling indigenes were built upon and refined for antipodean circumstances.

Acquisition of indigenous expertise was procured by many means, including employing Maori as individuals in the numerous and varied colonial police forces until their amalgamation in the mid-1870s, or even by assigning official policing duties to entire collectivities of Maori. After negotiating with the Crown, Maori individual or collective police would provide specified services: surveillance and/or muscle to enable, for example, the state to make inroads upon the independence of tribes resistant to the spread of 'settlement and civilisation'.

Why did many Maori wish to work as policemen for a highly Eurocentric state, and participate in the colonising and 'civilising' missions that aimed to virtually eliminate them as a people and a culture? The *rangatiratanga* discourse can shed light on this phenomenon. In particular, a number of state-based Maori policing activities can be seen as individual or collective contributions to the quest for *iwi*/tribal, *hapu*/sub-tribal, *whanau*/extended family or other modes of autonomy. Maori might enrol as police in pursuit of their collective interests against oppositional tribal groupings. The specialist geographical and cultural knowledge of indigenous police in the Hutt Valley in the 1840s, for example, assisted (in the cause of pursuing their own collective interest) the Crown's expulsion of other tribal forces (Wards, 1968: chs 7–9; Belich, 1986: 73–4; Hill, 1986: 237ff).

More broadly, soon after 1840 many Maori had realised that imperial might was so potentially overwhelming that they needed to negotiate with it to ensure survival. Many concluded that they had to *participate* in the processes of loss of *rangatiratanga* in order to limit the extent of that loss and retain a platform for rebuilding autonomy: negotiations for a modus vivendi with the government might well progress more smoothly from an 'insider' position, especially such an important one as policing. Despite the onrush of settlement, retention of a degree of *rangatiratanga* might be preserved, and autonomy even eventually enhanced, through an engagement that (among other things) led to acquisition of European skills and resources.

For such reasons the state seldom had difficulties gaining sizeable Maori policing assistance. Of course, Maori in the various policing systems had to enforce a number of requirements that cut across tribal customary laws, behaviours and aspirations. In particular, they were tasked with furthering a Crown agenda that continued through to the 1970s – that of full assimilation of Maori. This was something obviously incompatible with full exercise of *rangatiratanga*. In the interests of maximising their own groupings' chances of retaining any significant degree of *rangatiratanga*, then, many Maori leaders in effect engaged in a collaboration that meant sacrificing aspects of their own culture and modes of control. Not only would they assist governments to suppress tribes that were resistant to state control, they would provide policemen to discipline individuals or groupings in their own tribes who broke the most serious of the Pakeha codes of conduct.

Sometimes, they did not fully predict the consequences. 'Loyalist' chiefs found after the Anglo-Maori wars of the 1860s that the Crown could be as determined to supersede *their* authority and seize *their* ancestral land as it had that of the 'rebel tribes'. They would then seek new ways to reassert *rangatiratanga* and retain the land. Even tribes which had provided Flying Columns and Native Contingents to support the Armed Constabulary now steadily resisted state encroachment in various ways and found themselves confronted at times by policemen from other and even their own tribes.

After New Zealand was deemed to be fully pacified by the mid-1880s, and Maori to be behaving appropriately enough pending the dying out of their race and/or their culture, governments had little use for expert and specialist Maori knowledge and skills in policing. From this period, *rangatiratanga* was declared dead on a number of occasions by the Crown and by Pakeha commentators. The sole regular Maori constable left after 1886, when the police were split from the military and generally disarmed, had gone from the New Zealand Police Force within a year. The few Maori enrolled during the next eight or so decades were not taken on through any policy of acquiring specialist knowledge or skills. Maori people were now treated as if they had already assimilated: they no longer presented a collective threat to the state, with offending regarded as the action of individuals rather than collectivities. The paradigm for policing Maori was no longer that of a collectivised 'special case' requiring expert, insider skills of surveillance and coercion. Pakeha police could control individual Maori and Pakeha alike, and were considered to provide much better policing by being, for example, more amenable to both internalising and imposing discipline and regular rhythms of life.

Given that Maori did not die out, but made a remarkable demographic recovery from the beginning of the twentieth century, small numbers of part-time Native Constables were retained in remote areas to assist Pakeha police. But even this practice was steadily phased out, partly because local Maori police frequently resisted enforcing laws which encroached upon tribal customs – the right to fish, for instance. Such resistance constituted an indication that *rangatiratanga* was alive and well, and strengthened views that the 'Native temperament' meant that Maori should not be used for policing unless absolutely necessary. The institution of Native Constable was finally disbanded in 1945, in the early years of the great migration that turned Maori from a rural into an urban people. The long-standing state goal of full assimilation (under different names, from 'amalgamation' to 'integration') was now seen to be attainable; detribalisation would follow urbanisation, and the quest for *rangatiratanga* would disappear.

This did not happen. In fact, urban education contributed eventually to the Maori Renaissance. This, in turn, led to proactive efforts from the early 1970s to get more than a handful of Maori into the New Zealand police, partly to gain access again to specialist knowledge and skills under the rubric of 'community policing'. Such efforts increased as the quest for *rangatiratanga* put mounting pressure on the government. This pressure was so strong that, by the time of the nation's sesquicentennial commemoration in 1990, the government was officially declaring New Zealand to be a bicultural society, under the theme of 'a pact of partnership' between two peoples inhabiting one nation. Whatever the later developments in Crown–Maori relations, a strong indigenous presence within the New Zealand Police was clearly there to stay.

By 1990 Maori, numbering some 430,000, had clearly come a long way from their population nadir of a little over 40,000 at the end of the nineteenth century; their percentage in the population had more than doubled, and they had moved from being a predominantly rural to an overwhelmingly urban people. Yet even in the late nineteenth century, Maori had been engaged in a variety of self-determinationist strategies to promote *rangatiratanga*. One of these aimed at gaining state consent for a limited degree of autonomy, and Maori Councils set up by the Crown in

1900 attempted both to meet the demand and defuse its more threatening aspects (Hill, 2004; Lange, 2004). These new institutions, essentially refinements of earlier experiments, were to include policing regimes. Such agencies, collectively, comprised the second major mode of Maori engagement in policing. Just as the state's utilisation of expert knowledge and skill was intended to be (until the Maori Renaissance) a temporary phenomenon, pending full assimilation (or even disappearance) of Maori, so too was this second mode: policing as a component of institutions of indirect control by and of Maori.

There were two broad aspects of this method of control. The first was a holding operation by the Crown. Tribal authorities were used, in effect, to impose certain types of state-approved behaviour upon their people, especially those which assisted (or at least did not impede) commerce and settlement. The second was a degree of official supervision of the indirect control institutions aimed at establishing methods of preparing Maori for taking up European ways of doing things.

At first the concept of a holding operation predominated in state policy as the means of controlling indigenes. Pending the full penetration of Maori areas by settlers and the state, and with regular police focusing on the nucleated Pakeha settlements, policing directed by chiefs would (with some minimal state guidance) help create sufficient 'order and good government' to establish the conditions for colonisation. In fact, long before annexation of Aotearoa in 1840, chiefly policemen (some of them sworn in by the Sydney magistracy) acted as indirect control agents of the New South Wales state, exercising their *rangatiratanga* so that their tribes benefited from western trade and technology. After 1840, chiefs negotiating such arrangements did so out of similar motives, but more especially those of preserving some degree of *rangatiratanga* in the face of potential and actual imperial and settler might.

Chiefs (including the signatories to the Treaty) did not know initially that, in official eyes, all such partnerships, including their policing regimes, were designed to be temporary, pending the establishment of full and direct control. Even so, after increasing occupation of the interior by state and settler, and especially once colonists had outnumbered Maori some two decades after the Treaty, indirect control remained a significant state strategy – although greater guidance over it was implemented. Imperial models were introduced that aimed at preparing Maori to become 'well behaved' British citizens.

In the 1860s, for example, the colonial government encouraged tribes to transform their ruling *runanga* (councils) into elements of the machinery of state, complete with their own police forces (Ward, 1995; Hill, 1986: ch. 10; Pratt, 1992: ch. 2). However, those tribal governing and policing mechanisms which agreed to official status needed to gain Crown endorsement of their local laws. Officials and politicians were strongly suggestive as to what such laws should include – banning practices deemed 'repugnant to civilisation', or encouraging developments that would assist farming, such as fencing in animals – and they possessed the power of veto. For the government, official *runanga* were both holding and preparatory mechanisms of socio-racial control. They represented a state appropriation of *rangatiratanga*. Maori police chiefs, or Wardens, each heading numbers of *karere*/constables, were there to help (in a phrase used at the time) 'make Maoris parties to their own submission'. The aim, in short, was for Maori themselves to impose British rhythms of life and commerce upon the villages.

Yet, Maori who negotiated the official recognition of their *runanga* saw this as a way of asserting *their rangatiratanga* in the face of ongoing government encroachment, and of procuring Crown resources (including policing) to do so. In some cases, again, the indirect control regimes might supply policing and other resources to be used in asserting *rangatiratanga* against tribal enemies. Moreover, some *hapu* with official *runanga* escaped the fate of fellow tribal groupings which had resisted land selling and state authority – invasion, land confiscation (*raupatu*) and the imposition of occupation policing. As it turned out, the results of cooperation with the Crown often provided only a temporary respite. When the implications of a settler-dominated future became clear, tribes often changed direction in their quest for *rangatiratanga*. Indeed, the first formal head of the King movement (Kingitanga), which resisted official authority in the North Island from the late 1850s, had once been leader of the pro-government forces securing South Auckland. As King Potatau I, he was regarded by the Crown as leader of a rival sovereignty. Some *hapu* with official *runanga* decided to fight the Crown when it invaded Kingitanga territory in 1863.

Even tribes which remained 'friendly' to the government often assessed that the only immediately viable way of asserting *rangatiratanga* was to persuade the Crown to devolve a degree of power. A number of tribes acted together in pursuit of this aim from the 1870s, eventually establishing a Kotahitanga (Unity) parliament which met annually in the 1890s. So too did tribes whose land had been confiscated, establishing a Kingitanga parliament at the same period. It was out of such pressure that the new set of state mechanisms, the Maori Councils, originated in 1900. As with the official *runanga* of the 1860s, Maori saw these as a means for self-determination, while the government intended them to be temporary agencies of indirect control, preparing for either Maori disappearance or their full assimilation.

Maori Councils utilised state-approved constables to police the country villages where most Maori still lived. Possessing specialist community knowledge, they enforced state-guided laws whose prototypes were strongly influenced by the Young Maori Party – western-educated men who moved in government as well as tribal circles and who urged adaptation to many Pakeha ways. The Councils, and their constables (based at *marae*, the meeting places for Maori communities), also assisted regular police in their efforts to impose certain types of (Pakeha) standards upon tribal Maori. For Maori, none the less, the Councils – some of which lasted in various forms until the Second World War – were a chance to exercise a degree of *rangatiratanga*, however constrained. Their constables assisted with chiefly control, as well as helping impose certain state-approved modes of behaviour and discipline upon those who transgressed. In effect, Maori attempted to reappropriate the Maori organisational forms that the state had appropriated.

Another indirect control regime was attempted under the Maori Social and Economic Advancement Act of 1945. As in the past, the Crown's motivations were essentially to control, and put to official use, Maori autonomist aspirations. These had been heightened by devolved powers given the Maori War Effort Organisation, an official body which had been established to coordinate and channel the spontaneous Maori contribution to New Zealand's role in the Second World War. However, the 1945 Act clawed back much of the wartime authority that tribes had obtained. Under its Maori Welfare Organisation (MWO), which was responsible to the department controlling Maori affairs, tribal authorities could, however, authorise unpaid Wardens to carry out policing duties. The Crown wanted, in particular, to utilise insider knowledge and skills to suppress excessive drinking and disorder among Maori, a scheme which had worked in prewar Rotorua (Dunstall, 1999: 210–11).

As before, Maori leadership found a state-established system useful, and the Wardens were soon being used by tribal committees for many and varied purposes, including a number not covered by the Act. Within five years, tribal organisations in all areas of the country had opted into the MWO system. It became even more useful – for both Maori and the government – when urban migration picked up speed, and traditional tribal mechanisms of informal control found it difficult to survive the massive transfer of Maori population to the cities.

In urban spaces, in effect, Maori reconstituted their approach to *rangatiratanga*. This was sometimes in state-assisted ways which included mechanisms of indirect control. Politicians and officials saw urbanisation as an opportunity to finally decollectivise and assimilate Maori. But to their chagrin, the adaptation of *rangatiratanga* to the cities was often done in ways which complemented, rather than superseded, identification with rural *marae* and tribal/collective organisational forms. For Maori, the institutions of the 1945 Act and its successor legislation were, among other things, ways of obtaining state assistance for resisting full assimilation.

After participant observation among Maori Wardens, Augie Fleras suggested in 1980 that, while the state saw Wardens as social controllers of their own people, Maori communities saw them as devices for 'control and self-determination over those activities of importance to them'. Moreover, the Warden system reflected the increasing importance of women in Maori social and political life. Women appointees were in effect following up the success of female Maori welfare officers and the Maori Women's Welfare League, institutions seen by postwar governments as modes of indirect control – but viewed differently by Maori.

By the time of Fleras' observations, the socio-racial climate was changing enormously as a result of the Maori Renaissance. Official assimilationist aims were coming to be replaced by policies which reflected a bicultural discourse. Despite allegations of their being anachronistic, Maori Wardens still operate today because they are useful for both parties to that discourse. They are, for example, engaged by tribes to regulate *hui* (tribal gatherings), and they assist regular police in many ways. They can be seen as embodying both Maori *rangatiratanga* and a state response to it that aims simultaneously at utilising it and defusing its full expression.

As with all indirect control regimes, the fact that the very existence of Wardens depends on the support of the state – mediated from the early 1960s through the New Zealand Maori Council, the body formally representing all Maoridom – makes their role and future inherently problematic. When official efforts were made to abolish Wardens in the 1970s, on grounds that they were unacceptably separatist in a modern society, Maori leaders fought and won the battle – with the New Zealand Police being among their greatest supporters. However compromised the system might be by its association with the state, Maori organisations generally see it as a reflection of *rangatiratanga* – however much in need of reform – and so remain resistant to its removal (Fleras, 1980a; Fleras, 1980b; Te Puni Kokiri/Ministry of Maori Development, 1999).

Both the specialist knowledge of Maori police and their use in indirect control emphasise purposes related to potential or actual coercion. But the state has always had a third use for such personnel among its strategies for imposing or maintaining social conditions defined as order and regularity – that of being role models. Wardens, for example, were by the 1990s seen by some authorities as role models in a post-assimilation world – as an expression of biculturalism. Before the impact of the Maori Renaissance, however, the role model function of Maori policing was intended to be a way of assisting subjugation and assimilation.

After the founding of the colony, Maori police were expected to learn the ways and means of civilisation, and to pass these on to their people by dint of example. George Grey had become Governor in 1845 not only because of his military prowess, but also because he was considered an expert at ways of rapidly assimilating indigenous people. 'Civilising' by example, especially through young Maori leaders Europeanised by membership of police forces, was a key element in his plans. On arrival, Grey phased out the Pakeha-based Police Magistracy forces and established mixed race, paramilitary forces. Their Maori components had expert (including fighting) knowledge and skills to contribute. But they also had the task, especially after leaving the forces, of being key conduits for the 'civilising mission'. Their job, once they were programmed, was to turn the 'rude savage into the dutiful subject' – one who exhibited such characteristics as thrift, self discipline and regularity. This would be done through 'the skilful use of those powers which educated men possess over the wild or half-civilised savage'. Once back in their homelands, after their stint as police, they would be exemplars of good, Pakeha-type behaviour, some of them working as policing agents in indirect control regimes (Hill, 1986: ch. 4; Hill, 2003: 12).

Acting as exemplary conduits for civilised behaviour was also a requirement of Maori in successive state-based policing organisations: the Wardens and *karere* of the official *runanga* forces from the 1860s; Maori in specialist paramilitary police units like the Colonial Defence Force established in 1862, for which it was said that there would be 'no pains spared to imbue them with the views of the Government' (Hill, 2003: 12); Maori in the Armed (later, New Zealand) Constabulary Force; and the Native Constables in the Native Department and then (after 1882) the Police. By the later nineteenth century, regular police were also increasingly expected to be good-citizen role models. In effect, the handful of Maori police working from that time for the state had a parallel exemplary function among their own people. So too did the police of the various indirect control systems – although, as we have seen, they could also act as conduits for Maori leaders' attempts to retain and enhance *rangatiratanga*.

Participation in official social control mechanisms had helped Maori gain many benefits from the material and non-material culture of the Pakeha, while at the same time helping affirm their own *rangatiratanga*. Some Maori organisations combined both aspects by establishing their own internal policing mechanisms which adopted some European forms. Most leading, and many minor, political resistance movements and adjustment religions of the nineteenth century reflected this in their own police – the *pirihimana* of Ringatu, for example, or the *marae* police of Kotahitanga, or the *watene* of Kingitanga. And so too did major twentieth-century manifestations of *rangatiratanga*, such as the Ratana movement, with its *katipa*, who were originally headed by an Irish 'Chief of Police'. Often, local *marae* or community *komiti* (committees) would have their own laws and forms of policing, although an increasing amount of state intervention into Maori life from the 1920s made inroads into this practice.

On the surface, governments would not sanction the continuation or establishment of policing functions by non-state bodies. But in practice the state police and other authorities often tacitly encouraged, or at least tolerated, such dual control mechanisms in the interests of public order. In imposing the rules of their *rangatiratanga*, such unofficial police sometimes fell foul of the state police, especially when their attempts at coercion greatly exceeded their legal powers and promoted disorder rather than order – as with instances of *katipa* trying to impose discipline on Ratana Church members in the 1930s and 1940s (Dunstall, 1999: 210, 433). Usually, however, as was normal in the interaction between the state and Maori organisations, indigenous authorities and state agencies would negotiate to find a modus vivendi that accommodated (albeit temporarily) both *rangatiratanga* and official requirements.

We have discussed the policing intentions, motivations and processes of the two key parties engaged in the *rangatiratanga* discourse. Of course things did not always work out as planned. Governor Grey greatly exaggerated when he reported back to London in 1849 that 'probably no measure has been so totally successful in its results' as the civilising mission experiment with the chiefly policemen. It was hard to 'civilise' Maori chiefs when the policeman was 'constantly being called a nigger and a blackfellow to his face, and viewed as an inferior being' by the populace. Given that their white mentors in the forces were often rough and drunken labourers or tradespeople, some of the *rangatira* (chiefly) police succumbed to their ways: 'wending their way home to instruct their initiated brethren in the interior', not in the civilised virtues but instead in 'unmixed, unmitigated evil' (Hill, 1986: 268, 374; Hill, 2003: 13).

Some Maori policemen experienced great inner turmoil over their difficult role in mediating between two worlds – trying to respect tribal wishes that they work on behalf of autonomy, and at the same time spearheading inroads into that autonomy. Sergeant Karira of the Taranaki Native Police (his name was, suggestively, a transliteration of Creed) had devoted years to this dual cause. When he died in 1867, worn out, the European doctors said it was because of measles. But on his deathbed he had insisted that a devilish monster, a *ngarara*, had fastened upon his throat and would not desist until he expired – a customary punishment for violating tribal *tapu* laws (Hill, 1990: 217–18).

Early on, moreover, Maori police saw that however good they were at policing, and however incompetent their Pakeha colleagues might be, a hierarchy prevailed that always put white above brown. From this some took back a message that the much vaunted policy of 'amalgamation' of the races was likely to be entirely on Pakeha terms, and that the Crown really aimed at 'the assertion and preservation of British authority' – and imposing the cultural and other baggage that came with it. This message, taken home by men intended to be subverters of *rangatiratanga*, could strengthen Maori resolve to cling to it. Chiefly policemen might also use the western policing knowledge they had picked up to help supplement Maori social control measures.

On the other hand, 'failure' is a relative concept amid the complexities of the colonial frontier. Appropriation by Maori communities of British policing techniques might suit the colonisers well enough. Western policing skills could help chiefs impose forms of order that, while not ideal from the colonial government's perspective, helped impose preconditions for the penetration of trade and settlement. Alongside supporting customary law, Europeanised Maori police might well introduce *some* Pakeha ways that would assist the quest of successive governments for faster movement towards assimilation. In ongoing and often localised sets of negotiations, then, the two sides would interact to maximise their own benefits.

To conclude, since 1840 Crown–Maori relations have been fundamentally characterised, on the Maori side, by the struggle to retain or promote tribal or other forms of politico-cultural autonomy or self-determination. When two major resistance prophets died in 1907, the year that colonial status was cast aside, the government was convinced yet again that the quest for Maori self-determination had ended, especially since Maori had little land left and most now spoke English (Hill, 1991: 67). Yet, as much after as before 1907, Maori sought ways of revitalising *rangatiratanga*. State responses continued to involve varied agencies of policing in attempts to crush and/or appropriate strong expressions of *rangatiratanga*. In turn, Maori methods included reappropriating state appropriations of Maori organisational dynamism.

Eventually, towards the end of the twentieth century, successive governments came to acknowledge the need to forge some kind of partnership with Maori, and the assimilation discourse was abandoned in favour of a bicultural one. But in the first years of the new millennium the Crown was still far from fully acknowledging *rangatiratanga*, and the parliamentary Opposition was explicitly rejecting the concept of partnership between the Crown and Maori: endemic problems continued between the two parties to the Treaty of Waitangi. Accordingly, the relationship between police and Maori, always particularly complex, remained problematic.

References

Alves, D. *The Maori and the Crown: An Indigenous People's Struggle For Self-Determination*. Greenwood Press, 1999.

Ausubel, D. *The Fern and the Tiki*. Angus & Robertson, 1960.

Belich, J. *The New Zealand Wars and the Victorian Interpretation of Racial Conflict*. Auckland University Press, 1986.

Binney, J., Chaplin, G. and Wallace, C. *Mihaia: The Prophet Rua Kenana and His Community at Maungapohatu*. Oxford University Press, 1979.

Boenisch-Brednich, B. and Hill, R. S. 'Biculturalism in New Zealand/Aotearoa', in Csukas, G., Kiss, R., Kristof, I., Nagy, I. and Zsuzsa, S. (eds), *Times, Places, Passages: Ethnological Approaches in the New Millennium*. Budapest, 2004.

Byrnes, G. *The Waitangi Tribunal and New Zealand History*. Oxford University Press, 2004.

Cox, L. *Kotahitanga: The Search for Maori Political Unity*. Oxford University Press, 1993.

Dunstall, G. *A Policeman's Paradise? Policing a Stable Society 1918–1945*. Dunmore Press/Historical Branch, Department of Internal Affairs, Wellington, 1999.

Durie, M. *Te Mana, Te Kawanatanga: The Politics of Maori Self-Determination*. Oxford University Press, 1998.

Fleras, A. 'A Descriptive Analysis of Maori Wardens in the Historical and Contemporary Context of New Zealand Society', PhD thesis, Victoria University of Wellington, 1980a.

Fleras, A. *From Village Runanga to the New Zealand Maori Wardens' Association: A Historical Development of Maori Wardens*. Maori Studies Section, Department of Anthropology and Maori, Victoria University of Wellington, 1980b.

Head, L. 'The pursuit of modernity in Maori society', in Sharp, A. and McHugh, P. (eds), *Histories, Power and Loss: Uses of the Past – A New Zealand Commentary*. Bridget Williams Books, 2001.

Hill, R. S. *Autonomy and Authority: Rangatiratanga and the Crown in Twentieth Century New Zealand: An Overview*. Crown Forestry Rental Trust, Wellington, 2000.

Hill, R. S. *Introducing Policing into the Rangatiratanga Discourse: An Historical Overview of the Role of Maori Police Personnel*. Treaty of Waitangi Research Unit, Victoria University of Wellington, 2003.

Hill, R. S. 'Karira', in Oliver, W. H. (ed.), *Dictionary of New Zealand Biography*, vol 1. Allen & Unwin/Department of Internal Affairs, 1990.

Hill, R. S. 'Maori policing in nineteenth century New Zealand', *Archifacts*, 2, 1985, pp. 54–60.

Hill, R. S. *Policing the Colonial Frontier: The Theory and Practice of Coercive Social and Racial Control in New Zealand, 1767–1867*. Historical Branch, Department of Internal Affairs, Wellington, 1986.

Hill, R. S. *State Authority, Indigenous Autonomy: Crown–Maori Relations in New Zealand/Aotearoa, 1900–1950*. Victoria University Press, 2004.

Hill, R. S. *The Colonial Frontier Tamed: New Zealand Policing in Transition, 1867–1886*. Historical Branch, Department of Internal Affairs, Wellington, 1989.

Hill, R. S. *The Iron Hand in the Velvet Glove: The Modernisation of Policing in New Zealand 1886–1917*. Historical Branch, Department of Internal Affairs, Wellington, 1995.

Hill, R. S. 'The policing of colonial New Zealand: from informal to formal control, 1840–1907', in Anderson, D. and Killingray, D. (eds), *Policing the Empire: Government, Authority and Control, 1780–1940*. Manchester University Press, 1991.

Hill, R. S. and O'Malley, V. *The Maori Quest for Rangatiratanga/Autonomy, 1840–2000*. Treaty of Waitangi Research Unit, Victoria University of Wellington 2000.

Kersey, H. A. Jr. 'Opening a discourse on race relations in New Zealand: "The Fern and the Tiki" revisited', *Journal of New Zealand Studies*, October 2002, pp. 1–18.

Lange, R. *A Limited Measure of Local Self-Government: Maori Councils, 1900–1920*. Treaty of Waitangi: Research Unit, Victoria University of Wellington, 2004.

O'Malley, V. *Agents of Autonomy: Maori Committees in the Nineteenth Century*. Huia Publishers, 1998.

Orange, C. *The Treaty of Waitangi*, Allen & Unwin/Port Nicholson Press, 1987.

Pratt, J., *Punishment in a Perfect Society: The New Zealand Penal System 1840–1939*. Victoria University Press, 1992.

Te Puni Kokiri/Ministry of Maori Development, *Discussion Paper on the Review of the Maori Community Development Act 1962*. Ministry of Maori Development, Wellington, 1999.

Veracini, L. *Negotiating A Bicultural Past: An Historiographical 'Revolution' in 1980s Aotearoa/New Zealand*. Treaty of Waitangi Research Unit, Victoria University of Wellington, 2001.

Waitangi Tribunal, *The Taranaki Report: Kaupapa Tuatahi*. GP Publications, 1996.

Walker, R. *Ka Whawhai Tonu Matou: Struggle Without End*. Penguin, 1990.

Ward, A. 'The origins of the Anglo-Maori wars: a reconsideration', *New Zealand Journal of History*, 1, 2, 1967, pp. 148–70.

Ward, A. *A Show of Justice: Racial 'Amalgamation' in Nineteenth Century New Zealand*. Auckland University Press, 1995.

Wards, I. *The Shadow of the Land: A Study of British Policy and Racial Conflict in New Zealand, 1832–1852*. Historical Publications Branch, Department of Internal Affairs, Wellington, 1968.

Webster, P. *Rua and the Maori Millennium*, Price Milburn for Victoria University Press, 1979.

Chapter 14

'To make the precedent fit the crime': British legal responses to sati in early nineteenth-century north India

Jane Buckingham

Singha argues that from the earliest period of East India Company rule, the British in India functioned from a novel conception of 'sovereign right' (Singha, 1998: viii), a concept which 'negated the legitimacy of all other authorities in the exercise of force and violence in public life' (Singha, 1993: 181). Singha's assertion assumes that the colonial state saw itself as possessing sole legitimate authority over the life and death of its subjects. The question remains, however: who truly held jurisdiction over the indigenous body in the early colonial context – the Indian subject, the indigenous community or the state?

Here the validity of Singha's concept of sovereign right is assessed by considering how the British regulated forms of suicide customarily performed by widows and those suffering from intractable leprosy. I argue that until at least the establishment of the Indian Law Commission in 1834 to formalise the complex of British and Indian legal systems into a single Indian Penal Code (Smith, 1958: 526) the British colonial conception of 'sovereign right' was conservative rather than novel. The early colonial state recognised the traditional right of individuals to take their own life in certain circumstances. In developing legal control, the British in India attempted to follow closely the precedents established by *Brahmanic* tradition and those set by the Indian potentates – including the historical right of a sovereign power to control suicide.

Degree of British intervention in Indian criminal law

The degree to which the British adopted and intentionally transformed the pre-existing systems of Indian law is debatable. The East India Company felt its way in administrative and legal terms during the early nineteenth century. In terms of personal law, the avowed intention of the colonial state was to administer Hindu law to Hindus and Islamic law to the Muslims, reserving English law for the British and Company servants in India. The prevailing Islamic law of the Mughal sovereign was to be the basis of colonial criminal law. However, initial efforts to preserve the existing Islamic models of criminal law resulted in elevation and ossification of the textual legal tradition (Fisch, 1983: 5–7; Derrett, 1999: 225–320). Islamic customary law, hitherto applied by the Mughal emperors in conjunction with the *sharia*, was not adopted but only the ideal, theological and textual form of *sharia*. British procedural changes quickly modified the textual criminal law so that by 1817 the Islamic law had lost its influence. In many ways, Islamic law was lost the minute the British took it up. Well before the the Indian Penal Code (Act 45 of 1860) signalled a deliberate departure from Mughal legal precedent and embodied the emerging utilitarian-influenced values of the English penal system (Sen, 2000: 3–6), British adoption of Islamic law was – as it had been with the Hindu civil law – transformative rather than conservative (Fisch, 1983: 22–4).

By moving into the administration of criminal law at the close of the eighteenth century, the British symbolically displaced the Mughal emperor's right as ruler over the life and death of his subjects. Actual legal control was, however, never complete and was slow and difficult to implement. Colonial legal intervention in India only began to assume a coherent form with the promulgation of the 1860 Indian Penal Code (Fisch, 1983: 3–5).

Historiography of British legal intervention

Debate over the degree of British intervention in traditional Indian legal systems focuses on the transformation of civil law. However, the character-istics of the change are of equal relevance to both civil and criminal law. Following Sir Henry Maine's mid-nineteenth-century writings on Indian law, B. S. Cohn argues broadly for a transition from 'status' to 'contract' in Indian legal culture as the colonial power sought to establish procedures for dispute settlement and management of rights and obligations involved in property, individual, group and state relations (Cohn, 1990: 463). According to Cohn, the British-prompted transition in Indian law was not a coherent, clearly focused and inexorable movement but an ad hoc, unplanned and haphazard process. Despite their efforts, the British in India did not understand Indian culture as well as they believed, and their application of law was determined more by misunderstanding and pragmatism than any grand plan (Cohn, 1990: 479).

Focusing on the engagement of utilitarian ideals with Indian criminal law, K. K. Raman similarly argues for a limited British legal intervention. From the late eighteenth century, Benthamite legal reformers were convinced that the best means of reforming British society was by a radical restructuring of its legal system on 'rational' lines. When considered for application in Indian society, however, Bentham recommended that utilitarian conceptions of law be moderated according to the structures of the local culture. More than Cohn, Raman sees a more conscious and exact usage of the Indian legal idiom, and a more deliberate matching of utilitarian ideals to local Indian legal conditions, to ensure the legitimisation of British rule (Raman, 1994: 739–40). Representative of this restrained colonial response to indigenous legal culture is the persistence until 1834 of Persian as the language of court and administration (Smith, 1958: 649), the employment of Muslim legal advisers and the continued dependence, in some areas, on indigenous methods of administering justice and indigenous 'terms of reference' for the practice of the courts and judiciary (Raman, 1994: 790–1).

Early nineteenth-century Benthamites in India did not slavishly follow his model. They understood that the reform of law into a secular, rational and universal system was practically unachievable in India. Even James Mill who in the mid-nineteenth century had the opportunity to 'write upon the Indians as upon a blank slate' did not see his vision fulfilled (Raman, 1994: 757). Increasingly, from the mid-1830s, British adminis-trators were encouraged to pursue a scientific jurisprudence, 'abstract, universal, and secular in outlook' (Raman, 1994: 758). Yet their approach was pragmatic; they had no viable alternative to the continuity of many aspects of existing Indian law. Most legal disputes were resolved by customary means well beyond British reach. Even if the colonial administrators had wished to staff the legal system entirely with Company recruits, the Company could not afford such a policy (Raman, 1994: 746).

Novelty and completeness of British sovereignty

By contrast with Raman, Singha sees a far greater degree of British legal intervention in Indian life, claiming that British rule in India was qualitatively different from that of previous imperial states. Like Raman, she recognises the Company's linkage of the symbols of Mughal sovereign authority with its own emergent state power, thereby expressing legal continuities between the two regimes (Singha, 1998: 35; Raman, 1994: 790). Even so, Singha sees the British colonial displacement of Mughal legal authority as part of the unique usurpation of traditional patterns of rulership by the colonial intruders (Singha, 1998: x). Yet the British followed not only European but Mughal practice in supplanting the existing criminal law as an adjunct and aid to consolidating power (Fisch, 1983: 1–2, 5). Such appropriation of criminal legal power, with its attendant control over the life and death of the subject, was typical of any new regime, being regarded as necessary symbolically and for the maintenance of order (Fisch, 1983: 86, 122–5). Even Macaulay, who was confident of the British colonial right to assume legal control in India, asserted this right in terms of precedent. Implementing British criminal legal authority was understood as the duty of British conquerors as it had been the right of the conquerors who preceded them (Sen, 2000: 4).

Sen concurs with Singha's argument for 'novelty', contrasting colonial criminal justice with that practised in the eighteenth-century Maratha state. Drawing on Guha's work, Sen notes that the eighteenth-century rulers of the Maratha state did not reserve for themselves a monopoly on the 'right to punish' – possibly because their claims to sovereignty had always to accommodate individuals and groups who held substantial political power and considerable local autonomy and only temporarily fell under Hindu Maratha jurisdiction (Guha, 1995: 101–26; Sen, 2000: 3). The Maratha state either did not attempt or was not able to exert absolute centralised power over its subjects, but had always to recognise other political powers in order to remain 'sovereign' (Guha, 1995: 106–7; Sen, 2000: 7). With Singha, Sen sees, in the formation and application of law during the British period, a movement gaining momentum from the 1830s away from the pre-colonial state practices of `unpredictable intervention and shared jurisdiction' and towards insistence upon 'a monopoly of punitive authority' (Sen, 2000: 3).

While the Maratha rulers exercised a far from complete 'sovereign right' over their subjects, the evidence and arguments offered by Guha and Sen in their analyses suggest that the incompleteness of the Maratha state's 'sovereign right' was as much a matter of its limited power as respect for traditional forms of authority (Guha, 1995: 126; Sen, 2000: 3). In direct violation of traditional *Brahmanic* ritual authority and *shastric* prohibition of such violence against Brahmins by the state, the Maratha king Sambhaji executed Brahmins who threatened his assumption of the throne (Guha, 1995: 104). The distinction between British colonial authority and the Maratha state appears to have had little to do with a 'novel' British disregard for 'traditional forms' of punitive authority; instead it reflected the greater security of the colonial state. Able to gain power through military force and legitimacy through links with the long-established Mughal empire, the British were less susceptible than the Marathas to threats from local claimants to authority.

Focusing primarily on the legal history of Bengal, Singha represents the Company's degree of legal intervention in Indian life as extreme, and based on a novel conception of 'sovereign right' which 'negated the legitimacy of all other authorities in the exercise of force and violence in public life' (Singha, 1993: 181). She sees the exercise of this sense of 'right' as clearly evident in the British colonial legal response to traditional forms of assisted suicide, particularly the practice of *sati*, self-immolation by Hindu widows, and, to a lesser extent, of *samadh*, burial alive (Singha, 2000: 81–3).

Indigenous tradition of suicide – individual sovereignty

Whether wielded by the individual or the state, corporeal power is rarely if ever complete. In early nineteenth-century Hindu culture, suicide offered a legitimate alternative to a life of misery and social and ritual abandonment for those placed at the margins of society by widowhood or illness. Suicide was perceived by practitioners as a means of ending present suffering and a response to the ritual consequences of their condition, with implications for themselves and their family.

Whether or not a person could take their own life was as important an issue in indigenous *shastric* tradition as in British law. British reluctance to allow suicide among Indian subjects was not novel but consistent with *Brahmanic* opposition to self-destruction. Neither Hindu law-makers nor the early British state recognised suicide as an individual's right in other than exceptional circumstances. In the *Dharmasastra*, suicide was almost completely prohibited. It was rarely permitted as an act of individual authority over the body.

The *Brahmanic* position assumed a higher sovereignty over both flesh and spirit. Individual assumption of bodily autonomy had powerful ritual and religious consequences and was severely punished. Such an act was fundamentally a violation of *dharma*, duty or order, a breach of the fabric of community life. The *Brahmanic* law giver Manu, whose work was encoded in about the first century AD, refused funeral rites to assist the spirit of suicides in the after life, as did the *Vasisthadharmasutra* which prescribed in addition a 'penance' for even considering the action. Yama, emphasising the disruption of ritual authority inherent in suicide, argued that the

193

corpse of the suicide should be defiled (Sax, 1992: 203). Taking one's own life was not perceived as an individual's action in isolation. It was not only an action against personal *dharma* but was also construed as a fault in the fabric of Indian society and ritual.

Maintaining its authority over the ritual welfare of its adherents, the *Dharmasastra* prohibited suicide out of remorse, jealousy and such 'negative' states of mind. In certain circumstances, however, suicide was approved. Reflecting the essential concern of the *Dharmasastra* to preserve caste hierarchy, suicide was permitted for someone who had performed a heinous crime such as killing a Brahman. *Jauhar* mass suicide was permitted to preserve, for example, the honour of rajput women who would otherwise be defiled by the Mughal armies. (Bilimoria, 1995: note 10; Bayly, 1981: 174). In the *Dharmasastra*, suicide was also sanctioned, particularly for those who because of age or infirmity were no longer able to perform their religious duties (Sax, 1992: 203–5, 208). Looking outside the *shastras*, the pinnacle of Jain ascetic ideals was self-starvation to death (Babb, 1996: 2, 60). *Brahmanic* culture thus accepted the practice of suicide under certain conditions which the British similarly countenanced.

Brahmanic tradition also accepted forms of suicide which could be used to protect *Brahmanic* power. Suicide could be practised by someone with few economic or physical resources as a way of asserting power over another in redressing a grievance. The custom of *dharna* – according to which a person refused to eat and cast themselves on the threshold of another from whom they sought redress – could include the intention to fast to the death. Brahmins and ascetics could and did use such techniques of self-violence to great effect. As the highest in ritual status, suicide by such people posed a dramatic rending of *dharna* – the proper order of life. Suicide could be used against a transgressor, the bad karma of the Brahmin's death being transferred onto the person who had caused offence. This had dire consequences for the recipient since there was no expiation for the blood of a Brahman (Singha, 1993: 191) and the consequent rebirth was dire; to become 'a worm, dwelling in ordure for 60,000 years' was just one option (cited in Bayly, 1981: 171).

Early British attempts to control suicide as an act against the state

Like the Brahmin law-givers the British allowed suicide in some circumstances but opposed those forms which presented a direct challenge to their authority. The most obvious instance was Indian use of suicide to gain control over some aspect of colonial power relations. Long before Gandhi used the threat of fasting to the death in an effort to control British policy (Smith, 1958: 809), Indian subjects used the technique to evade the processes of British judicial and revenue systems. Where there was a conflict of interest between British maintenance of colonial authority and traditional practices of suicide, any acceptance of *Brahmanic* or customary precedent was put aside.

The British found Indian use of suicide in legal and administrative contexts frustrating and distressing, particularly when directed against revenue collectors and thereby hitting the East India Company's hip pocket (Singha, 1993: 190–1). J. Duncan, Resident in Benares, described the people of the region as 'addicted to suicide' in a letter to the Governor General in Council, Cornwallis, dated 17 December 1788 (*British Parliamentary Papers* (BPP), 1821 (749) XVII: 301). To curb the practice, he threatened the refusal of cremation to Hindus and of burial to Moslems who committed suicide in the process of judicial or revenue proceedings (Singha, 1993: notes 85, 87). Such refusals were a deterrent: the sufferers would be denied their rightful after-life and their families would endure not only emotional trauma but, in the Hindu tradition, would suffer ritual pollution from the incomplete disposal of the body.

Though in this period the policies of tolerance and respect for Indian tradition championed by the 'Orientalists' still held sway, Duncan found little to recommend or to justify preserving what he perceived among Indians to be a whimsical approach to life and death (Bayly, 1981: 171). Yet the gap between the state's theoretical and actual 'sovereign' power over the body was great. Duncan's threat was a desperate departure from the early British colonial policy of non-interference in Indian custom and religion (Cassels, 1965: 77). It reflected a tension between official respect for Indian custom and religion, grudgingly shared by Duncan, and the assumption that the sovereign state had a right of control over their subjects in life and death. Despite an increasingly secular conceptualisation of suicide in England (MacDonald, 1986: 76), Duncan's attitude reflected the persistence of a British Christian sense of suicide as against Nature and a sin against God, the ultimate abrogation of divine sovereignty over life and death (Bayly, 1981: 172). Duncan's reaction was among the earliest of British attempts to control Indian ritual and manipulative suicide and followed the practice of late medieval Christendom in refusing burial to those who inappropriately claimed sovereign right over life (Finucane, 1981: 56).

The later British legal response to *sati* and *samadh* reflected the increasing ambiguity of the British position. While reluctant to interfere in custom and religion, the British, partly due to missionary pressure, began to assume responsibility by the 1820s over life and death in contexts previously governed by family and caste concerns (Bayly, 1981: 171). In

1829, the colonial authority enacted legislation regarding *sati*, despite 'orthodox' *Brahmanic* opposition to the interference (Mukhopadhyay, 1958: 39–40). As in so many 'traditional' areas of family and community regulation, however, the legislation proved a far less effective deterrent than the British had hoped. Though Singha sees particularly in the British legal response to *sati* the exercise of a 'novel conception of sovereign right', the authorities strove to follow both *Brahmanic* and royal precedent rather than destabilise their nascent power with novel assertions.

British colonial assumption of *Brahmanic* legal authority

Assisted suicide, particularly as practised in the customary forms of *sati* and *samadh*, fitted uneasily into the developing British criminal law. Despite some instances of *sati* in South India (BPP, 1824 (443) XXIII: 371), neither *sati* nor *samadh* were common there and the British debates on the status of each practice and its practitioners developed principally through the deliberations of the North West Provinces, Bengal and Bombay governments. Colonial legislators could easily classify death by one's own hand as 'suicide'. However, these forms of suicide, which typically required assistance in the preparation of the fire or the digging and filling of pits, and occasionally a combination of fire and pit, could accommodate the concept of 'homicide'. Inevitably the British discussion over whether the individual had a sovereign right to take her or his own life was complicated by the further conviction that those assisting were not only parties to a suicide but possibly to murder.

At every level of colonial legal authority, the British took scrupulous, if sometimes inept, care to comply with what were perceived to be the *shastric* injunctions governing the appropriate taking of life according to Hindu tradition. Cooperating with *Brahmanic* court authorities, British legal authorities took on the *Brahmanic* role of interpreting and defending *shastric dharma* and, in so doing, affirmed the power of the *shastra* as a traditional authority within the framework of Islamic criminal law as bequeathed by the Mughal rulers.

The strength of *Brahmanic* precedent in guiding policy and actions at the higher levels of legal authority is evident in the attention given to precedent in a report of the *Nizamat Adawlut* (Supreme Criminal Court) to the Governor General in Council, responding to the urging by E. Watson, Fourth Judge, Calcutta Court of Circuit, for British suppression of *sati* and other 'murderous practices'. In his report on the cases of *sati* in the Calcutta Division, Watson argued that:

There is as little justification for a woman to burn herself with the remains of her deceased husband, as for a *raujkoomor* to destroy his daughters at their birth; burying alive for the leprosy, [sic] where the party is desirous to die; human sacrifices at *Saugor*; putting sorcerers to death, or killing a human creature by any other means, without justification or excuse – all of which are expressly made capital offences by the Regulations.

He continued that: 'The killing in all these instances (especially that contained in section 3, Regulation 8, 1799, where the desire of the party slain will not justify the killer)' were practices equivalent to *sati* in terms of 'erroneous prejudice and superstition, and perhaps of religion'. Therefore, since 'we do not find that the punishment of death, denounced against these crimes, has at all been considered by the people as an infringement of that complete toleration, in matters of religion, which it has been a fundamental principle of the British government to allow', Watson argued, 'there can be no doubt that the practice of suttee might be as easily checked and prevented, throughout the British territories, as any of the other murderous practices above referred to' (BPP, 1821 (749) XVIII: 393).

The *Nizamat Adawlut* was not convinced by Watson's claims, contending that while the stated forms of 'killing' appeared equivalent in Watson's eyes, there were clear differences between *sati* as a form of 'suicide' and the other forms of 'killing' which were essentially instances of 'murder'. Further, and this was the crux of the *Nizamat Adawlut*'s reluctance to endorse Watson's view, indigenous precedent clearly distinguished between *sati* and the other forms of 'killing' cited. The Court advised the Governor General in Council that:

Independently of the obvious distinction between the stated suicide of a woman burning herself or causing herself to be burnt, and the murder of another person, as in the case of a *raujkoomar*'s destroying his daughter, the sacrifice of children at *Saugor*, and putting to death persons supposed to be leprous, Mr Watson appears to have lost sight of the material circumstance, that in all these instances homicide, before it was declared murder by the Regulations, had no sanction of law either Hindoo or Mahommedan; whereas the burning of a Hindoo widow, with the body of her deceased husband, has the express sanction of the authorities, which are held sacred by the women who devote themselves as well as by the Brahmins and others who assist them in their voluntary sacrifice. (BPP, 1821 (749) XVIII: 403)

The *Nizamat Adawlut* noted that, according to the specific *shastric* authorities cited in their report (BPP, 1821 (749) XVIII: 419–20), the distinction of *sati* as a form of suicide was extended in indigenous tradition to assisted suicide of leprosy sufferers. In assuming *Brahmanic* authority in the application of *shastric* notions of who had the right to die, the *Nizamat Adawlut*, unchecked by the Governor in Council, was guided principally by the authority of *shastric* precedent.

Maratha precedent in the Bombay presidency

For regional governments, local royal precedent came into play. In the Bombay presidency, colonial responses to *sati* were guided by British understanding of Maratha sovereign authority. Company authorities believed that the precedent of 'sovereign right' had been established by the Maratha rulers and that, with regard to *sati* at least, the Marathas' exercise of this right was absolute. In their response to *sati* the Bombay government followed the Maratha precedent, as they understood it to be, with great caution and scrupulous attention to the dictates of local law and custom (BPP, 1824 (443) XXIII: 366, 368).

On 24 February 1822 the Collector and Magistrate for the Southern Concan, J. J. Sparrow, reported an 'illegal' case of *sati* by a Brahmin woman in the Rutnagerry Taluk. The *sati* had gone ahead, despite the interference and prohibition of the *sirkumaviesdar*, and was declared to be 'contrary to both the letter and the spirit of the Shaster, as handed down and inter-preted to us in the *bewastas* of the pundits of the *Sudder Dewanny Adawlut* at Fort William'. It was classed by the British as 'illegal' on the grounds of being practised by a Brahmin widow with the bones of her deceased husband rather than on his funeral pyre and because the required care arranged for the widow's child, who was under three years of age, was deemed inadequate. As the Magistrate for the region, Sparrow sought guidance from the Bombay government, particularly as to whether he should prosecute those involved in assisting in the *sati* or allow the breach of Anglo-Brahmannic law to go unpunished.

Sparrow had no doubt as to the legitimacy of British interference in the practice of *sati*. The Magistrate noted that under the previous Concan governments, '*no suttee* could take place, particularly in the Mahratta states, without the assent of the ruling power, which, according to its discretion, could either forbid or permit the ceremony'. Similarly, since British authorities had maintained this precedent during their occupation of the Concan, 'suttees have occasionally been abandoned through the interposition of our authority'. This precedent meant that it was 'no less the right than the duty of the ruling power to interfere and forbid, and even prevent them' when a *sati* was 'about to be proceeded with, contrary to law'. This 'right', the Magistrate argued, was not only sanctioned by the Bengal Circular Orders of the current British government in India but 'acknowledged by all under the late government'. While Sparrow believed in the appropriateness of British intervention, he was open to a government recommendation that the case be left unpunished, recognising possible merit in withholding judicial might. Perhaps, Sparrow suggested, 'in order to reduce the frequency of this horrid rite, it should be neglected and treated with as little notice as possible' (BPP, 1824 (443) XXIII: 369).

The Bombay government agreed with the Magistrate's understanding of the British sovereign right. It also shared Sparrow's willingness to set aside British concepts of the 'legality' or 'illegality' of a *sati* as detailed in the Circular Orders of 15 October 1818, and not to prosecute the instance of 'illegal' *sati* under discussion because the legitimate exercise of British authority seemed 'highly impolitic'. It was expedient to allow the 'illegal' *sati* to go unpunished rather than risk rousing 'a spirit of discontent, if not of opposition' among its subjects (BPP, 1824 (443) XXIII: 368). On paper at least, the importance of sovereign precedent in the British conceptualisation of 'sovereign right' had been asserted in this instance. Even so, the practice of their Maratha predecessors who had tempered their control over life and death by the need to retain their often precarious hold on power was also affirmed. The colonial government recognised the importance of modifying its own exercise of 'sovereign right' to minimise threats to its authority. Furthermore, the Presidency government had come to 'doubt the policy of the circular orders' issued from Bengal, recognising that significant regional differences existed in the authority of the written, particularly *shastric* tradition. While a British law based on Bengal's *shastric* authorities might be appropriate in that region, it could well be irrelevant for the Hindus of the Deccan. The Bombay government recognised that in some areas custom took precedence over the written law, and in such cases custom should be given the greater authority. Indeed the Bombay government cited Maratha custom regarding *sati* in confirming the Magistrate's action in leaving the case of 'illegal' *sati* unpunished (BPP, 1824 (443) XXIII: 369). In this case, both the government's expressed view of sovereign right and its practice complicate the arguments of Singha and Sen. Rather than being 'novel', the British notion of 'sovereign right' was strongly based in indigenous sovereign, customary and legal precedent. British sovereign practice, in the case of *sati* at least, seems as responsive and variable as that of the rulers who preceded them.

Individual *versus* state control over the life and death of the body

During the early colonial period, British assumption of criminal legal authority brought control over life and death – control over the body of the subject – in theory at least. This control had earlier been held by Hindu kings according to the right of '*danda*', whether *shastric* law was practised conscientiously or not (Guha, 1995: 103), and by the Mughal emperors who, like Hindu kings, held legal power over their people in accordance with their 'sovereign right' as rulers (Fisch, 1983: 19–21). For the British, as much as for the previous Hindu and Muslim rulers, state control over the subject's body – like the individual's perception and autonomy over their own body – was complicated not only by the occasional period of weakness in state power in relation to their subjects' strength (Guha, 1995: 105), but also by the significance of ritual, caste, family and community factors in guiding and even determining individual action. The colonial record indicates far more caution in the British assumption of 'sovereign right' than Singha would suggest. Early British administrators were clearly conscious of Hindu precedent in the practice of corporal and capital punishment and asserted the necessity of not violating the limits placed by local custom on the implementation of judicial control over the body. What distinguished British power was an excessive preoccupation with precedent – sovereign, legal and customary – in legitimising legal intervention in Indian society, rather than a unique interpretation of 'sovereign right'.

References

Babb, L. A. *Absent Lord: Ascetics and Kings in a Jain Ritual Culture*. University of California Press, 1996.

Bayly, C. A. 'From ritual to ceremony: death ritual and society in Hindu North India since 1600', in Whaley, J. (ed.), *Mirrors of Mortality: Studies in the Social History of Death*. Europa, 1981.

Bilimoria, P. 'Legal rulings on suicide in India and implications for the right to die', *Asian Philosophy*, 5, 2, 1995, pp. 159–80.

Cassels, N. G. 'Bentinck: humanitarian and imperialist – the abolition of suttee', *Journal of British Studies*, 5, 1, 1965, pp. 77–87.

Cohn, B. S. 'From Indian status to British contract', in Cohn, B. S. (ed.), *An Anthropologist among the Historians and Other Essays*. Oxford University Press, 1990.

Derrett, J. D. M. *Religion, Law and the State in India*. Oxford University Press, 1999.

Finucane, R. C. 'Sacred corpse, profane carrion: social ideals and death rituals in the later Middle Ages', in Whaley, J. (ed.), *Mirrors of Mortality: Studies in the Social History of Death*. Europa, 1981.

Fisch, J. *Cheap Lives and Dear Limbs: The British Transformation of the Bengal Criminal Law 1769–1817*. Franz Steiner Verlag, 1983.

Guha, S. 'An Indian penal régime: Maharashtra in the eighteenth century', *Past and Present*, 147, May, 1995, pp. 101–26.

MacDonald, M. 'The secularisation of suicide in England 1660–1800', *Past and Present*, 111, 1986, pp. 50–100.

Mani, L. *Contentious Traditions: The Debate on Sati in Colonial India*. University of California Press, 1998.

Mukhopadhyay, A. 'Movement for the abolition of *sati* in Bengal', *Bengal: Past and Present*, 77, 143, 1958, pp. 39–40.

'Papers relating to East Indian Affairs: viz Hindoo Widows, and Voluntary Immolations', 10 July 1821, BPP, 1821 (749) XVIII.

'Papers relating to East India Affairs: viz Copies or Extracts of all Communications and Correspondence Relative to the Burning of Widows on the Funeral Piles of their Husbands, Since the 23d March 1823', BPP, 1824 (443) XXIII.

Parekh, B. *Colonialism, Tradition and Reform: An Analysis of Gandhi's Political Discourse*. Sage, 1989.

Raman, K. K. 'Utilitarianism and the criminal law in colonial India: a study of the practical limits of utilitarian jurisprudence', *Modern Asian Studies*, 28, 4, 1994, pp. 739–91.

Rudolph, L. I. and Rudolph, S. H. *The Modernity of Tradition: Political Development in India*. University of Chicago Press, 1969.

Sax, W. 'Pilgrimage unto death', in Veitch, J. (ed.), *To Strive and Not to Yield*. Department of World Religions, Victoria University of Wellington, 1992.

Sen, S. *Disciplining Punishment: Colonialism and Convict Society in the Andaman Islands*. Oxford University Press, 2000.

Singha, R. 'The privilege of taking life: some "anomalies" in the law of homicide in the Bengal Presidency', *Indian Economic and Social History Review*, 30, 2, 1993, pp. 181–214.

Singha, R. *A Despotism of Law*. Oxford University Press, 1998.

Smith, V. A. *The Oxford History of India*. 3rd edn, ed. Percival Spear, Clarendon Press, 1958.

Chapter 15

'Everyday life' in Boer women's testimonies of the concentration camps of the South African War, 1899–1902

Helen Dampier

This chapter considers the idea of 'everyday life' in relation to Boer women's published testimonies of their experiences in concentration camps during the South African War between October 1899 and May 1902. It examines how 'everyday' experiences were 'forgotten' in favour of a nationalist version of events that represented the camps as places where the British carried out brutal mistreatment and even murder of Boer women and children. The notion of 'everyday life' in a concentration camp may seem anomalous, largely because of what the words 'concentration camp' have come to mean[1] (Stanley and Dampier, 2005, in press). The South African War concentration camps were vastly different in both kind and degree to Nazi camps: central to the concentration system in South Africa was the organisation and regulation rather than the destruction of 'everyday life'. In arguing for the importance of writing 'everyday life' back into the history of the camps, this chapter offers some alternative representations of camp life that depict the routine, domestic activities of the inhabitants and provide a counter to the dominant nationalist account.

War, the camps and women's testimonies

During the South African War between Britain and the Boer Republics, the British military authorities established concentration camps to accommodate Boer women and children rendered homeless by the scorched earth policy used to deprive Boer commandos of food and other resources.[2] By the end of the war, some 22,000 Boer children (particularly those under five) and 5,000 women had died in the camps. Death came mainly from measles, pneumonia, typhoid and enteritis. Such diseases reflected poor sanitation, inappropriate feeding and lack of access to clean water resulting from the hurried and haphazard establishment of the camps rather than deliberate neglect. Deaths in the camps were not the result of an intentional, genocidal project on the part of the British authorities, although this is frequently how they have been represented.

From September 1900, camps were established and administered by the British military who generally lacked the experience and skills needed to accommodate and provision large numbers of women and children before a civil administration[3] took over during 1901. The camps differed widely from one another and changed internally over the course of the war; conditions depended very much on the individual camp superintendent. Inhabitants were mostly accommodated in tents (some camps had tin or 'sod' houses), were provided with basic rations of food and cooking fuel, and sometimes clothing and bedding, although the quantity and quality of this varied.[4] Most camps permitted Boer inhabitants to keep servants, although servants were not always rationed and the number of private servants in the camps overall was small[5] (Stanley, 2004, 2005, in press). Hospitals, schools as well as shops where inhabitants could purchase additional food and other items were set up in each camp. Most had a resident clergyman who conducted church services. Some inhabitants worked either for the camp administration or for other wealthier inhabitants, and occupations included carpentry, gardening, brickmaking, shoemaking, clothes laundering, nursing and sewing. In certain camps, inhabitants received passes to work in nearby towns and, depending on the local military situation, inhabitants could also obtain passes to shop in town, visit the seaside or even attend the theatre and parties[6] (Concentration Camps Commission, 1902: 32). The concentration system was thus based on controlling, regulating and institutionalising everyday life as it sought to organise the several thousand women and children, as well as men, in each camp; it was not aimed at the destruction of the Boer people and their lives.[7]

Nonetheless, the terrible epidemics of illness in the camps, and the sometimes inept way these were dealt with, caused much public controversy in Britain.[8] In 1901 the British government appointed a committee of women, the so-called Ladies Commission, under the leadership of Millicent Garret Fawcett, to investigate camp conditions and the causes of the high death rates, and to recommend any necessary changes. By the time the Ladies Commission Report was published in January 1902, death rates had generally declined, partly because the camps were better established and more efficiently run by officials with greater understanding of what was required to organise them, and partly because the epidemics of measles and pneumonia had peaked in the second half of 1901. Levels and trends of camp death rates varied. Such variations can be attributed partly to the camp officials, but also to the difficult conditions under which they had to work, which included: obtaining suitably qualified medical staff, necessary hospital equipment and supplies and rations of sufficient quality and quantity, as well as maintaining standards of hygiene and cleanliness within the camp. The Commission also focused on Boer women's reluctance to admit their sick children to hospital, and their use of 'Dutch medicines' and home remedies, which included the administering of dog's blood as medicine and painting measles patients' skin with oil paint (Concentration Camps Commission, 1902: 17). Certainly many Boer families were unaccustomed to living in close and cramped quarters with others. Habits that had been relatively harmless on large isolated farms, such as emptying human excreta onto the open veld, could prove fatal in crowded camps where typhoid and enteritis were endemic. Boer children were especially vulnerable to infection because of their previous isolation on remote farms and were worst affected by the measles and pneumonia epidemics of 1901.

Whatever the complex epidemiological causes of the concentration camp deaths, this episode in South African history had a dramatic impact on Boer society, not least because an estimated 10 per cent of its population died in the camps. Significantly, Boer women's testimonies of the camps have been dominated by a strongly anti-British standpoint in seeing them as death camps where the British military deliberately set about trying to murder Boer women and children in a coordinated programme aimed at the eventual genocidal extermination of all Boer people. Such testimonies reveal little of everyday camp life, and focus in an exclusive and ritualised way on the 'murder' of the *volk* or people. This perspective has been uncritically incorporated into much of the historiography of the camps and is closely linked to particular political purposes[9] (for example, Van Bruggen, 1935; Steenkamp, 1941; Otto, 1954; Coetzer, 2000; Raath, 2003).

Immediately following peace in June 1902, women's accounts[10] of their war and camp experiences emerged. Emily Hobhouse's *The Brunt of the War and Where It Fell* (1902) contained brief women's testimonies she had collected during her relief work in the camps and was followed by a spate of other accounts (including Vis, 1902; De La Rey, 1903; Neethling, 1903; Van Helsdingen, 1903; Brandt-Van Warmelo, 1905). From the first, women's camp testimonies were linked to nationalist political purposes. Calls were made for women to remember and record their wartime experiences, as evinced by Johanna Brant-Van Warmelo's entreaty in *Het concentratie-kamp van Irene*: 'O, women of South Africa, write about everything you have suffered at the hands of our mighty oppressors. Nothing may be lost, nothing may be forgotten' (Brandt-Van Warmelo, 1905: 123).

From 1910, Afrikaans magazines such as *Die Brandwag* (*The Sentinel*, 1910) and *Die Huisgenoot* (*The Home Companion*, 1926) were established to popularise the language and encouraged women to contribute accounts of their concentration camp experiences. These focused strongly on the legacy of suffering endured by the Afrikaner people, and helped to generate the notion that this shared experience of suffering and hardship not only unified and strengthened Afrikaners, but also could provide them with a history of solidarity on which to build a sound, independent future state. In the decades following the war, women's published war and camp accounts played an increasingly formative role in the development of an Afrikaans cultural nationalist movement, culminating in a particularly fervent period during the late 1930s when many women's testimonies were re/published in association with the nationalist centenary celebrations of the Great Trek in 1938[11] (Neethling, 1938; Raal, 1938; Postma, 1939; Rabie, 1940). As Stanley has observed, Boer women's testimonies 'served *political purposes* by testifying within the framework of a nationalist political position *contra* the British imperialist one – the authors were all women committed to a nationalist and republican cause' (Stanley, in press).

After the camp accounts published at the end of the war, and the shorter magazine testimonies of the 1910s and 1920s, there were sporadic surges of publication, usually coinciding with moments of political significance and public interest. Many Boer women's camp testimonies or collections of testimonies were published by Nasionale Pers, a group of publishing companies linked to the National Party, and were then promoted, bought and distributed by women's national parties and organisations (for example, S. L. Le Clus's *Lief en Leed*; E. Hobhouse *Tant' Alie of the Transvaal*; letters from Emily Hobhouse to Mrs Steyn, 7 January 1923 and 1 July 1923; VAB, A156).[12] Besides women's published narratives, women's camp testimonies appear in sworn statements, letters to newspapers and private letters, as well as writings presented as journals and camp diaries but apparently written long after the war.[13] Three main collections of women's camp narratives are discussed here: E. Hobhouse, *War Without Glamour* (1927); E. Neethling, *Mag Ons Vergeet?* (*May We Forget?* 1938), and M. M. Postma, *Stemme Uit Die Verlede* (*Voices From The Past*, 1939).

War Without Glamour, introduced and edited by Emily Hobhouse, presents the testimonies of 31 Boer women, many of them well-known and influential, who describe their first-hand wartime experiences, though not all of them were in the camps.[14] *Mag Ons Vergeet?* contains 29 testimonies collected and edited by Mrs Neethling, who had been a camp inmate for a time. She used testimonies obtained by a journalist, Horak, who had advertised for women's camp accounts in the *Transvaler* newspaper.[15] After Horak's death, Mrs Neethling purchased his collection of accounts (now in the Van Zyl collection, State Archives, Pretoria) and published a selection. Her Afrikaans text in fact is a translation of her 1917 book, which originally appeared in Dutch as *Vergeten?* [*Forgotten?*]. Magdalina Margaritha Postma's *Stemme uit die Verlede* was preceded by an almost identical collection, *Stemme uit die Vrouekampe* (*Voices from the Women's Camps*), published in 1925 as a booklet for the Women's National Party. *Stemme uit die Verlede* gathers together 39 women's testimonies, some in the form of statements sworn before a magistrate.[16] While the women represented in Hobhouse's and Neethling's collections were generally members of elite, politically well-connected Boer families, Postma 'collected testimonies from a very wide range of people' (Van Heyningen, 2002: 189), albeit with political views that are remarkably consistent.

Both *Mag Ons Vergeet?* and *Stemme uit die Verlede* were republished in the late 1930s, when Afrikaner nationalism was experiencing a period of unprecedented growth. They depicted the camps as places where Boers had been subjected to oppression and mistreatment by the British, but where ultimately the Boer people's stoicism, bravery and patriotism had prevailed, paving the way for the emergence of a powerful and united Afrikaner nation, ready to re/claim *ons land*, our land – ostensibly achieved by the National Party election victory in 1948.[17] *Mag Ons Vergeet?* and *Stemme uit die Verlede* are inextricable from the nationalist context of their production, publication and distribution. Their nationalist intentions are made explicit in their 'Forewords' (Neethling, 'Foreword', 1938: v; Van Der Horst, 'Foreword II', in Postma, 1939: 8). *War Without Glamour* predated the fierce Afrikaner nationalism of the late 1930s. While Hobhouse was not an Afrikaner nationalist, many of the contributors to her collection were active in nationalist circles, and it was published by the Nasionale Pers and distributed by nationalist organisations.

While the precise meaning of 'everyday life' is dependent on circum-stances and what is considered normative, the exclusion of ordinary, daily activities and experiences from women's camp testimonies is a strikingly conspicuous feature of these collections. Boer women's camp narratives predominantly emphasise the barbaric and even murderous behaviour of both the British and black people towards Boer women and children. The testimonies frequently testify to identical incidents, share formulaic narrative schemes and replicate stock phrases, thus exhibiting what Gillis has called 'memory work' (Gillis, 1994). The absence of the 'everyday' in camp narratives is symptomatic of the close relationship many of these accounts had with the growth of Afrikaner nationalism. Narratives of illness, suffering and death in the camp testimonies replaced the concept of 'everyday life' itself, with the resulting perception that no normal life was possible in the camps. What, then, is the meaning of 'everyday life'?[18]

'Everyday life' in Boer women's narratives?

For Highmore, the idea of the everyday 'points (without judging) to those most repeated actions, those most travelled journeys, those most inhabited spaces that make up, literally, the day to day. This is the landscape closest to us, the world most immediately met' (Highmore, 2002b: 1). This approach is confirmed by Bovone's proposal that '[t]he term "everyday life" brings to mind daily rhythm: it would literally mean "that which happens every twenty-four hours"' (Bovone, 1989: 41). From this viewpoint, extraordinary events such as natural disasters or wars do not readily seem to be part of the 'everyday'. However, 'ordinary' and 'extraordinary' are of course socially constructed categories and the content and meaning of everyday life are also culturally determined. Highmore goes on to point out some of the complexities associated with the concept:

> Everyday Life is a vague and problematic phrase. Any assumption that it is simply 'out there', as a palpable reality to be gathered up and described, should face an immediate question: whose everyday life? […] To invoke the everyday can be a sleight of hand that normalises and universalises particular values, specific world-views. (Highmore, 2002a: 1)

In addition, those who experience the 'extraordinary' – wars or natural disasters – still have to continue with the business of daily life, although in dramatically changed circumstances; what constitutes 'everyday life' becomes both modified and structured by changed social conditions. If 'everyday life' is interpreted as Bovone's 'daily rhythm', the ordinary, routine practices that make up day-to-day existence – such as sleeping, walking, working, cooking, eating, family life and socialising in the extraordinary conditions of wartime South Africa – then there is very little, if any, writing about of everyday wartime life in Boer women's narratives.

The three collections under discussion, and also the wider number of archived testimonial writings, purport to present the stories of ordinary suffering Boer women, who are presented as wronged mothers who stoically bore 'the brunt of the war'. Yet they display a curious silence about the commonplace aspects of camp life such as cooking, cleaning, childcare, schooling or socialising – though for most women these activities must have taken up the majority of their time. Instead, the testimonies largely conform to a grand narrative: each is structured in a similar way, and there are specific incidents and emphases that recur across the accounts, indicative of shared 'memories'. Hobhouse took these similarities as a confirmation of the veracity of the women's accounts (Hobhouse, 1927: 5); but there is another way of reading these similarities.[19] By the time women's accounts were being published – many of them as a more or less explicit part of the Afrikaner nationalist project – only 'certain' narratives about the camps were encouraged into the public domain. Writing about memories of trauma, death and hardship with an overtly political anti-British tone were favoured.

While these things – trauma, death, hardship – certainly made up part of daily life for *some* women in *some* camps at *certain* times, their ubiquitous appearance in the testimonies suggests that the official nationalist campaign to 'remember' led to a distorted emphasis on only certain types of experiences and memories. While almost all camp narratives decry the widespread 'murder' of children by starvation and mistreatment in the camp hospitals, for example, only 23 of the 99 women whose stories appear in the three published collections had children who died in camp.[20] These were nationalist women making political capital from the personal losses of others.

The basic narrative structure common to most of the accounts is revealed in the overlap between the testimonies, with the writers repeating, corroborating and reproducing their own and one another's testimonies. Four main aspects of war and camp experience are focused on: capture by British soldiers; the journey to camp; mistreatment by the British in camp, with particular reference to poor or tainted rations, starving children, the 'murderous' camp hospitals and the numbers of deaths in camps; and making sense of these experiences as part of the Afrikaner nation's history of suffering and sacrifice, while looking forward to the time when these sacrifices will result in national liberation and independence from oppressive British imperialism. The following extracts are typical of these emphases.

Capture

> They [British soldiers] threw our wheat and corn in front of the door or in the ditch. I saw nothing more of my chickens, and the yard was full of feathers. The pigs screamed as they were shot or stabbed to death. (Mrs Du Toit, in Neethling, 1938: 40)[21]

> On 3 August when I went to my house, I found everything there destroyed. The animals had been cut into pieces while still alive; the yard was painted with blood ... everything they could take, they took, and then they set the house on fire. (Mrs Makwayer, in Postma, 1939: 63)

> In a moment they [British soldiers] sprang from their horses and beat to death all the animals there were; yes, they did not mind even though the animals crept amongst us, but they beat them dead, they were so cruel; and we must just look on ... When they were gone we found nothing but pieces of the pigs. (Mrs Meijer, in Hobhouse, 1927: 45)

Interestingly, a large proportion of many of the testimonies devote more space to the capture by the British soldiers and the subsequent journey to camp than they do to camp life itself (see, especially, the testimony of Mrs Albertyn, in Hobhouse, 1927: 44).[22] Descriptions of capture emphasise the brutality of British captors as they set about enforcing the scorched earth policy, burning crops and farmsteads and killing farm animals. The killing of animals motif centres on the stabbing and cutting up of livestock, especially pigs, often when still alive; it symbolises the purported savagery of the British. Women's accounts also emphasise their destitution after capture: having 'nothing but the clothes on our backs' is the most common image of being left homeless and penniless after a British raid and capture.

Journey

> On the way there [to Brandfort camp] my youngest child died, and the most heart-breaking thing was no white person, but three kaffers had to bury her. (Mrs Wolvaardt, in Postma, 1939: 28)

> In three vans and open trucks we left Middelburg ... The worst for us was to hear the Kaffirs shouting at us and their provocation at all the stations. We had no way of defending ourselves. We heard the Kaffirs say: 'Boers, that is good enough for you!' Can Afrikanders stand

that? Again we trusted the Lord would avenge us. (Mrs Van Den Berg, in Hobhouse, 1927: 31)

We got given nothing to eat until the evening, and then it was raw meat, which we quickly had to cook … We had to sleep next to the wagons without any protection other than our blankets, while the kaffers slept under the wagons and still complained that they were hindered by the crying of our children. (Mrs Du Toit, in Neethling, 1938: 83)

Tales of the journey to the camps are permeated with indignant disapproval of black people assisting the British with the capture and transportation of Boer women to the camps. Women express fear and anger at the presence of threatening racial 'others' who have transgressed the racial order by conspiring with the British against their 'rightful' Boer superiors[23] (Dampier, 2003). An emphasis on hunger, especially the deprivation and hunger suffered by children, appears in the narratives.

Camp life: rations and vitriol

We got nothing other than corned beef, white bread and black coffee, and there wasn't enough of anything to still our hunger; we nearly died of hunger … We also got blue vitriol in the flour and something else that made red flecks in the bread. (Mrs Du Toit, in Neethling, 1938: 88)

The meat that was given to us, was that of sick animals and in the flour there were pieces of vitriol. (Mrs Alberts, in Postma, 1939: 91)

I myself took vitriol out of the sugar and hooks out of the tinned meat. (Mrs Scheepers, in Postma, 1939: 146)

Great stress is placed in the testimonies on poor, insufficient rations, with frequent claims that vitriol was added to rations to poison camp inhabitants. That the British tried to murder Boer women and children by adding hooks to tinned meat is a common allegation. In fact the tinned meat distributed in the camps was imported from North America, and the hooks story relates to a particular incident concerning one of the large tins of corned beef found to contain some meat-hooks[24] when opened in Pietersburg camp (DAC 6: Papers received, Pietersburg camp, May–December 1901). 'Crystals' in sugar and flour, assumed to be vitriol, were additives to stop the rations going hard in high humidity. Specific stories were generalised, gained currency and were repeated as evidence of the British plot to wilfully murder the Boer people.

Starving children

> After a few days, one [of my children] died with the words: 'Mother go to Jesus and ask for food for me'. (Mrs Wolvaardt, in Postma, 1939: 28–9).

> Here and there [in the camp hospital] one saw a child sitting up with outstretched hands and tears streaming, crying 'bread, bread, I am so very hungry'. (Mrs Roos, in Hobhouse, 1927: 126–7)

> Many people in the camp were so debilitated by hunger that they had to be taken into hospital. And many people died of hunger in the hospital. Once I asked a child of about twelve years old how he was. He said: 'Fine, but I am almost dying of hunger'. (Mrs Bronkhorst, in Neethling, 1938: 22)

In women's camp narratives, children appear exclusively in relation to starvation, sickness and death. One device used to give impact and authenticity to claims made about hunger and starvation among children is the use of children's 'own' direct speech about this. Some children, notably those suffering from gastro-intestinal diseases such as enteritis, were placed on starvation diets in hospitals to bring the illness under control. Boer women who did not share the same medical culture as the British camp doctors usually regarded these starvation regimes not as a cure but a form of murder[25] (Van Heyningen, 2002). In the camp narratives, there is a total absence of memories of children playing, being mischievous, attending school or going about their daily routines.

'Murderous' hospitals

> Most of the people who used the doctors' medicine, died. I also lost one child in this manner, but the other children who did not make use of the doctors' medicine, all stayed alive. (Mrs Alberts, in Postma, 1939: 92).

> The hospital was a place of horror to us, we dreaded it like death, especially the children, who had to be forced to go. (Mrs Viljoen, in Hobhouse, 1927: 63).

> It was generally known: in the hospital, all the children die, if not of sickness, then of hunger. (Mrs Truter, in Neethling, 1938: 195)

A key theme about hospitals and illness is that all who entered the camp hospitals were more than likely to die, and that the best way of avoiding death was to keep out of hospital. This notion is *not* borne out in the camp records, which indicate that the majority of patients treated in camp hospitals survived, and that the overwhelming number of deaths occurred in the tents. Many women also describe the sadness and pain of being separated from their children who were frequently taken to hospital by force. Actions that seemed to some Boer women to be needless cruelty on the part of camp authorities were based on the urgent necessity of preventing the further spread of disease by keeping all the sick isolated from other inhabitants.

Deaths

> In my eyes the camp was nothing other than a murder camp. I saw that in one night 37 bodies were brought to the mortuary. (Mrs Barnard, in Postma, 1939: 94)

> At the end of August the daily load of coffins on that transport wagon had increased to 22 in number. Sometimes there were 2 corpses in one coffin. They often put as many as eight coffins in one grave. (Mrs Rossouw, in Hobhouse, 1927: 96)

> Almost every day there were up to thirty deaths. (Mrs Pienaar, in Neethling, 1938: 92)

Many testimonies attempt to convey the scale of the camp deaths by describing how many people died at a particular time or each day, and how many were buried together in multiple graves.[26] Little sense of individual sadness, personal loss or private mourning emerges from the narratives. Instead, the numbers of dead are related in a rather routine way and are rallied as conscious sacrifices made by the Afrikaner nation for its ultimate independence. That the large majority of camp deaths occurred among children under the age of five renders as distinctly dubious attempts to cast their deaths as knowing sacrifices made for the *volk* or nation.

Making sense

> Our trials began when our loved ones – husbands, brothers, sons – were called up. Yet they went willingly, like heroes, to give their lives for freedom and for justice. (Mrs Wepener, in Neethling, 1938: 100)

> The Afrikaner woman carried herself very bravely. Was it not for people and fatherland that she suffered, and would it not have been

more than enough reward if she kept her independence? (Mrs Kriegler, in Neethling, 1938: 124)

How can there still be Afrikaans mothers who suffered still more and now go along with the arch enemy? But we trust that our People will once again be united. (Mrs Wolvaardt, in Postma, 1939: 29)

Several women's accounts end by reworking Boer suffering during the war – camp deaths and those of Boer men on commando – into part of a preordained 'rise of the Afrikaner Nation'. The phrases 'for freedom and for justice' or 'for freedom and fatherland' recur across the texts, and some women anticipate the future Afrikaner Nation by writing: 'we trusted the Lord would avenge us' (Mrs Van der Berg, in Hobhouse, 1927: 31) and 'we trust that our People will once again be united' (Mrs Louw, in Neethling, 1938: 29).

Forgetting the everyday in narratives of 'traumatic' pasts

The almost total absence of 'everyday' memories in women's testimonies examined here needs to be seen in the context of Afrikaner nationalism, with the accounts being produced during a period of intense nation-building. Vogelsang (2002) has explored the process of remaking history in former Soviet states – her study focuses on Simferopol in the Crimea – through a 'remembering the forgotten' that has occurred since the end of Soviet rule in 1989. She argues that the practice of re/creating history in the context of building a 'new nation' encourages people to remember 'correctly' the traumas they suffered under Soviet domination now that they have the freedom to do so and are no longed oppressed and silenced by an authoritarian regime. These stories of past oppression, long denied and suppressed but now brought to the surface, constitute the new history of a now-liberated nation, whose people are bound together by their shared experience of past injustice.

Vogelsang holds that this has led to the assumption that there was no 'normal life' under Soviet rule, and that all legitimate or authentic memories about the past are those that are traumatic and were repressed. Memories of ordinary people going about the daily business of everyday life, in spite of the oppression of Soviet rule, have now become 'forgotten' in favour of 'worthy' memories of suffering. Vogelsang insists that official campaigns of remembering always involve official campaigns of forgetting. In the South African context, women writing their testimonies 'forgot' memories of everyday camp life in producing their narratives, because these were produced expressly for political, nation-building purposes.

That the testimonies in the three collections under discussion do not generally narrate details of 'everyday life' stands in contrast to the many contemporary *photographs* that have been archived. These *do* testify to the ordinary domestic routines around which camp life was organised. Photographs show families with their possessions posing for pictures outside their tents, children attending school or catechism classes, and camp inhabitants playing sport, cleaning, working, cooking, at Sunday church services and receiving rations. Many of these photographs were taken by travelling photographers at the request of camp inhabitants themselves, often to send to absent relatives. A few camp photographs are reproduced here, and show some aspects of everyday life that are not represented in women's testimonies.[27]

Photograph 1 shows a group of children gathered at a camp soup kitchen to receive their soup ration. Soup kitchens for children, the elderly and the infirm were started in most of the camps in the wake of the Ladies Commission visits. Photographs 2 and 5 both show camp inhabitants participating in sports activities. Sports days were sometimes held in camps, and a few camps had rough tennis courts. Photograph 3 depicts a group of camp school children with their teacher. By the end of the war all

Photograph 1   Soup kitchen in a camp

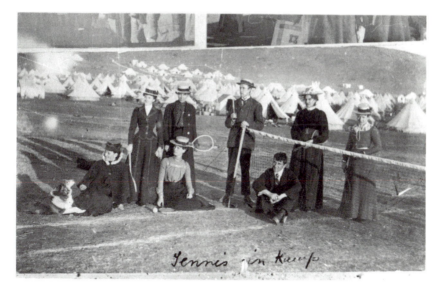

Photograph 2   Tennis in Winburg camp

Photograph 3   Schoolchildren in a camp

Photograph 4 Two young women outside their tent

Photograph 5 Sport in Bloemfontein camp

Photograph 6   Shoemakers in Winburg camp

the camps had established schools, although the quality of schooling varied from camp to camp and greatly depended on the ability of the camp authorities to recruit qualified teachers. The two young women posing outside their tent with some of their household possessions in photograph 4 is typical of many of the camp photographs which often show family groups gathered outside their tents, sometimes with their pets and belongings. The men in photograph 6 are shoemakers in Winburg camp, where other occupations for male inhabitants included brick-making and carpentry.

While these photographs, like the testimonies, are situated in a particular historical context and can be 'read' in a variety of ways to deconstruct their multiple meanings, they were nevertheless taken at the time and in the context of the war. They were thus less subject to the retrospective reworking so evident in women's testimonies written after the war. The photographs portray camp inhabitants grappling with the changed circumstances of their everyday lives. While they show everyday life structured by the camp system, they depict individuals experiencing and negotiating an institutionalised everyday life by, for example, choosing to represent themselves in a very particular way in this context – as in photograph 4. It is a sense of this negotiation of the very specific kind of everyday life, organised by the camp system, that is so absent in the written representations of the camps. What appear instead in the testimonies are the stylised, ritualised narratives of nationalism that emphasise only death and suffering.

Many commentators, such as Brink (1990: 279) and Grundlingh (1999: 22), have stressed the significance of concentration camp memories of victimhood and suffering to the formation of Afrikaner nationalism. The testimonies in *Stemme uit die Verlede* and *Mag Ons Vergeet?*, in particular, were closely associated with the Afrikaner nationalist project. To remember 'the worst' aspects of camp life and describe the camps as places of 'murder', where Boer women and children were martyred in the nationalist cause, best served their political aims. This is not to suggest that memory of such things was nothing other than a nationalist construction – as Werbner points out in relation to Zimbabwe, this reduces memory to 'an artefact of the here and now, as if it were merely a backwards construction after the fact' (Werbner, 1998: 2). What is interesting, however, are `the processes by which memory lives, gets realised or ruptured, is textualised, becomes buried, repressed or avoided, has its effects, and is more or less transformed (Werbner, 1998: 2); and how the nationalist context resulted in only traumatic and 'politically correct' memories being 'textualised' and brought into the public domain, at the expense of other more everyday memories, shown so graphically in the photographic representations.

By explicitly re/producing in a ubiquitous way narratives which inscribed collective death and suffering in place of the everyday experiences of individuals, the greatest political capital could be generated by those seeking to further a nationalist agenda: this was postwar 'memory work'. Gillis stresses that memory work is always 'embedded in complex class, gender and power relations that determine what is remembered (or forgotten), by whom, and for what ends' (Gillis, 1994: 3). In this instance, nationalist politicisation of the concentration camps led to visions of British cruelty and barbarism and Boer suffering replacing memories of ordinary, everyday life in women's camp testimonies.

Notes

1 For a discussion on the power of the words 'concentration camp' see Stanley and Dampier, 2004.
2 The camps were situated along railway lines for military reasons and for ease of provisioning.
3 The camps in the Transvaal, Orange River Colony and Cape were granted civil administration in March 1901 and the Natal camps in November 1901.
4 In some camps local committees carried out 'relief' work which included distributing clothing and medical comforts. Some of these items were

supplied by the camp administrations, while various relief committees privately donated others.

5   Apart from black people who lived in the so-called 'white' camps as servants of Boer inmates, there were black people who lived in these camps as employees of the camp administrations. There were also separate black camps (which later became about 60 farms), and estimates of the deaths in the black camps range between 14, 000 and 20, 000. On black people in the 'white' camps see Stanley 2004 and 2005.

6   For example, the Ladies Commission commented, 'The [Pietermaritzburg] camp was out of bounds for the military camp, but the people were free to go into town as much as they pleased up to 6 p.m. After that hour they required a pass, which Mr Struben not infrequently granted if there was anyone wanting to go to the theatre or to a party.' (Concentration Camps Commission, 1902: 32).

7   The numbers in each camp were constantly changing with new arrivals and deaths, and people were also moved from camp to camp. Bloemfontein had the largest camp population, with the combined population of the 'old' and 'new' camps standing at 6660 in September 1901 (Concentration Camp Commission, 1902: 39). There were also numbers of Boer men in the camps, although this is seldom mentioned in nationalist literature about the camps, where it is implied that all adult men were fighting on commando. Apart from the very young and the very old, men in camp included those who had surrendered, those who were neutral and those who worked directly for the British.

8   This was further fuelled by a speech given in June 1901 by British Liberal M.P. and leader of the party, Sir Henry Campbell-Bannerman, when he denounced Britain's conduct of the war in South Africa as 'methods of barbarism'.

9   Much of the secondary camp literature fails to challenge many of the apparently proven 'truisms' so frequently repeated in women's testimonies about the camps as places of deliberate mistreatment of the Boers by the British. To varying degrees these texts present uncritically nationalist versions of these events, and this historiographical tradition continues up to the present time. Some key examples include Van Bruggen 1935, Steenkamp 1941, Otto 1954, Coetzer 2000, and Raath 2003.

10 These included Vis 1902, De La Rey 1903, Neethling 1903, Van Helsdingen 1903 and Brandt-Van Warmelo 1905.

11 Many Boer women's accounts were re/published around the time of the 1938 Great Trek centenary celebrations, and these include Neethling 1938, Raal 1938, Postma 1939 and Rabie 1940. The so-called Great Trek refers to the events of 1836–38, when a group of Dutch-speaking 'Voortrekkers' left the Cape Colony and journeyed into the interior of Southern Africa, partly to escape British rule. In 1938 these Voortrekkers were commemorated as brave, hardy, heroic pioneers in a series of triumphalist nationalist celebrations which included a re-enactment of the Great Trek.

12 For example, bulk orders were made of both Mrs Le Clus' *Lief en Leed* and Hobhouse's *Tant' Alie* by the Women's National Parties, which arranged for

the promotion, sale and distribution of these books amongst their members. See letters from Emily Hobhouse to Mrs Steyn 7 January 1923 and 1 July 1923. (VAB, A156).

13 Most of the documents presented and archived as camp diaries show signs of being written up long after the war itself and are therefore not diaries in the usual sense.

14 Not all the testimony-writers in *War Without Glamour* or the other collections were actually in camps; some describe wider wartime experiences.

15 The full collection of women's testimonies obtained by Horak and later bought by Mrs Neethling is now in the State Archives in Pretoria (Van Zyl collection W19).

16 *Stemme Uit Die Verlede* appeared in a slightly 'updated' form of Afrikaans, and significantly included one additional testimony by Mrs S.C. Scheepers, mother of Boer commandant Gideon Scheepers, who had been controversially executed as a war criminal by the British military on 17 January 1902. Scheepers was later valorised as a hero and martyr of the republican cause.

17 Political control of South Africa by the National Party ended in 1994 with the first democratic elections.

18 In the PhD research on which this article draws, I question the referentiality of memory in Boer women's wartime women's testimonies by drawing on Stanley's re/working of Hirsch's term 'postmemory' as post/memory, a concept which recognises the mediated, unstable nature of all memory. See Hirsch, 1997; Stanley, 2005, in press, and Dampier, 2004, in progress.

19 In the preface to *War Without Glamour*, Hobhouse states: 'The universality and similarity of experience is striking. Had every woman of the two Boer Republics (apart from the few big towns) recorded her experience, the result would have been but a general repetition of these statements with minor variations of detail.' (Hobhouse 1927: 5).

20 In *War Without Glamour*, five out of 31 testimony-writers experienced the deaths of their children in camp. In *Mag Ons* the proportion is six out of 29 and in *Stemme*, 12 out of 39.

21 I have translated all quotes taken from *Mag Ons Vergeet?* and *Stemme Uit Die Verlede* from Afrikaans into English.

22 For instance, in *War Without Glamour* the four pages of Mrs Albertyn's testimony are almost entirely concerned with this, with only the last short sentence making a brief comment about entering Aliwal North camp and her feelings of relief because, 'My troubles were by no means at an end, but the worst was past' (Mrs. Albertyn in Hobhouse 1927: 44).

23 See Dampier (2003) for an analysis of 'race' matters in Boer women's testimonies.

24 On the Pietersburg meat hook incident, see DBC 6: Papers received, Pietersburg camp, May–December 1901.

25 For a detailed discussion of the conflict of medical cultures in the camps see Van Heyningen 2002.

26 In some camps during the height of the epidemics, there were occasions when several people were buried in a single grave. Black and white people were sometimes buried in the same grave, although this has not been acknowledged or commemorated officially.

27 The six photographs here are from the archive of the War Museum of the Boer Republics, South Africa, and are reproduced with their kind permission.

References

Free State Archives Depot (VAB), Bloemfontein:
   A156 – Steyn collection.
State Archives, Pretoria:
   W19 – Van Zyl collection.
   DBC 6: Papers received, Pietersburg camp, May–December 1901.
Bovone, L. 'Theories of everyday life: a search for meaning or a negation of meaning?', *Current Sociology*, 37, 1, 1989, pp. 41–59.
Brandt-Van Warmelo, J. *Het concentratie-kamp van Irene.* Hollandsch-Afrikaansche uitgevers-maatschappij (HAUM), 1905.
Brink, E. 'Man-made women: gender, class and the ideology of the volksmoeder', in Walker, C. (ed.), *Women and Gender in Southern Africa to 1945.* David Philip, 1990.
Coetzer, O. *Fire in the Sky: The Destruction of the Orange Free State, 1899–1902.* Covos-Day Books, 2000.
Concentration Camps Commission. *Report on the Concentration Camps in South Africa by the Committee of Ladies appointed by the Secretary of State for War, containing reports on the camps in Natal, the Orange River Colony and the Transvaal*, CD. 893. HMSO, 1902.
Cuthbertson, G., Grundlingh, A. and Suttie, M. (eds) *Writing a Wider War: Rethinking Gender, Race, and Identity in the South African War, 1899–1902.* David Philip, 2002.
Dampier, H. 'Reading "Race" in Hendrina Rabie-van der Merwe's testimony *Onthou! In die Skaduwee van die Galg'.* Paper presented at the Auto/Biography Conference on 'Witness, Testimony and Confession', University of Manchester, January 2003.
Dampier, H. 'Women's Testimonies of the Concentration Camps of the South African War', unpublished PhD thesis, University of Newcastle, 2005.
De La Rey, Mrs (trans. Lucy Hotz). *A Woman's Wanderings and Trials During the Anglo-Boer War.* T. Fisher Unwin, 1903.
Gillis, J. R. (ed.) *Commemorations: The Politics of National Identity.* Princeton University Press, 1994.
Grundlingh, A. 'The bitter legacy of the Boer War', *History Today*, November 1999, pp. 21–5.
Highmore, B. (ed.) *The Everyday Life Reader.* Routledge, 2002a.
Highmore, B. *Everyday Life and Cultural Theory: An Introduction.* Routledge, 2002b.

Hirsch, M. *Family Frames: Photography, Narrative and Postmemory.* Harvard University Press, 1997.

Hobhouse, E. *Report to the Committee of the Distress Fund for South African Women and Children.* South African Conciliation Committee Distress Fund, 1901 (reprinted in Raath, 1999, pp. 35–117).

Hobhouse, E. *The Brunt of the War and Where It Fell.* Methuen & Co., 1902.

Hobhouse, E. *Tant' Alie of the Transvaal, Her Diary 1880–1902.* Allen & Unwin, 1923.

Hobhouse, E. *War Without Glamour. Women's War Experiences Written By Themselves, 1899–1902.* Nasionale Pers Beperk., 1927.

Le Clus, S. L. *Lief en leed: 'n verhaal van huis – en kamplewe gedurende die Anglo-Boereoorlog, van 1899 tot 1902.* Nasionale Pers (1920).

Maffesoli, M. 'The sociology of everyday life (epistemological elements)', *Current Sociology*, 37, 1, 1987, pp. 1–16.

Neethling, E. *Should We Forget?* Holland: AF Publishing Co (Hollandsch-Afrikaansche uitgevers-maatschappij (HAUM), Dusseau & Co., 1903.

Neethling, E. (as 'The widow of H. L. Neethling'). *Vergeten?* De Nasionale Pers, Beperkt., 1917.

Neethling, E. *Mag Ons Vergeet?* Nasionale Pers, Beperkt., 1938.

Postma, M. M. *Stemme uit die Vrouekampe.* Unknown publisher, 1925.

Postma, M. M. *Stemme uit die Verlede.* Voortrekkerspers Beperk, 1939.

Otto, J. C. *Die Konsentrasiekampe.* Kaapstad, Bloemfontein, Nasionale Boekhandel, Beperk, 1954.

Raal, S. *Met Die Boere in die Veld.* Stormberg Publishers, 1938, republished 2000.

Raath, A.W.G. (ed.) *The British Concentration Camps of the Anglo-Boer War 1899–1902: Reports on the Camps.* War Museum of the Boer Republics, 1999.

Raath, A. W. G. *Die Boerevrou.* Privately published, 2003.

Rabie-Van der Merwe, H. *Onthou! In Die Skaduwee van die Galg.* Nasionale Pers, 1940.

Stanley, L. 'Black labour and the concentration system of the South African War.' *Joernaal vir Eietydse Geskiedenis/Journal for Contemporary History*, 3, 28(4), pp. 190–213.

Stanley, L. *Mourning Becomes ... Post/Memory and the Concentration Camps of the South African War.* Manchester University Press and Rutgers University Press, 2005, in press.

Stanley, L. and Dampier, H. *Aftermaths: Post/memory, Commemoration and the Concentration Camps of the South African War 1899–1902.* European Review of History.

Steenkamp, W. *The Soldiers.* Cape Town, 1941.

Van Bruggen, J. R. L. *Bittereinders.* H. W. Hyser, 1935.

Van Helsdingen, J. *Vrouewenleed: Persoonlikje Ondervindingen in den Boereoorlog.* Hollansch-Afrikaansche Uitgevers-maatschappij, 1903.

Van Heyningen, E. 'Women and disease: the clash of medical cultures in the concentration camps of the South African War', in Cuthbertson, G., Grundlingh, A. and Suttie, M. (eds), *Writing a Wider War: Rethinking Gender, Race, and Identity in the South African War, 1899–1902.* Ohio University Press and David Philip, 2002.

Vis, W. R. *Tien maanden in een 'Vrouwenkamp'*. D.A. Daamen, 1902.

Vogelsang, I. *Remembering the Forgotten: Researching a Repressed Past – Some Theoretical Thoughts*. PhD thesis, University of Manchester, 2002.

Walker, C. (ed.) *Women and Gender in Southern Africa to 1945*. David Philip, 1990.

Werbner, R. (ed.) *Memory and the Postcolony*. Zed Books, 1998.

Chapter 16

Codification of the criminal law: the Australasian parliamentary experience

Jeremy Finn

This chapter considers the diverse parliamentary histories of codification of the criminal law in the Australasian colonies in the period 1870–1900. Three conceptually different kinds of criminal law statutes were proposed. Firstly the true 'code', as exemplified by the Code Napoléon of France, which in a relatively brief single statute set out all the relevant principles of an area of law. Only the Victorian General Code Bill in the 1880s was of this nature.[1] More common was 'consolidation' of statutes – bringing together *without substantive change* provisions previously scattered over a number of different statutes, as with the Victorian Crimes Act 1890. Consolidation of this kind was often seen as a necessary prelude to true codification. More complex, and rarer, were 'criminal codes' which combined existing statutory law – usually with some limited reform of problem areas – with a reduction to statutory form of substantial elements of the relevant common law. The Criminal Code Act 1893 (NZ); Criminal Code 1899 (Queensland) and Criminal Code Act 1902 (Western Australia) are in this class; the Criminal Law Amendment Act 1883 (NSW) has some elements of both consolidation and reform without claiming to be a code.

The English and imperial background

The history of the attempts to codify the English criminal law is well-known.[2] Much of England's penal law was consolidated in the 1820s and again in 1861. These consolidations were drawn on by Macaulay for the Indian Penal Code, in turn followed by the 'Stephen' Code, which developed from the work of James Fitzjames Stephen and the report and draft Criminal Code prepared by a royal commission (on which Stephen sat) which recommended legislation which set out in fairly concise terms much of the existing statute and common law rules, and a coherent statement of the relevant rules of criminal procedure. Bills embodying the Stephen Code were regularly introduced into the British Parliament from 1879, but were defeated by fierce opposition from conservative lawyers and judges.

A rival code, the work of E. D. Lewis, a London solicitor, was introduced in 1880, but failed to progress (see White, 1986: 357). A third code, written by Robert Wright for the Colonial Office in 1870 was, after scrutiny by Stephen himself, circulated to some colonies lacking self-government and was adopted in some West Indian colonies (Friedland, 1981; O'Regan, 1988: 108, note 19). Canadian efforts to codify the statute law had commenced at an early date and many provinces had adopted a process of regular revision and consolidation by way of re-enactment of their statutes. The most notable element of codification is the Criminal Code Act 1892.[3] Legislators could have drawn on this material, and on Italian, Californian and New York codes – the latter were apparently brought to public notice because Dudley Field, the author, visited Australia in 1874 (Woods, 2002: 292).

New Zealand and the Criminal Code Act 1893

Until the 1880s, New Zealand had done little to amend its inherited English law apart from adopting, in 1867, the English reforms of 1861. The Reprint of Statutes Act 1878 provided for commissioners (Alexander Johnston, a judge of the Supreme Court, Walter Reid, the Solicitor-General, and an assistant) to collate the statutes for reprinting. They reported that mere collation by way of reprinting would be wasteful and unhelpful, and the government responded by a new bill to allow the commissioners to consolidate, without change, the existing statute law. The principle of consolidation in this form received general support, but it is also notable that one MP, Downie Stewart (of whom more below), drew the government's attention to the writings of W. E. Hearn in Melbourne, and his intention to codify the entire law. That, suggested Stewart, was the model which the government should follow.[4]

Johnston and Reid were appointed as Commissioners to prepare a Criminal Code in 1879. They largely worked from the English Bill of 1880, but excluded historical or peculiarly English offences, as well as any offences under Imperial statutes expressly stated to be in force in New Zealand. The Commissioners recommended waiting until England had legislated, and they deliberately expressed no opinion on the proposal (incorporated in the English Bill of 1880) that the accused be able to give evidence at his or her own trial, but did recommend firmly against the English proposals for a more structured system of criminal appeals and re-trials.[5] Notable features of the Criminal Code Bill were the abolition of the distinction between felonies and misdemeanours and the statutory definition of a number of offences (especially offences against property) and some defences. Procedural rules were also radically simplified.

The Bill was first introduced into Parliament as a government measure in June 1883, 11 days after the Commissioners reported, only to be withdrawn by the government after it passed the second reading, allegedly because of insufficient time to deal with it.[6] The then premier (and prominent lawyer) Frederick Whitaker spoke enthusiastically of the benefits of codification generally, specifically mentioning both the French and the New York codes. The Bill received a reasonably sympathetic hearing, although critics seized on the Commissioners' recommendation for delay. Other objections included a concern, later often resuscitated, about the inclusion of a statutory offence of blasphemous libel. The debate also saw the only call made during the entire decade's debate on the Code for it to be submitted to the legal profession and the judiciary for their views. It will be noted that at no time was there any formal process in New Zealand for further consultation with the legal profession and the judiciary; the latter only were later consulted (White, 1986: 365). In 1884 the Bill was again introduced, only to be discharged a week after the first reading.

A third attempt was made in 1885, with the significant difference that the Bill was introduced into the Legislative Council by Patrick Buckley, the Colonial Secretary and a successful lawyer, later to be Attorney-General and briefly a judge of the Supreme Court. The Bill again met with a mixed reception, with concern being expressed as to the blasphemy offence and the provision allowing the accused to give evidence. The peculiar politics which hampered the Bill's passage are well shown in the committee stage debate, where Whitaker, the Bill's sponsor in 1883 but a political opponent of Buckley, spoke in support of the Bill but voted against its passage. Critics of the Bill deplored the (real) overlap with the Police Offences Act 1884 and the inclusion of blasphemy or urged delay until England legislated. The Bill passed the committee stage narrowly, and the third reading more comfortably.

The Bill then went to the House of Representatives where Joseph Tole, the Minister of Justice, somewhat intransigently informed the House that as this was a 'technical' bill, he would withdraw it if the House sought to debate it clause by clause. There ensued the best informed and most wide-ranging debate of any in Australasia on a code Bill. W. Downie Stewart, a Dunedin lawyer, criticised much of the Bill, drawing comparisons with the Indian Penal Code and the French code. He welcomed the provision allowing an accused to give evidence but, citing a study he had done on American law when travelling there ten years earlier, urged the adoption of a provision, widespread in the American states, that failure to give evidence could not be commented on by prosecution counsel or by the judge. Such protections were later enacted.[7] Another speaker wanted the age of consent to be raised to 16, as had occurred in England. The most vehement opposition to the Bill came from a Mr Moss, criticising the retention of whipping and flogging on the basis New Zealand had no permanent criminal class requiring such punishments. The Bill passed its second reading, but again a lack of parliamentary time for the committee stage caused the Bill to be abandoned.

It was several years before any version of the Code would progress so far. The government tried again the following year, and again flogging was attacked – and defended – while concern was expressed as to the age of consent in sexual offences, criminal libel, private prosecutions and the extent to which the Bill provided for certain matters to be dealt with as questions of law for the judge rather than matters of fact for the jury. This latter point regularly reappeared in later debates, with speakers on each side appealing to American law or legal journals. Much of the opposition was clearly purely party politicking, and the Bill was defeated, more or less on party lines, at the committee stage.

This defeat ended the first phase of attempts to enact a Code. Nothing was attempted in 1887, and although in 1888 Buckley again moved it, he was on the opposition benches. Although the Bill passed the Legislative Council after being sent to a Select Committee – with debate again focusing on the blasphemy provisions and on the need to provide for an accused to give evidence – it did not progress past the first reading in the lower house. No further attempt was made until 1891, although the Criminal Evidence Act 1889 did provide for an accused to give evidence.

The Liberal victory in 1891 transformed the position. Buckley, now Attorney-General and Colonial Secretary, introduced the Bill that year, and it passed through the Legislative Council comfortably. Although it passed the second reading in the House of Representatives – after a debate where the bigamy and criminal libel provisions were criticised and the allegedly superior drafting of the New York and Californian codes extolled – the Bill was a casualty of the early termination of the session consequent on the Legislative Council's rejection of other measures. In 1892 the Bill died in the committee stage for reasons which are obscure, but in 1893 Buckley returned to the charge. The Bill passed through both houses quickly, all opposition crushed by the Liberal majority voting on party lines. It has been argued (White, 1986: 374) that the key reason for the passage of the Bill is that the leading lawyers of the time, persons who were generally in positions of power, supported the Bill. There is some factual basis for this view, but it takes no account of the opposition to the Bill shown by other lawyers and the rather ambiguous role played by Whitaker. Nor does it explain why such leading figures failed to ensure adequate parliamentary time to debate the Bill. An alternative view is that, while the support of leading lawyer figures is important, the long-drawn out passage of the Bill reflects a decade of partisan politics, where the strong proponents of the Bill were almost entirely drawn from the ranks of the Liberals, and the opponents largely from more conservative political factions. While liberal governments of 1883–86 almost managed to pass the Bill, the overwhelming strength of the Liberals in 1893 guaranteed its passage.

Victoria

Victoria saw two quite different aspects of the consolidation and codification debate.[8] The statute law was consolidated in 1864–65 and again in 1889–90, each consolidation being very largely the work of George Higinbotham, quondam Premier and later Chief Justice. No bill specifically aimed at codifying the criminal law as such was ever put forward, but Victoria saw the only attempt at a 'Code' on the European model – a statutory restatement of all the existing common law and statutory rules.

W. E. Hearn, the Dean of Law at Melbourne University, laboured for much of the 1870s and 1880s (with some belated government support) over a draft code, intending to put in succinct form the entire statute and common law of general application. His Substantive General Law Consolidation Bill 1884 (later re-titled the General Code Bill) was drawn in part from the Victorian consolidations, and also from English statutes, the Stephen Code and the English Bills, as well as the Indian Contracts Act and Indian Succession Act. The Bill, among other things, sought to codify the substantive criminal law – both offences and defences – though not criminal procedure. Debate, however, generally focused on the principle of codification with little discussion of the criminal law as a specific topic.[9] It was introduced by Hearn in the Victorian Legislative Council in 1884 but did not proceed after a select committee issued a lukewarm report, suggesting so many amendments that Hearn withdrew the Bill.

In 1887 Hearn returned to the issue, successfully moving that a joint select committee of the legislature be appointed to consider how best the law might be codified. The committee was appointed with Hearn as its chair, and after examining various witnesses, including Hearn himself, the committee recommended enactment of Hearn's General Code Bill. However, the combination of negative responses from eminent legal personages asked to comment on the Code and Hearn's death in April 1888 meant the voices of caution overrode what remaining enthusiasm there was for full-scale codification. The government, quite probably prompted by Higinbotham, opted to defer any attempt at codification in favour of a fresh consolidation of the statutes, which was speedily accomplished in 1889–90. The Crimes Act 1890 (Vic) consolidated the statute law of the colony, although some significant changes were made by the Crimes Act 1891, which dealt with simplifying the law of attempted murder, raising the age of consent in sexual offences, making provision for incest to be a crime as well as amending the law relating to theft, to perjury and making the accused and his or her spouse competent but not compellable witnesses.

Queensland

The Queensland Criminal Code is known almost universally as the Griffith Code, after its principal author, Samuel Griffith, the state's Chief Justice. While Griffith drew on Stephen's work, he also acknowledged his indebtedness to the New York and the Italian penal codes.[10] The passage of the Bill incorporating the Griffith Code through the Queensland Legislative Assembly presents a most remarkable comparison with the drawn-out process in New Zealand, with the Bill passing all stages in the (unicameral) Queensland Parliament in less than five weeks in 1899.[11] The debates show the Bill enjoyed a broad degree of cross-party support and a ready allocation of parliamentary time.

The second reading took place the day after the Bill was introduced, with Rutledge, the Attorney-General and main driver of the Bill, referring to codification having taken place in New Zealand and in America. He laid out the history of the move for codification and mentioned Griffith's acknowledgment of drawing on the Italian and New York codes. Rutledge specifically mentioned provisions dealing with cross-border crimes and with provocation as a defence for assaults. In all this Rutledge was clearly following and echoing Griffith's views. Yet not everything in the Bill did so. Rutledge alluded to removal of the death penalty for sodomy – which brought Queensland's law into line with that of South Australia, Western Australia, New Zealand, Tasmania and Great Britain itself – indicating this was his own view and that Griffith and another Commissioner did not agree with the relaxation.[12]

The debate then adjourned for almost a week, at which time a number of members ventilated such points as the Crown's power to stand aside jurors, the desirability of keeping a sentence of solitary confinement and the problems of false pretences offences in country districts where cheques were the normal medium of exchange. There was only one speech of real substance, in which a Mr Lesina first criticised extensively the punishment of flogging which was provided for various offences, and secondly argued for the abolition of capital punishment on the basis of various supposed miscarriages of justice.

The Bill entered the committee stage a week after its second reading began and eight days from its introduction. Rutledge suggested that he would move all 708 clauses of the Bill as one block, unless members wished to nominate specific provisions for later debate. This proposal was not accepted, and the Assembly began to work through the Bill, clause by clause. There was some significant debate about offences relating to obstructing the course of justice and the like. In total that day the Assembly passed 21 clauses, a rate which did not bode well for completion within the session.

When committee stage debate resumed on 3 October, progress was much faster, with for the first time clusters of clauses (up to 14 in one case) being passed as a block. The only matters occasioning debate were whether it was necessary or desirable to have the death penalty for capital treason by killing the sovereign and, less dramatically but perhaps more relevantly, about possible restrictive or unfair effects of the unlawful assembly provisions on labour disputes. The following day's resumption of the committee stage debate saw abandonment of any clause-by-clause debate – sections of the bill of up to 55 clauses being moved and passed as a unit. Only the piracy provisions received any substantial mention. Progress was even more rapid on the following day, when over 170 clauses went through the committee stage, with only four matters being raised for substantial discussion, including the vagueness of the obscene publications provisions and, more vigorously, about the use of arms by police against persons resisting arrest.

The Bill continued in for a fifth day in committee on 10 October, with over 300 clauses being passed after scant consideration – for instance, the entire property offences section was passed as a block without debate. The only substantial debate was on the provision for the imposition of flogging as a punishment, which drew more attention than any other clause in the Bill.[13] The sixth and last committee stage day saw the last 42 clauses dealt with quickly. The Bill then passed its third reading on 24 October uneventfully. Thus the Bill had passed through the Assembly entirely in 34 days, of which six were completely or partially taken up with the committee stages. There was little substantial debate at second reading or elsewhere as to the merits of the Bill – except for Rutledge's regular references to the work of Griffith and the fact the Bill largely represented his work.

Western Australia

The Western Australian Criminal Code owed an enormous debt to the Griffith Code, but there was significant local input in the consolidation of earlier Western Australian law, a task largely performed by T. F. Sayer, former Secretary of the Law Department and Commissioner of Titles, later MP for Claremont, and later still Parliamentary Draughtsman for Western Australia. The strong support of the Premier, George Leake, and of the influential parliamentarian and future premier, Walter James KC, was essential in the Bill's speedy passage.[14] However, it does appear that support was widespread rather than based solely on a 'government' party.

The process of debate on the Bill[15] shows there was by no means an unquestioning acceptance of the Queensland model, and a number of distinctly local views were ventilated as the Bill progressed. Some of the matters which drew comment in other colonies – such as the raising of the age of consent, provision for the accused to give evidence and a court of criminal appeal – had been ventilated in earlier years and did not reappear in the debates on the Code. The Code Bill was introduced by Walter James in the Legislative Assembly on 3 September 1901; it completed the legislative process on 7 February 1902. The Western Australian legislature apparently spent even less time, though over more sitting days, on the Code than did the Queensland Parliament.

The first, rather perfunctory, debate took place at the second reading in the Legislative Assembly. The (slightly contradictory) emphases were on portraying the Bill as a consolidation of existing law, but also as almost a reproduction of the Queensland Code Act. Sayer emphasised the convenience of a code:

... if we desire our criminal law to be a written law, we should pass this code and enable any person to ascertain what the law is, which he could not do except by getting textbooks and copies of the English statutes.[16]

The Bill then passed the committee stage with scant amendment after only two full days of debate. From the start large parts of the Bill were being moved en bloc, and often passed with little debate. On the first day in committee, only two issues occasioned any serious debate – the criminal liability of, and maximum penalty which could be imposed upon, spectators at a prize fight, and the provisions dealing with corrupt electoral practices. James sought to focus attention on getting the Bill through, suggesting contentious provisions should simply be omitted.

A new and much more substantial issue was then raised as to provisions relating to 'bawdy houses' and whether it was necessary to outlaw brothels. Here, for the first time in the debate, supporters of the Bill all defended the clause as being identical with that currently in force in England.[17] From there the debate moved to gaming houses, with critics of the Bill claiming it created heavier penalties than anywhere else in Australia. Gambling in other forms was also discussed. A number of other parts of the Bill passed without discussion, and there ensued a fairly wide-ranging debate on various provisions, including the punishing of 'garrotting' (disabling to enable robbery) by whipping. Members then raised the offence of desertion of children by parents. The Western Australian Bill made this unlawful if the children were less than 14 years of age, and it was pointed out that Griffith's original draft provided for an age of 16 (it being claimed that the Queensland Parliament had altered the figure). An amendment, quickly agreed, raised the age to 16.[18] Griffith's authority was again invoked on the subject of criminal defamation, with statements that the Bill represented Griffith's reform of earlier Queensland law. The debate, which throughout appears to have been characterised by a remarkably friendly and cooperative spirit, concluded with discussion of two matters – fraud related to mining royalties and whether majority verdicts should be possible in criminal cases – which owed nothing to Griffith or to the Code. The third reading took place a few days later, so that the Bill had passed through the lower house in seven weeks, though only seven sitting days were involved.

The passage though the Legislative Council took longer and was less straightforward. The Bill went to the Council three weeks after passing the Assembly – a surprisingly long time after the third reading in the Assembly by comparison with other jurisdictions – and more than two months elapsed before the second reading in January 1902. The delay reflects a brief period of intense political instability. The degree of political upheaval which occurred makes the cooperative atmosphere of the debates all the more remarkable.

The, very brief, second reading debate in the Council included the only challenge to the wisdom of codification. H. S. Haynes pointed to the failure of Code Bills in England and challenged the attempt to define the common law offences. He moved successfully for the Bill to be sent to a select committee which was to report back a week later. Any hopes of delaying or substantially modifying the Bill were short-lived, with Haynes later moving for the committee to be discharged as its members were concerned they would be held liable for any defects in the Code. The members therefore recommended any amendments to the Bill occur at committee stage, but nothing of importance arose. There was a substantial, if not particularly logical, debate on the provision which removed the death penalty for rape, substituting life imprisonment with or without whipping, and an amendment on a technical matter as to appeals. The last stage of the debate came with attempts to reopen the question of bawdy houses. When the Bill was re-committed to allow some minor amendments to be made, J. D. Connolly, claiming to represent the views of the Kalgoorlie Municipal Council, sought unsuccessfully to include a provision to forbid prostitutes soliciting in a public place. This proposal elicited a range of responses, some sympathetic in principle but arguing the Police Offences Act was the proper legal vehicle, others that such a provision was not necessary or was not fair to women. The final acts of the process took place in the first week of February 1902.

The other Australian jurisdictions

New South Wales provides an interesting contrast to the 'code' jurisdictions. In 1871 a Law Reform Commission, chaired by Chief Justice Alfred Stephen, recommended enactment of a Criminal Law Amendment Bill to consolidate the existing statute law, with some changes, and to incorporate major English developments. Stephen, the dominant figure in the reform debate, believed reform of this kind was practicable and codification impossible in the prevailing parliamentary conditions (Woods, 2002: 261–63 and 308). That Bill, passed only in 1883, was not a true code in that it did not define many of the offences, but it was more than a mere consolidation in that it made significant changes to a number of areas – partly by adoption of the English statutes of 1861, but also by significant reform of the law relating to criminal procedure and evidence.

A few parliamentarians did seek more far-reaching reform and true codification, with the Stephen Code, the New York Penal Code and the Indian Penal Code being urged as alternative models. Many issues were touched on in the long years of debate. Some, such as the age of consent in sexual offences and provision for an accused to give evidence, mirror debates in other jurisdictions. Others such as providing for challenges to jurors, trespassing on land to hunt deer or hares and the cutting of timber on private land were not debated elsewhere. More attention focused on the 'larrikin' provisions for offences involving public misbehaviour offences than any other issue in the whole Bill, perhaps because this provided a flashpoint for the discussion of whipping as a form of punishment. The 1883 Act was re-enacted as the Crimes Act 1900, a purely consolidation statute.

South Australia moved much later and less decisively. A local judge, Richard Pennefather, was commissioned by the South Australian government to draft a criminal code, which was introduced into the South Australian Legislative Council in 1903 but never debated, as a new Attorney-General did not favour it (Taylor, 2002). Tasmania did even less at this time, with the Criminal Code only being enacted in 1924.

Conclusion

The history of codification of the criminal law in Australia is quite disparate. On one hand there are the failed attempts, as with Hearn's and Pennefather's codes. At the opposite end of the spectrum lie the very rapid enactment of the criminal codes of Queensland and Western Australia. New Zealand lies somewhere between these two, given that eventually the criminal code was enacted, but the ten years it took clearly differentiate the New Zealand experience from the other code jurisdictions.

These remarkably different parliamentary histories suggest that speedy codification was only likely where there was a broad consensus in favour of the legislation. Both the Queensland and the Western Australian debates show a very general harmony of purpose; the New Zealand debates regularly descend into political point-scoring. In the latter climate, enactment of the code required both political will and political might; not until 1893 were the two sufficiently allied. The partisan nature of opposition to the Bill may have contributed to the generally much livelier and more sustained debates in the New Zealand parliament, especially the not uncommon reference to American law – something which has no counterpart in the Australian debates.

There are, however, some similarities within the discourse in the parliaments. The difference in timing of the legislation masks the common concern that the law be reformed to allow an accused to give evidence, and the widespread sentiment that some proper form of appellate review of convictions was needed. It is clear that in none of the code jurisdictions did the legislators scrutinise the conceptual framework of major crimes against persons or property – except in relation to the age of consent for sexual offences. There is in all cases some element of concern as to the offences which covered interaction between society and state – unlawful assembly, drilling and sedition were all clearly capable of giving rise to concerns as to the limits of legitimate political action. The concern in New Zealand and Western Australia as to criminal libel may be similarly categorised. The remarkable New Zealand concern with blasphemy is not, as yet, readily explainable. There was clearly a widespread concern as to the nature and severity of punishment appropriate to criminal offending, although attitudes within the legislatures varied widely. Rutledge in Queensland appears to have been more 'progressive' in this regard than his equivalents in other jurisdictions, yet it is not clear how widely his views were shared.

Why did the codification movement find backers in New Zealand, Queensland and Western Australia, and not in the other jurisdictions? Clearly there was the influence of certain leading proponents and influential lawyers such as Rutledge, Buckley, Sayer and, indirectly, Griffith himself. Yet other jurisdictions had leading lawyer figures and no such reform occurred. Perhaps the answer lies in the combination of strong leadership and parliamentary majorities open to significant change in the law. The governments at the time of enactment of a Code were all of a distinctly progressive or liberal hue. Codification in advance of England required a willingness to assert the intellectual independence of the colonies, something more common among radicals and liberals than among the conservatives. Secondly, reform often required substantial lay support. Where, as in Queensland and Western Australia, lay support was widespread, codification came quickly. In New Zealand it ultimately required a disciplined parliamentary majority, while lack of broad support meant codification in Victoria hardly moved from the theoretical. Successful, and unsuccessful, codes were the work of lawyers; their success or failure seems to have depended on the balance between opposition from other lawyers and support from laymen.

Notes

1. The term 'code' was also used on occasion for statutory restatements of settled common law principles, as with the Bills of Exchange Act 1882 (Imp) or the Sale of Goods Act 1893 (Imp). These have no criminal law equivalent.
2. The literature is extensive. For a convenient discussion see Bentley (1998).
3. Perhaps surprisingly this Act was never specifically referred to in any Australasian discussion of a criminal code. The most accessible account of the 1892 Code is Parker (1981).
4. New Zealand Parliamentary Debates, 1879, vol. 34, p. 783.
5. The Commissioners penned a memorandum to accompany the Bill of 1883. The Memorandum is reproduced in the 1908–31 Reprint of the New Zealand Statutes, vol. 2, 176–81. By far the most useful source on the Bill and the Parliamentary debates is White (1986).
6. The principal source for this section is the New Zealand Parliamentary Debates; significant debates are reported in vol. 44, 1883, pp. 44ff; vol. 45, 1883, pp. 578ff; vol. 51, 1885, pp. 56ff; vol. 52, 1885, pp. 206ff; vol. 53, 1885, pp. 407ff; vol. 55, 1886, pp. 454ff; vol. 61, 1888, pp.143ff; vol. 72, 1891, pp. 322ff; vol. 77, 1892, p.104; vol. 81, 1893, pp. 590ff.
7. Criminal Evidence Act 1889 (NZ), s.4; Criminal Code Act 1893 (NZ), s.400.
8. The debates are reported in Victorian Parliamentary Debates; see in particular vol. 47, 1884, pp. 1310ff; vol. 54, 1887, p. 425; vol. 57, 1888, pp. 511ff and vol. 58, 1888, pp. 1735ff.
9. No good account of Hearn's activities as a lawyer exists; his life and economic thought is recounted by Copland (1935). A copy of Hearn's 1885 Draft Code for Victoria, bearing Hearn's annotations for 1886–87, is preserved in the Australian National Library. See also Moore (1934: 184–5). The Report of the Joint Select Committee 1887 is printed in Victorian Parliamentary Papers 1887, no. D7. Higinbotham's evidence before the Select Committee urged the passage of the Hearn Code as a viable starting point for codification, but expressed thorough disagreement with its arrangement (see Report, 16). That comment was seized upon by opponents of the measure. For Higinbotham's career see Morris (1895).
10. A useful and scholarly account is O'Regan (2002). Unfortunately no study has considered whether Griffith also drew on the New Zealand Act of 1893, but there are a few notable similarities, as with the provocation provision and some of those relating to the criminal liability of children.
11. The principal sources for this section are the Queensland Parliamentary Debates (QPD) for 1899 and 1900. Significant debates are reported in 1899, pp. 104ff, pp. 149ff, pp. 196ff, pp. 222ff, 265ff, pp. 281ff, pp. 325ff, 522ff; and 1900, pp. 119ff, 1218ff.
12. QPD, 1899, p. 112. The reduction mirrors the English 'Labouchere' reforms of 1885.
13. QPD, 1899, pp. 332–5.
14. Russell (1980: 234) erroneously describes James as the Premier at the time of the Bill's passage.

15. The principal source for this section are the Western Australian Parliamentary Debates (WAPD). Important debates are reported in vol. 19, 1901, pp. 1101ff, pp. 1363ff, pp. 1399, 1401–2, 1574ff; vol. 20, 1902, pp. 2447ff, 2643ff, 2768ff.
16. WAPD, 1901, vol. 19, p. 1101.
17. WAPD, 1901, vol. 19, pp. 1404–5.
18. WAPD, vol. 19, p. 1408. The author's reading of the Queensland debates could not identify any such amendment, but as committee stages were not fully reported the statement is credible.

References

Bentley, D. *English Criminal Justice in the Nineteenth Century*. Hambleden Press, 1998.

Brown, D. H. *The Genesis of the Canadian Criminal Code of 1892*, Osgoode Society, 1989.

Castles, A. *An Australian Legal History*. Law Book, 1982.

Copland, D. *W. E. Hearn, First Australian Economist*. Melbourne University Press, 1935.

Friedland, M. 'R. S. Wright's Model Criminal Code: a forgotten chapter in the history of the criminal law', *Oxford Journal of Legal Studies*, 1, 1981, pp. 307–46.

Kercher, B. *An Unruly Child. A History of Law in Australia*, Allen and Unwin, 1995.

Manchester, A. H. 'Simplifying the sources of the law: an essay in law reform. Part II – J. F. Stephen and the codification of the criminal law in England and Wales' *Anglo-American Law Review*, 2, 1973, pp. 527–50.

Moore, W. H. 'A century of Victorian law', *Journal of Comparative Legislation and International Law*, 16, 1934, pp. 175–200.

Morris, E. E. *A Memoir of George Higinbotham*. Macmillan & Co., 1895.

O'Regan, R. S. *New Essays on the Australian Criminal Codes*. Law Book, 1988.

O'Regan, R. S. 'Griffith and the Queensland Criminal Code', in White, M. and Rahemtula, A. (eds), *Sir Samuel Griffith: The Law and the Constitution*, Law Book, 2002.

Parker, G. 'The origins of the Canadian Criminal Code' in Flaherty, D. (ed.), *Essays in the History of Canadian Law*, Vol. 1. University of Toronto, 1981.

Russell, E. *A History of the Law of Western Australia*. UWA Press, 1980.

Taylor, G. 'Dr Pennefather's Criminal Code for South Australia', *Common Law World Review*, 31, 2002, pp. 62–102.

Thomas, J. 'Griffith at work (1893–1903): a snapshot' in White, M. and Rahemtula, A. (eds), *Sir Samuel Griffith: The Law and the Constitution*. Law Book, 2002.

White, S. 'The making of the New Zealand Criminal Code Act of 1893: a sketch' 16 *Victoria University of Wellington Law Review*, 16, 1986, pp. 353–76.

Woods, G. D. *A History of the Criminal Law in New South Wales: The Colonial Period 1788–1900*. Federation Press, 2002.

Index

Hawai'i
'colonizing project' 100–1
'contract' or indentured labourers
96
head constables
of borough police forces 122
of county police forces 123
hereditary criminal communities 3,
79–80
Het concentratie-kamp van Irene 205
Highlands of Scotland, property
acquired through settlement 48
historical research, 'genealogical'
method 32–3
history
practice of re/creating 213
Whig interpretation 11, 13, 27
see also Australian frontier histories;
colonial histories; legal histories;
transnational history
*A History of Australia, New Zealand and
the Pacific* 94
history of crime and criminal justice
11–12, 13, 16–17
History of English Criminal Law 25–8
sources 27
'history of the present' 33
history of punishment 25–39
contribution of Radzinowicz 25–8
Elias and the civilising process
34–7
Foucault and histories of the
present 31–4
new directions and histiographies
37–9
sociological inquiries: the legacy of
Rusche and Kirchheimer 28–31
The Home Companion (*Die Brandwag*)
205
Howard, John 20
human sacrifice 80
'humble foresters' 30
Hunt, Samuel 151–2

Imperial Germany, re-establishment of
the death penalty 16

imperialism, European *see* European
imperialism
imprisonment
link to the capitalist mode of
production 29
see also lifetime incarceration; mass
imprisonment
indentured labourers 99
in Queensland 95–6, 101
see also female indentured labourers
India
archives of colonial lunatic asylums
98–9
British legal responses to *sati see*
British legal responses to *sati*
colonial state 86–7
criminal tribes *see* criminal tribes of
north India
degree of British intervention in
criminal law 190–3
and legal pluralism 3
rural elites 80–1
Indian Law Commission 189
Indian Penal Code 3, 189, 190, 225
indigeneity in colonies of settlement
61
in South Australia 61–2
indigenous peoples vii
colonial law's relation to 59–60
extermination in Tasmania 44
response to settlement 44
violence towards 43
see also Aborigines; American
Indians; Maori
individual sovereignty 193–4
industrial 'frontier towns'
applicability of Fairburn's model of
the colonial social pattern 142
see also Crewe; Middlesbrough
inebriate institutions 162
infra-judicial methods of justice 9
and agents of the new state 18–19
International Criminal Anthropology
Congresses 20–1
International Penitentiary Congresses
20